Structure and Insight
A Theory of Mathematics Education

DEVELOPMENTAL PSYCHOLOGY SERIES

SERIES EDITOR

Harry Beilin
Developmental Psychology Program
City University of New York Graduate School
New York, New York

A complete list of titles in this series is available from the publisher.

Structure and Insight
A Theory of Mathematics Education

PIERRE M. VAN HIELE

Dr. Beguinlaan 64
2272 AL Voorburg
The Netherlands

1986

ACADEMIC PRESS, INC.

Harcourt Brace Jovanovich, Publishers

Orlando   San Diego   New York   Austin
London   Montreal   Sydney   Tokyo   Toronto

ACADEMIC PRESS, INC.
Orlando, Florida 32887

United Kingdom Edition published by
ACADEMIC PRESS INC. (LONDON) LTD.
24–28 Oval Road, London NW1 7DX

LIBRARY OF CONGRESS CATALOGING-IN-PUBLICATION DATA

Hiele, Pierre M. van.
   Structure and insight.

   (Developmental psychology series)
   Translated from the Dutch.
   Includes index.
   1. Mathematics—Study and teaching (Elementary)
2. Cognition in children.   I. Title.   II. Series.
QA135.5.H56   1985   372.7   84-18611
ISBN 0-12-714160-X (alk. paper)
ISBN 0-12-714161-8 (paper)

PRINTED IN THE UNITED STATES OF AMERICA

86 87 88 89   9 8 7 6 5 4 3 2 1

Contents

Preface   vii

Introduction: The Roots of My Theory   1

1   Preliminary Questions   7

2   How Do We Meet a Structure?   9

3   How Do We Recognize a Structure?   13

4   Rigid and Feeble Structures   19

5   What Is a Structure?   23

6   Properties of a Structure   27

7   The Media in Which Structure Acts   33

8   Levels of Thinking   39

9   The Consequences and a More Exact Analysis
    of the Theory of Levels of Thinking   49

10 A Psychological Approach to Levels of
    Thinking   59

11 Intuition   71

12 Reality, Individual, and Language   77

13 Structures at Different Levels   83

14 Consequences of the Languages at Different
    Levels   89

15 The Development of Number   93

16 Levels of Structure in Argument   109

17 The Intuitive Foundations of Mathematics   115

18 Direct Reactions to Visual Structures   127

19 Direct Interactions between Reality and
    Common Human Knowledge   129

20 Switching Over from One Structure to Another   131

21 The Relations among the Media of Structure   137

22 Is it Possible to Test Insight?   151

23 A Phenomenal Introduction to Geometry   163

24 The Significance of Intention in the Learning
    Process   175

25 The Problem of Motivation in Education   187

26 System Separation and Transfer   195

27 The Relation between Theory and Problems in
    Arithmetic and Algebra   199

28 Proportion and Fraction   205

29 Objectivity   217

30 A Step in the Direction of Philosophy   227

    References   240
    Index   243

Preface

The approach to instruction based on the levels of thinking now commonly known as "the Van Hiele levels" was introduced in the United States by Izaak Wirszup in a lecture entitled "Some Breakthroughs in the Psychology of Learning and Teaching Geometry." Since that lecture, given at the Closing General Session of the National Council of Teachers of Mathematics in 1974, the levels of thinking approach has been the focus of increasing interest in the United States and many people have asked me to provide more details of it. I am sympathetic with this interest because the levels of thinking approach originated from my wish to improve teaching outcomes and my theory is useful only after the background of it has been made clear.

The goal of this book is to contribute to the improvement of teaching. Yet there is, of necessity, considerable theory in it: an understanding of how the levels can be used in practice requires an understanding of the theory behind it. There are ways to ascend from one level to the next and the teacher can help the pupil to find these ways. To be able to do this we need a theory, and practice follows from it. I was never much interested in the question of how many levels can be identified in a certain topic because it is possible to improve teaching without answering this question.

When I developed my levels approach it was aimed at the teaching and learning of geometry. This is an unnecessary restriction, however; the teaching and learning of other topics can be improved equally well with the same levels approach.

In the Netherlands I have written textbooks of mathematics in the levels of thinking framework. It is not necessary to provide a full description of those books here because their content is for the most part determined by the country in which they are used. Still, if an attempt is to be made to improve teaching with the help of the levels of thinking framework, and it is desirable to do so, then textbooks used here will have to be changed.

If my levels are used well, it is possible to start the teaching and learning of geometry—and many other topics—at a much earlier age than is now usually done. Making such a change is a policy matter and requires the cooperation of the educational authorities. Such an attempt has been made in the Soviet Union and I think it is worth trying to advance the teaching of geometry in other countries as well, using the levels approach. Even without changes in educational policy on a national scale, teaching in the new way will still have a positive outcome.

Some psychologies lay much stress on the learning of facts. The learning of structures, however, is a superior goal. Facts very often become outmoded; they sink into oblivion because of their lack of coherence. In a structure facts have sense; if a part of a structure is forgotten, the remaining part facilitates recall of the lost one. It is worth studying the way structures work because of their importance for the process of thinking. For this reason a considerable part of my book is devoted to structures.

In some chapters I am critical of certain aspects of Piaget's theory. Some critics of my earlier articles, however, have recognized that my opinion of Piaget is essentially positive. They are right: being critical of a theory is only meaningful if one agrees with the greater part of it. There is even some reason to claim that my levels originated with the theories of Piaget. That they bear my name can be explained by my working with them in quite a new way.

Many original ideas can be found in this book. I came upon them in analyzing dubious theories of both psychologists and pedagogues. It is not difficult to unmask such theories: simply test them in practice. Often this is not done because of the prestige of the theory's proponents.

The most important part of a teaching–learning process is discussion. With this book I initiate such a discussion. I see my role in this work as that of a teacher who has been learning for a long time.

Introduction: The Roots of My Theory

Even when young I was interested in teaching. I liked to help pupils of my class and of lower classes with their difficulties at school. When they seemed to lack all understanding, I was curious about the causes. I was not convinced of the infallibility of teachers; my father liked to write letters to my teachers when he thought that they had made mistakes. I remember that I did not like those letters: I was not surprised that they made mistakes; everybody does, even my father.

I had the notion that algebra textbooks were not well written. At the beginning of the book many operations were introduced at once, and it was difficult to realize immediately $3a + 5a = 8a$ but $3a \times 5a$ is not $15a$ but $15a^2$. And you also had to take care not to write $a^3 \times a^5 = a^{15}$. So even in the lowest class of secondary education I intended to write a new algebra textbook in which all those difficulties would be separated: I wrote it many years later.

I had great difficulties with geometry, though I got good grades, because I did not understand what axioms and definitions were good for. When after some time I began to understand, there were new difficulties: my understanding turned out to be misguided. "Every new thing in geometry should be introduced with axioms or definitions," the teacher had said, but triangles were lifted and laid down on their other side and in the axioms and definitions nothing could be found about "lifting," "laying down," and "other side." I know now that if I had asked the teacher about those things he would have answered that he had made omissions on purpose, but the lessons were not arranged in such a way that I had the courage to ask.

1

After some years, I began solid geometry. The teacher told us that with plane geometry he had made omissions, but that from now on he would mend his ways. Soon he gave the proof that two planes having one point in common must have at least a straight line in common. In the proof was talk of the two parts that space is divided into by a plane, and because the axioms mentioned nothing of those two parts, I did not understand the proof. It is easy to understand why later I was interested in axiomatics, and with the axiomatics of Pasch my problem was solved.

When I became a teacher I intended to do much better. With algebra this was not too difficult: I only had to analyze the operations and present them one after the other, and the results were much improved. I now know that it is possible to do it much better, but that is on the grounds of my theory of levels of thinking. However, with geometry I had very little success. At that time geometry textbooks were written with the purpose of building geometry from a true set of axioms. Some were still missing, but nevertheless the books were much too difficult. Most of the pupils did not understand them at all. I gave many additional lessons to pupils working with such textbooks, so I knew very well the difficulties that originated from them.

It was obvious that beginning with a sufficient set of axioms would not improve the results. But another new idea was also introduced at about this time: Begin geometry with a propaedeutic curriculum. This was a good idea, for such an introduction might be a link between reality and geometry. After the pupils became accustomed to space, they would understand the necessity of bringing order to all the properties they had become acquainted with. Then a real start in geometry could be made. The results were better, but still bad. Many of the pupils did not understand the point of axioms and definitions. They really did their best, but it did not help. And afterward, when after a long time they finally understood, they would say, "Now we understand, but why did you explain it in such a difficult language?" Soon I understood it was not the language that was so difficult, it was the pupils who had changed. It was an annoying situation: It seemed as if the teacher was unable to do anything; the pupils found their way themselves. But still, if the teacher had done nothing, the pupils would never have found their way.

From 1938 until 1951 I worked at a Montessori secondary school. On one hand, this was fortunate, for at such a school one can choose their own textbooks. It was even acceptable to write them oneself. If the teacher made mistakes, the pupils usually did not suffer for it, because the contacts between teacher and pupils were so frequent that it was always possible to correct the mistakes. On the other hand, the work was especially difficult: Teachers were expected to help pupils after school hours. The preparation of study material took a great deal of time.

In my Montessori period, it occurred to me to write a dissertation on a didactic subject. I thought that many pupils were underevaluated; I had seen many occasions when even those with very little initial success finished with reasonable results. So I thought it would be worth following a number of pupils for several years and reporting everything they did in connection with their performances in mathematics. I still think such an investigation might have remarkable results. However, the difficulties are innumerable. Though you teach a student one year, you cannot rely on being his teacher for the following years.

Teaching in a Montessori school has many advantages for the teacher who wants to know something about the way pupils think. They speak constantly with teachers about their difficulties, and the information disclosed is often astonishing. In the beginning, they understand much less about the subject matter than you might have expected, even when they have good grades. At the end, the results usually exceed expectations. From this you may conclude that it is very difficult to predict results at school.

I was in contact with many other teachers. Frequently we had meetings under the guidance of H. Freudenthal and T. Ehrenfest-Afanassjewa. On one occasion a new textbook, by Bos and Lepoeter, was introduced; according to A. D. de Groot this book was a consequence of Selz's psychology of thought. It was a geometry text based on problem solving. If one had to prove the equality of two angles, the book taught them to look for parallel lines, an isosceles triangle, an isosceles trapezoid, a parallelogram, and so forth. It had a recipe for every situation one might meet in an ordinary geometry problem. We did not like the book; most of us thought that problems were means, not ends. And if problems are a means to show whether one understands a structure, why should they learn all the elements of the structure separately? Of course, if solving problems is an end in itself, training for it may be very useful; but if it is only a means to demonstrate that the learning process is going well, it supplies little information once the training is over.

It was worth investigating what Selz's theory contained. In *The Laws of Productive and Reproductive Working of the Spirit* (Selz, 1924) I found what I was looking for. Thinking, according to Selz, is determined by constant problem solving. For solutions, the recall of things you know already is necessary. You need expedients for such recall, and better thinking may be obtained by knowing more expedients.

Of course it is true that solving geometry problems will be improved by learning many methods of solution. But before we can decide if we want such improvement, we must determine what problem solving in geometry is for. And to determine this, we must first know the purposes of teaching geometry, and whether transfer is possible from problem solving in geometry to problem solving in general.

In order to find the answer to the first question, I talked with many who were interested in this subject, such as Freudenthal and Ehrenfest-Afanassjewa. The results of this investigation can be found in Chapter 23. The answer to the second question I found in Mursell's *The Psychology of Secondary-School Teaching* (1939). Mursell talked of "transfer of training" and he gave examples in which it can be seen that the learning of certain abilities in one field usually does not imply that those abilities have also been acquired in other fields. So the ability to solve many problems of geometry might not imply an ability to solve other sorts of problems.

Again we might ask: Why do teachers like problem solving in geometry so much and why are certain psychologists so happy with it? The answer to the first question is complicated. Geometry problems often have a long history. Many parts of the theory of geometry have their roots in important technical problems that had to be solved long ago. Furthermore, many people like puzzles, and once you have solved a puzzle you can continue enjoying it by putting it to other people. So geometry teachers often like problems because they themselves are able to solve them. Problems do, of course, serve some functions in education. These are examined in Chapter 27.

The satisfaction of psychologists with problem solving can be explained by the experiments of psychologists themselves. A great part of Selz's theory is based on the results of problem solving. Experimental subjects were given a concept like 'tree', for instance, and then were asked to respond with a part of this concept, such as 'branch'. After giving their answers, subjects had to explain how they arrived at them. The expedients subjects used to find answers were recorded, and those who had difficulty were induced to learn the others' expedients. In *Attempts to Raise the Level of Intelligence* (1935), Selz describes this method and shows that many gains can be made. But his examples, problems of continuing sequences of numbers, are of little significance for education. After some time many of his subjects are able to continue sequences reasonably, but what is this ability good for? Real learning implies the control of structures, and the structures Selz works with are of too little extension to be interesting. I admit that Selz had little choice; I do not dispute his results. But his followers have mistakenly supposed that the subject matter of his experiments might also serve as subject matter for instruction. Learning nonsense words is important for the study of some learning processes, but learning such words in instruction is just a waste of time.

In 1951 I became a teacher at a non-Montessori school, and soon I was immersed in a struggle about insight. Because I had understood that the learning of facts could not be the purpose of teaching mathematics, I was convinced that development of insight ought to be the purpose. But the approach of the school was otherwise; it was thought best that the teacher taught facts and methods, even if the pupils did not understand them. Because of this conflict, I began a dissertation on insight under the guidance of Langeveld and Freudenthal. The former brought me into contact with the works of Gestalt psychologists, from which I learned that insight might be understood as the result of perception of a structure. At first I thought this simply a transposition of difficulties, for what is a structure? Afterward I began to understand the very important slogan: Structure is what structure does. First see how structures work, and afterward you will understand what structures are. In this book I have put this idea into practice.

Most of the ideas of structure I have developed in this book are borrowed from Gestalt theory. But I still agree with the objections Selz has against it. The great leaders of this theory, Wertheimer and Köhler, tried to explain human thinking with the help of physiological laws, and for the present such attempts seem to me quite unfruitful. If we want to explain human thinking, we will have to deal with concepts like 'will' and 'opinion', and so far there are only very few, very poor links between those concepts and physiology. But if we want to apply psychology to didactics it is not at all necessary to decide such questions. If you want to use your television set, it is not necessary that you know how the apparatus has been constructed; if you want to use structures in instruction it is not necessary that you know how the brain makes use of structures. Structures are subject to general rules, and it is sufficient to know these rules. Piaget's *Structuralism* (1968) gave rise to my writing about structure.

In 1954 I read Koning's dissertation: *Some Problems in the Didactics of Natural Sciences, Especially in Chemistry* (1948). In this book he cited a paper by Piaget (1927) that mentioned levels. This lead to my setting up of the theory of levels of thinking. After having read Piaget's original papers, I at first opposed to them, especially *The Development of Number* (1941), which might suggest that the transition from one level to the next is a biological development and cannot be stimulated by a learning process. I must admit that this statement was not exactly made by Piaget himself. But some of his followers did draw this conclusion. In any case, an important part of the roots of my work can be found in the theories of Piaget. It is important then, too, to emphasize the differences:

1. The psychology of Piaget was one of development and not of learning. So the problem of how to stimulate children to go from one level to the next was not his problem. It was mine.

2. Piaget distinguished only two levels. In geometry it appears necessary to distinguish more. Some of Piaget's results would have been more intelligible if he had distinguished more than two levels.

3. Piaget did not see the very important role of language in moving from one level to the next. It was occasionally suggested to him that children did not understand his questions. He always answered that they did understand; this could be read from their actions. But, although actions might be adequate, you cannot read from them the level at which children can think.

4. According to Piaget, human spirit develops in the direction of certain theoretical concepts. He was not aware that those concepts are only human

constructions, which, in the course of time, may change. So development with some theory as a result always must be understood as a learning process influenced by people of that period.

5.   Piaget did not see structures of a higher level as the result of study of the lower level. In my theory, the higher level is attained if the rules governing the lower structure have been made explicit and studied, thereby themselves becoming a new structure. In Piaget's theory, the higher structure is primary; children are born with it, and only have to become aware of it.

6.   In my theory, a structure is a given thing obeying certain laws (borrowed from Gestalt theory); if it is a strong structure it will usually be possible to superpose a mathematical structure onto it. In Piaget's theory the mathematical structure always defines the whole structure.

So we see there are many important disagreements between us. But it was still significant that Piaget first introduced levels: the experimental person at the lower level not understanding the leader at the higher level. But in another aspect, too, Piaget distinguishes himself from other psychologists. The learning material supplied by Piaget consisted of whole structures, whereas the other psychologists always occupied themselves with elements: meaningless words, coordinated concepts, sequences of numbers, and so on. We may be sure that by disputing Piaget I also learned much from him.

In my dissertation study I also met the work of Van Parreren, particularly *Intention and Autonomy in the Learning Process* (1951). This book opposed the idea that learning must always be accompanied by an intention. In his experiments, Van Parreren demonstrated that a very adequate learning of actions is possible just by learning to do, without any rational thinking. This idea too was of great importance for my theory; it induced me to pay more attention to visual structures in which thinking is unnecessary, structures on which one can base conclusions without further reasoning.

For the last twenty years of my study I have had much support from H. J. De Miranda. After becoming acquainted with the theory he became a fervent supporter, and in working out the details he has made many important contributions. In this volume, I have tried to mention him at such occasions, but I am sure I have sometimes unintentionally failed to do so.

1

Preliminary Questions

To study the essence of human thinking, you must deal with questions of many different kinds, questions that have more to do with each other than you might have thought. I will mention some of these problems:

1. In Gestalt psychology the following kind of statement is made: "Insight is brought about by a structuralizing of perception." Is this merely a jump from the difficult concept of 'insight' to the new, hazy concept of 'structuralizing', or can we really proceed in the problem by using the notion of 'structure'?
2. Mathematics is applied in many sciences to give the solution of problems a numerical foundation. Does this prove that mathematics forms the base of those sciences, or is mathematics only a means to form a model, like that of atomic theory in chemistry in the era before the twentieth century?
3. There are many concepts, like 'causality', about which there are many differences of opinion. Some people maintain that those differences only exist because such concepts are vaguely stated. Is it possible to clarify such concepts? How should we proceed to do so?
4. Many research workers describe phases in the processes they are studying, whether of a child learning to understand a complicated conception, or of the development of a disease. Opposing researchers say that these phases do not happen so often, and that the discoverer of the phases manipulates his results in such a way that those phases always appear, whether they are essential or not. Is such manipulation the normal way in

research, is it inherent in all scientific descriptions, or is it an exception? Is there a method to reduce such verbal license?

5. When you study a very new subject, it very often happens that you are not able to understand the line of thought of the author. Must your conclusion be that you are too stupid to understand the material, or may you hope for the possibility that the author has not given careful arguments?

6. In arguments of some questions, it may happen that someone says, "I know it because I see it." Is such an argument always objectionable, is it always necessary to use deductive arguments?

In this book you will find a description of a theory of cognitive levels. I show you how levels of thinking demonstrate themselves, how they come into existence, how they are experienced by teachers and how by pupils. You will also see how we can take account of those levels in writing textbooks.

Man is inclined to take for granted the things he has always done, the things his great teachers have always enunciated. For those with a pioneer spirit, such truths are not so certain; for those people there very often exist other possibilities. If this book results in the strengthening of the critical sense of the reader, I will have attained my objective.

2

How Do We Meet a Structure?

Many people have written about structures. It is of little use to mention them here, because most of their works are constructed in the traditional terms of deduction, and if I were to discuss them I would also be obliged to reason with these terms. The course of this book demonstrates why I avoid thinking in terms of the constructions of deduction in the beginning.

I cannot begin with a definition of *structure*. A definition of a concept is only possible if one already knows, to some extent, the thing that is to be defined. In this case there is a very great chance that the idea you have of structure is quite different from the concept I want to develop.

An important medium in which you find structure is language. Language is very important to thinking. Without language, thinking is impossible; without language, there is no development of sciences.

I know you may have objections. Many years ago, when my children were young, two of them were quarreling. They asked me to be an arbiter. The first had said: "Every time we do not sleep, we are thinking." The other said: "This is not true; it may be that I am walking in the woods and I see the woods, but I do not think." The first: "You are thinking then, for you know it is the woods you are walking in, and to be able to know that you must have been thinking." The other: "Maybe, but for such knowledge I have not used words in my mind, so I have not been thinking."

At that time my idea was that the first child was right. You can act without thinking in words, but to do the right thing, it seems that thinking is necessary, even if without words. I told the story to H. Freudenthal and he agreed with the second girl. He said: "You can do adequate things without thinking in words, but real thinking is arguing, and that you can't do without words." I now think that he and the second daughter were right, although an opponent may maintain that it is only a question of choice. Later in this book I defend this view.

Language has a structure. Young children discover this structure by building up sentences they have never heard. I remember my eldest daughter discovering the word "indeed." She used the word in different sentences for a whole day.

The world in which we live has many structures. This world I will, in accordance with Popper, call World 1. Of course, you may say that such a world has no reality, that this world is only a construction of our mind (Popper calls the mind World 2), that the structures we see in World 1 are only structures of ourselves. This is a tenable conception but not very practical. It is very difficult to talk to a person, to discuss the things you see around you, if you want to express at any time in your discussion that neither he nor the things around you exist.

So to make it easy, we accept the existence of World 1 and we see the structures of this world. But still there is a difficulty: If we see a tree, we deal with a structure. For we know that it is a tree, even if we have never seen this particular tree before. But in forming this structure, language has taken part. We have been in many discussions before about trees. We have seen many sorts of trees and we know that a shrub is not a tree. In our mind we have an idea of 'tree' that is connected with 'growing up', 'leaves', 'branches', and all those notions have been built up by using a language. So someone might suppose that the structures of World 1 are only structures of the language.

Most conceptions of things we see in World 1 are mixed up with structures that are built up with a language. But this is the end of a long process. Young children who have not yet developed a language for certain things can still react to them in a sensible way. They see the structure and they give an adequate answer by their actions. So there is no doubt that World 1 has a structure of its own.

An animal, having no language, reacts directly to the structures of World 1. Most of its reactions are stereotyped: It reacts as if it were a part of the surrounding world. A human answer is usually encapsulated in a verbal structure; for us it is very difficult to react to World 1 directly.

When we are teaching, we very often forget that such a direct way exists. To bring a pupil in contact with World 1, we give him an explanation. By doing so, we give our interaction a deductive character. But usually this is much too early. A child first needs a direct communication with the material.

In scientific discussions we always use a language of deduction. We leave the direct communication of the human mind (World 2) with World 1 out of consideration. By doing so we promote a verbal knowledge in which we do not know the reality of our subject.

In this book I show how it is possible to improve communication in scientific discussions. This method can also be used in education. It is for this reason that concepts that are necessary to my explanations will be made clear by examples and not by definitions.

The pictures in Figure 2.1 are photographs I have taken myself. They were chosen to show you what structures are. I could have chosen any photograph whatever, for everything that has something to say has it because of a structure. But those I have chosen are very clear; they will give you little difficulty. The structures you see are structures of World 1. If you ask me: ''What must I see in such a picture,'' you are on the wrong road. For in that case you are trying to explain the structure with the help of World 2; you are asking for a structure in that world.

The photographs were not taken specifically for this book. I took them only because I liked the structures in them. When I took a picture, I did not try to explain the structure; I simply took the picture because I said to myself: ''Oh, how beautiful things are.'' If you like them too, without understanding why, you have understood the structure.

3

How Do We Recognize a Structure?

Some examples of structures are given in Figure 3.1. They are all visual structures. I begin with them because it is easiest to see the properties of such structures.

The first thing to be observed in these structures is that they can be extended. It is very easy to extend a structure of squares: If you give a young child a set of square tiles, he will in most cases be able to extend the pattern. So if you want to start geometry with a well-known structure and the child is no younger than 6 years, you can always begin with the structure of square-grid paper.

It is not necessary that a structure be infinitely extendable. Figure 3.2 shows a structure (left) that is completed on the right. Of course you can go on with adding triangles, but then you are creating a new structure.

Sometimes there are several ways to extend a structure, such as those in Figure 3.3 and 3.4.

Structures of numbers can also be extended in different ways. The following sequence of numbers is given: 1, 1—1, 1—2—1, 1—3—3—1, 1—4—6—4—1. How should you continue this sequence? Perhaps you see in it the beginning of Pascal's triangle and will continue with 1—5—10—10—5—1. But there is another possibility. You may think it is the beginning of the powers of 11, first 11^0, then 11^1, and so on. If this is your idea, you will continue with 1—6—1—0—5—1.

Some psychologists test your intelligence by giving you a sequence of num-

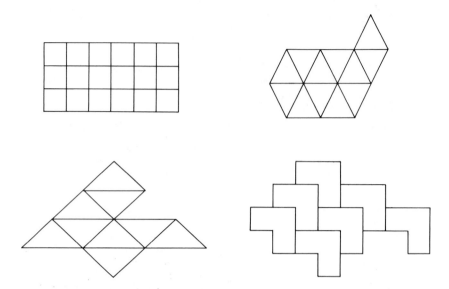

Figure 3.1

bers and asking you to continue it. Usually the continuation is very easy. A psychologist (George Sand) gave the following sequence: 2, 3, 5, 8. A mathematician might follow with 13, 21, 34; for $2 + 3 = 5, 3 + 5 = 8, 5 + 8 = 13, 8 + 13 = 21$, and so on. This is called the Fibonacci sequence. But the "right" continuation could have been 12, 17, 23; For the psychologist's idea could have been $2 + 1 = 3, 3 + 2 = 5, 5 + 3 = 8, 8 + 4 = 12, 12 + 5 = 17, 17 + 6 = 23$, and so on. It is a custom with some psychologists that there be no explanation afterward; there is no time for it. So a mathematician sometimes has less chance of success. A very clever subject might find a continuation the psychologist

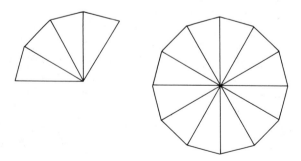

Figure 3.2

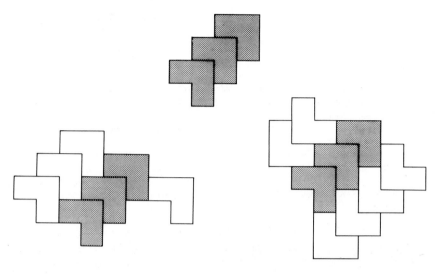

Figure 3.3

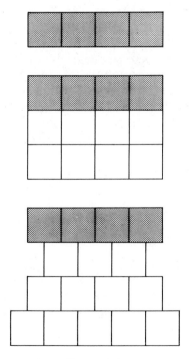

Figure 3.4

never thought of: Still it could be rejected. Testing in this way promotes conformity.

Let us be clear about what conformity is. A dictionary might give something like this:

> **conformity** (Latin *conformis* = similar): adaption to norms that are in force in a community in relation to the values, customs, and rules. Conformity is found in all human groups and has many causes. The most important of these are *identification* with important or powerful people; *indoctrination*—being exposed to specific and mostly partial information, with screening from other influences; *social pressure,* the extortion of conforming behavior through threat of punishment, expulsion, or other sanctions. The extent to which people are inclined to conform depends on characteristics of the personality. Those who conform comparatively fast are characterized by less intelligence, less resolution, less spontaneity, less confidence, and a greater emotional dependance on other persons.

We can see that it is very bad to promote conformity by testing, no matter what the reason. In a later chapter I deal with the question of how structures are spread in human knowledge. One of the most important impediments to such spreading is conformity—in many forms.

1.   There are many well-known examples in which Church and State have made people conform. Everyone knows of art which has been called "degenerate"; everyone knows of the difficulties Galileo, Copernicus, and Darwin had when they introduced their unconventional theories.

2.   Of the same sort, and perhaps more important, is the indoctrination done by teachers. Often pupils are not allowed to ask why their teachers tackle a problem in the way they do. On examinations the pupils usually must abstain from criticism of the subject matter they have been taught, for if they criticize, they reduce their chances to pass.

3.   Commerce uses indoctrination with great success. "Master's Dog Food is the only correct dog food, for it contains verogen, and verogen is just what your dog needs." Such advertising always does well, even though no one knows what verogen really is. The slogan makes a very scientific impression and that is enough.

4.   When you are engaged in a great concern, you must avoid every pronouncement that does injury to that concern. Such indoctrination we consider self-evident.

5.   The most extended indoctrination proceeds from groups. "The judgment of questions of this sort you can better leave to men": In such a way women are indoctrinated. People who are not impressed by the wisdom of such groups can be amazed by the frequency with which these groups practice indoctrination, and by the lack of evidence with which other people endure it.

The construction of visual structures in our mind very often does not need a language. You can ask a child to continue a given structure (as in the preceding pictures) and he or she will succeed without having learned a language that accompanies the structure. There are many structures to which animals can respond and thus behave successfully in nature.

In many cases in which language does play a part, the continuation of a structure is not found by applying a rule. A child who says "leaved" instead of "left" uses a rule he has learned by practice; he shows that he has understood a structure of a part of the language. It is well known that children are very sensitive to such structures. In this phase of understanding, the influence of adults is very little, and it can surely not be intensified by the mention of a rule.

In *Variations on a Theme of Haydn,* Brahms builds a structure. It is not necessary to know very much about music to notice and to appreciate the structure. So appreciation of a structure does not implicate understanding of the structure.

In chemistry there are structures with the character of a model. They have the function of making visual rather abstract concepts. Such models, in the beginning, are only tools that enable one to calculate in terms of the concepts. Molecules, for instance, were in the nineteenth century things you could use in your calculations, but their existence was not sure. The same thing was true in the beginning of the twentieth century with the atomic model. Later, when science recognized more and more data about atoms that were in agreement with each other, the existence of molecules and atoms became more and more accepted.

You can see in this case that there are structures that can only be understood by using a language. Here is a difficulty I discuss in a later chapter: The structures of molecules and atoms are not directly visible, and therefore it takes a long time to learn to see them in a visual way. But chemists and teachers of chemistry do see molecules and atoms when they write down formulas of chemical substances and equations for chemical reactions. They see these particles as realities and they therefore are inclined to underrate the difficulties of beginning students of chemistry. It is true that models of atoms and molecules make a visual impression. But they are very complicated, and it is worth investigating to see if there are easier ways to begin chemistry.

4

Rigid and Feeble Structures

If you know a sufficient part of the structures in Figure 4.1, you can extend them without making mistakes. Such structures we will call *rigid structures*.

If you are acquainted with 20 pictures or so of Dufy, Rembrandt, Fra Angelico, or Cézanne, you will be able to recognize other pictures of those painters. You will come to your opinion by operating in a structure. Of course you may make mistakes, if, for instance, you are looking at an early work of an artist or an imitation. From just these examples we can learn that we are dealing with real structures: You do not recognize the early work, because it does not have the structure of the mature work; you are deceived by the imitation because the imitator has tried to copy the structure. It is difficult not to make mistakes; you

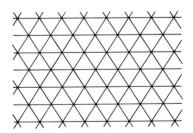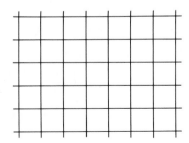

Figure 4.1

must see a great many of the works of the painter to be quite sure. Therefore, I will call such structures *feeble structures*.

The tiled track in Figure 4.2 is a rigid structure: You can continue the structure with great certainty. Mathematical structures are very rigid if the rule of the structure is given. But they lose their rigidity if the rule is not given, if you have to guess. The Fibonacci sequence 2, 3, 5, 8 is very easy to continue, if you know it is the Fibonacci sequence. If this is not given, there are other continuations.

My wife and I were once composing a textbook of algebra and we wanted to introduce sequences geometrically. In Figure 4.3 you see the left half of a square. With this half you can build whole squares. You can do it with 2, 4, 8, and 16 half-squares, as the figures illustrates. This is a beautiful sequence and we thought that it would continue with 32, 64, and so on. To be sure that it was not too difficult, we asked our daughter of 10 to continue the building. To our astonishment she found a square of 18 half-squares (Figure 4.4). In this figure you see that the sequence 2, 4, 8, 16 may be continued with 18, 32, 36, 50. If you know how the sequence is constructed, it is a very rigid sequence. But you can be sure that such a solution would be rejected on most psychological tests.

Even if structures seem to be very rigid, there are often possibilities for different continuations, and they can give rise to great tensions if groups of people want to force their favored continuation.

It may be that you do not like feeble structures because they tend toward insecurity. Many people do not like them. It is often said that feeble structures are not structures at all; some people only want to deal with structures with a rigid mathematical foundation. It is true that every time we work with feeble structures there is some insecurity. But, still, nature is full of such structures. The cat lying in wait and the blackbird in danger of the cat—they both live in a feeble structure. The man who is driving a car in heavy traffic also lives in a feeble structure. Still, most of the time he knows the right continuation; otherwise there would be many more accidents. So if we eliminate the feeble structures from our study, most human and animal behavior cannot be understood.

The structures in Figure 2.1 are generally rigid. Strictly rigid is the structure of Islamic architecture. Also rather rigid is the structure of the winding staircase. The structure of the fallen leaves is avowedly feeble. Still it is a structure, for if I place the leaves in a neater construction, most people like it less.

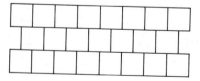

Figure 4.2

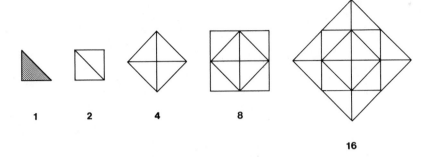

Figure 4.3

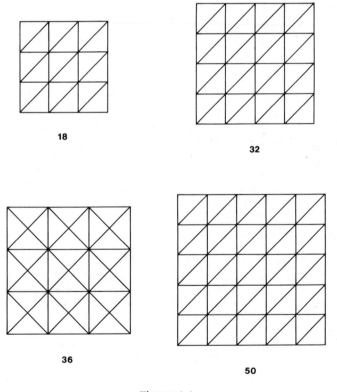

Figure 4.4

5

What Is a Structure?

In the preceding chapters we have seen structures recognizable because of their rigidity. If the structure is feeble it is not easy to react adequately; very often you only can say: "This is a bad continuation; that might be a good continuation." So you see that the most important property of structure is this: A structure can be extended because of its composition.

Here we see a correspondence between man and world. We have expectations. If you show me a picture and you say it is made by Dufy, I may be shocked because I think it seems like a painting by Picasso. A picture by Picasso cannot be forced into the structure of the pictures by Dufy. Still, such a structure permits quite an array of expectations; we might speak of a pattern of expectations. But with the word *pattern* we express the same thing as with the word *structure*.

If I ask a person to continue the structure of a tiled track, there is an expectation. The person adds a tile and I am disappointed if he does it in the wrong way. Here we see the second property of structure: Structures have an objectivity, different people continue a structure in the same way.

Development of habits by stimulus–response training does not exclude the forming of structures. When a parrot expresses his desire to eat from what has been placed on the table by whistling, a structure is built up. The person who comes forward with the food fulfills the expectation of the parrot; man and animal know how to act in accordance with the structure.

Some people are suspicious of speaking of a parrot "having an expectation" and "wanting to eat something." They dislike the attribution of human properties to parrots. But even behaviorists can agree with the above description. There is something in the behavior of a parrot we can call expectation and something in its behavior that expresses its desire for food.

If you continue the sequence 2, 4, 8, 16 with 18, 32, 36, 50, you might not act in accordance with the expectation of a psychologist, but you do act according to a structure, even a very rigid one. There can be accord with the psychologist—if he is willing to listen to you.

Structure is an important phenomenon: It enables man and animal to act in situations that are not exactly the same as those they have met before. Structure saves man and animal from a never-ending life of trial and error. Structure enables people to understand each other. People see the same structure and they can express their harmony by continuing the structure in the same way.

In Gestalt psychology you might find the following statement: "We are sure of insight when the person (or the animal) you are studying comes to a conclusion on account of a mental structure." In my dissertation, "Begrip en Inzicht" (Conception and Insight), of 1957, I wrote: "Insight exists when a person acts in a new situation adequately and with intention."

The Gestalt psychologist and I say the same thing with different words. When the Gestalt psychologist speaks of a structure, he presumes an expectation on the strength of which one is able to act adequately. With the word "adequately" is implied the relevance of objectivity. For before we can speak of adequacy, there must be some agreement about what is adequate. After the agreement has been attained, there is also objectivity. The Gestalt psychologist speaks of a mental structure and so transfers from the structure of World 1 into the structure of World 2 (the mind). "On account of a mental structure" supplies the parallel with my "intention." A person who acts with intention does not act at random, he acts according to the structure he perceives, corresponding to his mental structure, the structure of his expectation.

My description of the way you can recognize insight has proven to be successful. It is a workable description. Gestalt psychologists have given the same description, but with other words.

The analysis, at any rate, brings us to an important question. We spoke of a "mental" structure, and so we might have to exclude insight when animals are under discussion. In my description we found the corresponding phrase "with intention." In animal psychology, intention of animals is recognized by the starting of a movement. If we admit such an intention without requiring thinking, we may speak of insight of apes, on account of the experiments of Köhler. We also may say that rats demonstrate insight in a maze. The notion of animal insight can be useful. It can reflect on the insight of man. When you use a typewriter you need not know where the various keys are: Your fingers go to the keys on their own. As in animal psychology, we could state that this is the starting of a movement showing an intention. Still, you are acting as result of a structure of action and not as a result of a mental structure. This is in contradiction with usage: If our fingers go to the keys without a mental structure, we say, "They go by themselves, I had no intention." How will we resolve this? Will we speak of insight in this case or not? If we reject insight in this case, we must also reject it in the case of a pianist reading music whose hands go to the keys in the right position. We must also reject most animal insight.

This is not the place to resolve this issue. The primary importance of the problem is not a resolution of which of the above situations exhibits insight. It is important for the concept of insight and intention. From the examples we may learn that man often shows adequate reactions to situations in which thinking is not necessary.

6

Properties of a Structure

We have not yet found a definition for structure. This is to be expected, because it is only possible to give a definition when we are quite sure what structure really is. But we have made some progress. We have found some properties of structure:

1. A man or animal can act on account of a structure in new situations.
2. Structure is objective: Other people see (hear or smell) a structure just as we do. Other people are able to react to a structure just as we do.

Before I continue the properties of structure, I will mention the characteristics Piaget (1968) gives of structure. For Piaget there are three characteristics:

1. Structure has a totality.
2. Structure is achieved by transformations.
3. Structure is autoregulating.

Piaget does not give examples. So we will have to interpret those characteristics ourselves.

The first characteristic implies that with a given structure, all elements of the structure are always given. And there is another notion: Each structure can be seen as a totality. In the first idea there is the possibility of an extension of the structure in only one way. The second expresses the truth that, mentally, structures are experienced as a whole. Still, this is not a constituting fact; it is an experience.

The second characteristic is more a method to study structures than a real characteristic. Of course, many structures allow transformation from one element to another. But if we deal with feeble structures, such transformations are not easy. And if Piaget recommends looking at every structure for mathematical or logical laws, there is a great danger that feeble structures will have no place in his theory.

With the last characteristic, Piaget says that structure and its boundaries are maintained by intrinsic laws. I suggest that the laws a structure is subjected to are more a result than a part of the definition. It is clear that Piaget, with his three characteristics, has already given a conception of the development of structures. By doing so he has blocked the investigation of the development of structures at a higher level. And he banishes from his study all structures that are mathematically difficult to express but still worth studying.

It is very important that a structure can be seen as a totality; a structure is more than the sum of its elements. In Figure 6.1 you see a tile. You can make a floor with such tiles. We have made a floor with four rows of three tiles (Figure 6.2). There are many regularities in the floor you would not have expected by only seeing the single tile.

In structural psychology (Gestalt psychology) there are four important properties that govern structure:

1. It is possible to extend a structure. Whoever knows a part of the structure also knows the extension of it. The extension of a structure is subjected to the same rules as the given part of it.
2. A structure may be seen as a part of a finer structure. The original structure is not affected by this: The rules of the game are not changed, there are only enlarged. In this way it is possible to have more details take part in the building up of the structure.
3. A structure may be seen as a part of a more-inclusive structure. This more-inclusive structure also has more rules. Some of them define the original structure.
4. A given structure may be isomorphic with another structure. In this case the two structures are defined by rules that correspond with each other. So if you have studied the given structure, you also know how the other structure is built up.

Figure 6.1

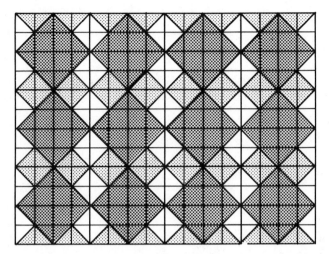

Figure 6.2

To apply the first rule, for example to the concept "human skeleton," we may suppose that we become acquainted with the human skeleton by looking at such a skeleton. The extension of the structure may happen when we realize that we have such a skeleton ourselves. The thought process necessary for such an extension is very easy: There are no new elements in it.

The second rule, the construction of a finer structure, is also easy to illustrate with this example. We get a finer structure by giving names to parts of the skeleton. The constructions of a language enable us to recognize these parts, and after that it is possible to study the mutual position of the parts and their function.

The third rule is used if we begin to study skeletons of animals and to compare them with the human skeleton.

The rule of isomorphism of structures is also used when we compare the skeleton of man with the skeleton of an animal. Generally we can use the same names for the bones. It is also possible to use a global isomorphism. In this case only a few of the rules of the structure are applicable in both structures. Such global isomorphism is used if we speak of the skeleton of a building, for instance a Gothic cathedral. In this case the isomorphism is not mathematical at all. Still, there is a system of pillars, beams, and other elements by which the whole building is supported.

In mathematics, isomorphism is the most rigid. I give one example: addition and multiplication.

Addition in the set of real numbers is defined by five rules:

1. For every two numbers a and b there exists a number $a + b$.

2. There exists a number 0 with the property that for every number a, $a + 0$ $= a$.
3. For every number a there exists a number $-a$ with the property $a + (-a)$ $= 0$.
4. For every two numbers a and b, $a + b = b + a$.
5. For every three numbers a, b, and c, $a + (b + c) = (a + b) + c$.

Multiplication in the set of real numbers is with the exception of 0 defined by the following five rules:

1. For every two numbers a and b there exists a number $a \times b$.
2. There exists a number 1 with the property that for every number a, $a \times 1$ $= a$.
3. To every number a there exists a number a^{-1} with the propery $a \times a^{-1}$ $= 1$.
4. For every two numbers a and b, $a \times b = b \times a$.
5. For every three numbers a, b, and c, $a \times (b \times c) = (a \times b) \times c$.

The two structures are the same. You have only to change (1) the set of the real numbers with the set of the real numbers with exception of 0, (2) + with ×, (3) $-a$ with a^{-1}, and (4) 0 with 1.

In all cases of isomorphism, from mathematical isomorphism to global isomorphism, the understanding of new situations can be simplified to a considerable extent. If the isomorphism is mathematical, the correctness of it can be proved by analyzing both structures and by demonstrating that the constituting principles of the ordering of the structures are the same. After that you may transfer all rules from one structure to the other. If the isomorphism is global, the resemblance in the beginning is only external. It is then necessary to study which of the constituting principles of one structure can be transfered to the other. In any case, global isomorphism may give starting points to make a new structure understandable.

When in 1941 Germany began its war with the Soviet Union, many people thought of Napoleon's invasion of Russia. No more than a global isomorphism existed between the two structures, but still there was hope or fear of a similar result. For example, De Jong (1974, p. 170) writes:

> In Haarlem, in the Netherlands, there was a stove dealer who made of his show window a great snowfield strewn with miniatures of broken trucks, bodies of horses, and corpses of soldiers; in the center he placed a base burner with a three-cornered hat on it, like Napoleon wore, and the passers-by understood it and were pleased by it. The German security police understood it, too, and the stove dealer was arrested.

A global isomorphism can be understood so clearly that it leads to an arrest.

The first- and the fourth-mentioned properties of structure generally show themselves directly: They are innate in man. For the second and third properties, on the contrary, a study is usually necessary. If education is directed at the development of insight, it should stimulate pupils to develop their recognition and use of the second and third properties.

The photographs in Figure 2.1 show various visual structures. The rigid structures on which these things are based can easily be distinguished because they can be extended in only one way. It is easy to see even the feeble structures, though they can be continued in different ways. From the photographs of the cabbages and the road-roller, the structure is so obvious that one needs only a part to know the whole.

Do we now know what structure is? I think so. We know the properties of it. We know that we need structures in order to act adequately and because we usually act adequately, there must be structures everywhere. But then, structure must have a very wide signification. Is there danger that this signification is too wide? I do not think so. For in all situations, we may count on the four properties of structure.

I have given a definition of insight. We have seen that structure and insight are very closely related. So if you desire, you can construct a definition for structure now. I will not help you with it. I can go on without such a definition.

7

The Media in Which
Structure Acts

It is not immediately clear in which media you can find structures. To begin with, we may consider five media:

1. Reality, the world in which we live (Popper's World 1).
2. The human mind, if we speak of mental structures (Popper's World 2).
3. The mind of humanity; There are many structures made by mankind. Often we do not possess these structures ourselves, but we can get access to them by asking, reading books, and so on (Popper's World 3).
4. Language; For the construction of many structures, especially of World 3, language is necessary.
5. Human action; There exist structures in human action that are not governed by a structure of human thinking.

To demonstrate that structure of reality exists, imagine two individuals looking at the same thing. Sometimes they see a rigid structure and are able to continue it in the same way. There is an agreement in their reactions to the structure, and therefore we may conclude the existence of a structure with an objective character.

If you have any inclination to deny the existence of mental structures, consider the following: An individual has the ability to anticipate the continuation of a visual structure, and he is able to do this before he begins action and before he has seen the continuation of the structure. The possibility of such anticipation enables us to conceive reality and to act adequately in new situations. A mathematician is able to have a whole theory in mind (mental structure) before he writes it down, adding it to World 3.

The communication of an individual with other people is incomprehensible if we conceive of such a communication as only the sum of communications between two special individuals. Someone attending a colloquium does not do this to be informed of the personal ideas of the leader of the colloquium. He attends because he expects to acquire knowledge that belongs to common human thought.

Of course 'common human thought' is an unattainable ideal. It is closely related to objectivity and we know objectivity is dependent on time, space, and group. Still, though 'common human thought' cannot be exactly defined, this notion is indispensable; a great part of individual thinking is acquired by communication with common human thought. Common human thought is highly structured, for it enables people to act adequately in many new situations.

A part of the structure of common human thought is stored in common customs. If you obey the proverb "When in Rome, do as the Romans do," you are ready to obey structures of human thought of a very local character. Very much of common human thought is embodied in reference books, pictures, scientific treatises, photographs of the starry sky, and calculators. With the aid of these things, an individual can enrich, correct, and coordinate his own mental structures.

In the interaction of the three media, language plays an important part. Still, we have already seen that language is not always necessary.

Language is very inappropriate to transfer a visual structure from one person to another. Transferability sometimes will be a thousand times better if a part of the real structure can take over the task of language. I will give some examples.

Once, busy with practical work in physics, a pupil was astonished by the fact that two objects having the same temperature could be very different to the touch, one unremarkable, the other cold. Another pupil said: "Feel that iron rod, how it gives a cold touch!" The first pupil did not need a further explanation: He understood at once that it was the conduction of heat that gave the impression of a cold touch. By having been shown a situation that was typical of heat conduction, all was made clear to him.

In a botany lesson a pupil had difficulties with the identification of a sprig of *Impatiens nolitangere*. Another pupil saw his troubles and said: "Can you identify that plant there in the window sill?" The first pupil then said: "I don't know, but I know that it is called 'balsam' [*I. balsamina*]." He saw the resemblance of his plant and balsam, looked "balsam" up in a reference book, and saw on the same page an illustration of his plant: *I. balsamina*. The illustration gave much more information than the formal system of identification, for language poses many difficulties for explaining visual structures.

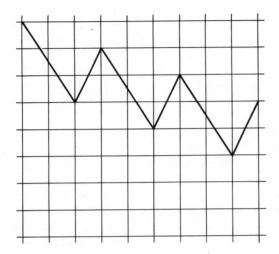

Figure 7.1

In Figure 7.1 you see a figure that is easy to continue. Yet it would be difficult to give a description of it, and definitions would be required. For instance you might speak of vectors **a** and **b** and you might define the succession **a b a b** as a saw. Then you may say: Continue the saw that is formed by the vectors **a** = (2, −3) and **b** = (1, 2). You must know something about mathematics to be able to understand this description. So you see, the continuation is much more difficult to describe than to accomplish.

If a structure is seen in World 1, it is reasonable to give it a name. We have done so above, with the name "saw." Such a name giving is important; it makes the structure more accessible. In this situation, it is important that language has a structure of its own. Language makes it possible to connect a given structure with other structures. Here language makes use of the fourth property of structure: global isomorphism.

If you say to someone: "Such an idea does not belong to his pattern of thinking," it is not necessary to explain what you mean by "pattern of thinking." It is sufficient to know what "pattern" in common language means, even though the word "pattern" is here used figuratively.

From this discussion you can conclude that language not only functions as medium of communication between individuals but also enables individuals to think independently. Several types of transfer to another structure (global isomorphism) are facilitated by language, even by only one symbol of language. The importance of this must not be undervalued.

In the above I have demonstrated that we can only understand structures by taking account of tree media: reality (World 1), human mind (World 2), and common human mind (World 3). There is also a fourth medium: language. There are interactions between the first three media in which language is not necessary. On the other hand, language can, with name giving and with its own structure, create innumerable new possibilities for the constitution of structures. It is important to mention that language is rather useful in describing visual structures. I draw your attention to the interaction between different media in later chapters.

I now discuss the fifth medium: action. Initially you might say that this medium has nothing to do with thinking and is therefore not necessary to our analysis. We first had to give a justification for placing the medium "reality" next to the structures of "mind," "common mind," and language. All those structures were linked with thinking. If we now consider the medium of action, we have a medium that has some independence from the other media.

We can recognize structure in the action especially when thinking is left out. Van Parreren (1951, pp. 49–54) expresses this in the following way: "when you leave your hand alone, doing things without your mind." Such structures of action occur in playing the piano, writing, manual labour, cycling. All these actions will be disturbed if you begin to think about your actions while doing them. When you are beginning to learn cycling, the first thing you have to do is keep on pedaling. The kinesthetic reactions to keep balance happen by themselves. If you begin to reflect on these reactions, you will never be able to cycle.

However, there are also structures of action that are formed rationally: for instance, simplifying expressions in algebra. If you have to do complicated things, the action is very often accompanied by thinking; sometimes, after having done such things many times, a structure of action will be formed.

There are many people who tell you that it is better to think before you act. Indeed, it is best not to set to work hurriedly. But, on the other hand, there are people who tell you that mental structures very often come into existence by action (Piaget, Montessori). This latter view is also important. I have seen teachers busy for an hour with a problem they expected to solve by thinking, whereas they might have solved it in only a few minutes by handling the material.

It seems that the structures of action are just as important for man as the structures of mind. Still, there is a great difference between those two media. Some animal psychologists speak of animals "thinking without words" because they do not give enough attention to the differences in media. Compared with the thinking of man, such a thinking is very poor, and it is rather confusing to speak of thinking in this case.

The question might be asked, is it really necessary to make use of the last two media: language and action? Are they not part of the first three media? The answer is that we cannot determine to which medium they belong. Language might be understood as a part of World 1: Many people can hear it in the same way. But language is also directly connected with the mind: Only by language do we know what someone else has thought. And language is certainly connected with World 3, for it is by language that World 3 is for the most part constituted. Just the same points can be made about action. Action also, though not as strongly, is associated with the first three media. Therefore, I prefer to retain the notions of language and action as media. If I did not, we would at many times have to ask: "Are we speaking of the right medium?"

8

Levels of Thinking

When I began my career as a teacher of mathematics, I very soon realized that it was a difficult profession. There were parts of the subject matter that I could explain and explain, and still the pupils would not understand. I could see that they really tried, but they did not succeed. Especially in the beginning of geometry, when very simple things had to be proved, I could see they did their utmost, but the subject matter seemed to be too difficult. But because I was an inexperienced teacher, I also had to consider the possibility that I was a poor teacher. And this last annoying possibility was affirmed by what came next: Suddenly it appeared that they understood the subject matter: They could talk of it very sensibly. But very often they said: "It isn't so difficult, but why did you explain it to us with so much difficulty?" In the years that followed I changed my explanation many times, but the difficulties remained. It always seemed as though I were speaking a different language. And by considering this idea I discovered the solution, the different levels of thinking.

I first introduced my discovery in the following way (van Hiele, 1955, p. 289):

> You can say somebody has attained a higher level of thinking when a new order of thinking enables him, with regard to certain operations, to apply these operations on new objects. The attainment of the new level cannot be effected by teaching, but still, by a suitable choice of exercises the teacher can create a situation for the pupil favorable to the attainment of the higher level of thinking.

You see my attempt to clear myself from not being able to give sufficient instruction; you also see the solution: a suitable choice of exercises. Indeed, it has turned out that by changing the text books all difficulties could be swept away. So my introduction of the levels was not only a statement, it was also a program. You see also the influence of Piaget: the old and the new levels were attached to operations. A new level of thinking could be attained by performing certain operations. Later, especially with the collaboration of J. de Miranda, I came to understand that a new language was involved. I elaborate this idea in a later chapter; here I restrict myself to the first acquaintance with the levels and continue with that original article.

> Further, you can say that the potential of the pupil has been much increased by the attainment of the higher level, and also that whereas subject matter can be easily forgotten, it is unlikely for a pupil to fall back to a lower level.
>
> Now we see why it is important to know which levels of thinking are necessary for which subject matter: Until a pupil has attained the needed level, the performing of his task is impossible. This line of thought has important consequences.
>
> In the first place, according to this idea it is very doubtful that one should choose a development in terms of logic as a directive for a geometry curriculum. The difficulties persist, even if the usual axioms are given up and replaced by a system of axioms simply consisting of all propositions the pupils regard as evident. Doing only this, no essential changes have been made: The reasonings that follow still use concepts like 'proof,' 'premise,' and 'conclusion,' and these certainly belong to a level the pupil has not yet attained.
>
> In the second place, it is evident that at this stage the teacher indeed has to realize the difficulties a pupil experiences when studying geometry, that he indeed has to make a careful choice of the subject matter; but on the other hand, he cannot preclude the crisis of thinking; he cannot avoid it, for by this crisis the transition to the higher level will be born.
>
> In the third place, it is obvious that the teacher has to take into account the heterogeneous composition of the class, even when he has had the advantage of an ideal selection method. A group of pupils, having started homogeneously, do not pass to the next level of thinking at the same time. At times, one-half of the class will speak a language the other half is unable to understand: This is unavoidable (van Hiele, 1955, pp. 289–290).

This was written by my wife and me some 30 years ago, and these views and our knowledge of this subject matter have since changed a little. At that time, it was very common to begin the teaching of geometry with axioms and definitions; you knew it was not really possible, but at least you had to try. To gild the pill, a propaedeutic curriculum was sometimes given as an introduction, but with a 6-week duration it could have no effect whatever. Nowadays in Holland it is possible to ignore the axioms and definitions for approximately 2 years: It is not quite in agreement with the curriculum established by the authorities, but they do not interfere, because of the much better results. But the evaluation of the results to be strived for have changed. We now know that an axiomatic approach to geometry is not the way to give pupils an opportunity to make use of geometry as fast as possible. But beyond this we can ask: for what part of the pupil population is logicist teaching of geometry useful? This is a question I did not have in 1955, but after having unsettled the logicist approach of geometry, it is easily understood that this question would follow.

I now continue the article of 1955. Tracing of levels of thinking that play a part in geometry is not a simple affair, for the levels are situated not in the subject matter but in the thinking of man. After continually ordering tasks, we at last came to the following result:

> A new level is attained when the pupil is able to apply operative properties of a well-known figure. [This level we now call *second level*] For instance, if a pupil knows that the diagonals of a rhombus are perpendicular, after having reached the first [second] level he must be able to conclude that if two circles have two points in common, the segment joining the points of intersection and the segment joining the centers of the circles intersect each other perpendicularly. It may be that he does not directly see the rhombus in the figure, but he should be able to finish after his attention has been drawn to this rhombus. On the other hand, the pupil not having attained this level does not see the importance of the knowledge of the figure containing a rhombus. If we denote a child not having attained the first [second] level as a child being in the first period, and a child having attained that level as being in the second period, it is clear that a child of the first period cannot understand any series of reasonings containing elements of the above-mentioned type. We see that it is not, as frequently thought, the number of links that is important, but the nature of the links (p. 290).

In the article of 1955, what was spoken of as the first level is now spoken of as the second level. So in the continuation of the article, what was spoken of a second level, we now speak of as a third level, and so on. The difference is caused by our not having seen the importance of the visual level (which is now called the first) at that time. Still, at that time there were people (like Joh. Wansink) telling me: "I think your levels of thought are very interesting; still I am anxious to know what is at level zero."

Nowadays the appreciation of the first level has improved. I give here a part of an article written by Kees van Baalen in *Euclides*, a Dutch periodical on the teaching of mathematics.

> The second level is, if I understand you correctly, that conceptions are pointed out by their mathematical names and are put in formal connections. Of the first level it is said: "direct visual things are concerned . . . like reality presents itself to the pupil, like the pupil talks about it." Afterward you emphasize the danger of the pupil parroting the teacher at the second level while still continuing to think at his own level without being able to make connections between the levels.
>
> So far I agree with you [Bram Lagerwerf and Van Hiele] and I appreciate your anxiety for education and pupils, but still I think the Van Hiele theory makes use of an unstated assumption, namely that, whereas natural numbers are ethically indifferent, still in giving the names *first level, second level,* and so on, there is really an estimation of value. That means that the second level is valued higher than the first level. Mention is also made of "the teacher descending to the level of the pupil" and of the help given the pupil to rise to the level of the teacher.

My opinion, against that of yours, is that the order of succession of values has to be reversed. In this sense the first level is the highest and the other levels are subordinate to it.

The first level is the level at which people (including the pupils) think in their daily life, with which they have their experiences, and with which they make their decisions. The other levels (in my eyes lower levels) are those in which, from a limited perspective, parts of the matter used at the first level are chosen to make models as an *aid* for thinking and deciding at the first level. (van Baalen, 1980/1981), p. 429)

Van Baalen is quite right when he supposes that in founding my theories in 1955 I had the idea that the higher the number of the level, the more it had to be valued. At that time it was for most teachers of mathematics an important task to make pupils understand abstract theories. So by having found the levels, we hoped to conquer the barricades. Now, since it has become clear that by taking account of levels of thinking it really is possible to make abstract theories understandable to many pupils, we have begun to question whether it is really worth reaching such high levels. So now there is no difference between Kees van Baalen's opinion on this matter and my own.

I continue my article of 1955 (pp. 290–295):

A second level [1981 notation: third level] is attained when a pupil is able to operate with known relations of figures known to him. That means that a pupil having attained this level is able to apply congruence of geometric figures to prove certain properties of a total geometric configuration of which congruent figures are a part. It means that also the pupil can deduce the equality of angles from the parallelism of lines.

The latter example requires an explanation, which at the same time should indicate how the [third] level has to be understood. It is quite possible to present a theorem in such a way that it logically relates to parallelism, whereas the pupil, for the comprehension of the theorem, need not have attained the [third] level, because the theorem has been formulated in such a way that in it parallelism is not seen as a needed relation between lines. There is, for instance, the theorem: In a quadrangle having two consecutive right angles, the two other angles together equal 180°. When it has not yet been proved that the sum of the angles of a quadrangle equal 360°, you may think the use of parallelism is inevitable. You might expect the following reasoning: If in a quadrangle two consecutive angles are right angles, two sides of the quadrangle are parallel, for we have defined the parallelism of two lines by the existence of a third line being perpendicular to both of them. The other two angles are interior angles on the same side of the transversal, so they have a sum of 180° degrees. But if a pupil is only at the [second] level, he can help himself out of the distress by considering the figure as a totality. He sees a trapezoid with two right angles and he has learned the other angles have a sum of 180°.

In a similar way the pupil can be helped by the introduction of structures: Alternate interior angles are recognized as part of a Z-form, interior angles on the same side of the intersecting line are recognized as part of a U-form, and corresponding angles are recognized as part of a F-form. In this way the relation between angles and lines is reduced to the properties of one single figure, e.g., the Z, the U, or the F. Such didactic expedients can be used when certain logical results have to be attained and the pupil is still on the [second] level. Perhaps they may be a stimulus to attain the [third] level. But in fact a pupil using this expedient who is not yet at the [third] level has not progressed by using it. Moreover, this method can turn out to be harmful if the teacher, in his zeal for quick results, has these structures *learned* by the pupils. For by doing so he weakens the necessity for the pupil to come to a higher order of thinking, he avoids the crisis of thinking.

Still there are teachers who never or scarcely ever meet the above-mentioned difficulties. How can we account for this? There are two methods to solve these problems in such a way that, at least in the first year, you will never meet them. The first method is to explain theorems at school and afterward have them learned by heart at home. You can also demand that the pupils be able to give proofs with the figures in different positions than they have seen at school. The pupil not yet at the required level can help himself by simply learning by heart the order of the steps in the proof. It is very difficult to determine if the pupil understands the proof, for he knows exactly which properties of the geometric figures he must use. If he is not at the [third] level, he does not know why he has to use them, but he is not asked why. And he also knows what relations he must use. If he has not attained the level, he does not know why, but he is not asked why. The teacher, after proposing a new problem, will state that the pupil has a lack of ingenuity; he is not aware that the pupil is not at the level at which he would be able to make use of such ingenuity.

The second method is that the teacher changes the subject matter to such a form that the thinking activities needed by the pupil remain limited to a lower level. The self-deceit on the part of the teacher by acting so is much smaller than with the first method; now the teacher knows he will have to continue remodeling the subject matter at a lower level for his pupils; he knows that for the time being he will have to expect little ingenuity.

It is clear that the above-mentioned methods are not real solutions to the problem: The crisis of thinking is avoided by them and this is exactly what is necessary for the development of thinking of the pupil. But on the other hand, in our education, where everything is ruled by schedules, there is little time for a thinking crisis. The pupil asks the teacher for an explanation; this is a reduction to a lower level, and the teacher, happy to be able to keep the lesson going, readily gives it.

If we closely examine the various theorems coming up for discussion in the beginning of geometry, many difficulties met with by the pupils can easily be explained. Even if we do not know if a certain theorem needs the attainment of the [third] level or not, the explanation remains in force.

Theorem: The bisectors of the base angles of an isosceles triangle enclose, with the base, a new isosceles triangle. To be able to prove this theorem you have to know that in an isosceles triangle the base angles are equal; therefore, in the new triangle the base angles are also equal. If in a triangle two angles are equal, then the triangle is isosceles. Usually the pupils cannot perform such reasoning. The theorem is usually presented very early therefore (1) because they have not yet attained the [second] level, they are not able to operate with the properties of a geometric figure; (2) because they have not attained the [third] level, they are not able to operate with very easy relations like the equality of angles; (3) because they have to operate with two theorems, one being the converse the other—'isosceles triangle → equality of angles' and 'equality of angles → isosceles triangle'—there may be an interference that can only be eliminated after a still higher level than the [third] has been attained. You see that the uncertainty about the nature of the difficulty hinders us from predicting at what time the difficulties will be over, but we are certain that the moment at which the problem is given is misplaced.

Theorem: When two lines intersect, vertical angles are equal. The difficulties presenting themselves with the proof of this theorem are attributed now to the self-evidence of the theorem, now to the asymmetric presentation of a common adjacent angle. Still, it turned out that the results are much better if the problem is given at a later date, when the majority of the pupils have passed to the [third] level. There is no doubt that the results would be much more improved if the problem was postponed.

When pupils have become acquainted with the theorem about congruence of triangles, they generally are unable to apply this knowledge in order to prove the equality of elements in a given geometric figure. If we wait a year or so, it appears that the same pupils have no further difficulties with such proofs, even if the congruence has not been repeated. After attaining the [third] level of thinking, the operation with relations has become possible for them.

It is very tempting to generalize the theorem and to extend the [third] level to algebraic operations and perhaps other relations. Without a closer inquiry this is not permitted: We found the above-mentioned two levels [second and third] by ordering the subject matter of *geometry*; in this research algebra was not included. There is a possibility of levels of thinking in algebra. It may seem that in primary school pupils have learned to operate with relations between arithmetic quantities, but it is a question whether this learning has been successful, and if not, perhaps the pupils have been helped by a level reduction introduced by the teacher. Such speculations I do not wish to engage in now. [The levels of arithmetic will be dealt with in another chapter.]

There remains the important question of how the necessary crisis of thinking can be initiated and how the pupil can be induced not to avoid it, but on the contrary to surmount it. Education is not now geared to such a working method; everybody expects the teacher to do his duty in such a case, that is, to give an explanation, or in other words to apply reduction of level. The obligation to have finished a task that can be done by every pupil who is not too dull is in complete contradiction with the demand that a pupil has to be induced with appropriate subject matter to a thinking crisis at the right moment and with the recognition that the duration of this crisis cannot be legislated. The obligation to have the homework finished forces the teacher to have the pupils work continually at the same level, or if this is impossible, to have the pupils present the results of other pupils.

The above reasoning might lead to very negative conclusions about education. In practice, however, we see that thanks to education nearly all pupils attain the two levels [second and third] sooner or later. This is not the case with the higher levels. A [fourth] level must be connected with the possibility of comparing, transposing, and operating with relations. This level is necessary for operation without help with extensions of theorems, with indirect proofs, etc. One of the simplest proofs at that level is of the theorem having the premise, the medians of a triangle intersect in the proportion 2 : 1, and the conclusion, the three medians of a triangle have one point in common. In practice we find that many pupils never attain this level. Still, there is a great possibility to obtaining a good grade on the final examination without ever having attained this level. I have no scruples about this, but it shows that the final examination gives no reliable prognosis for a continued study of exact sciences, because for pupils going to the university, this higher level is indeed needed.

Since 1955 our point of view has changed. In 1955 we were sorry for the pupils if they could not understand us; we went on with our expositions, the pupils were very unhappy, but fortunately their unhappiness came to an end:

After having attained the level, all misery was over. Now we know teaching can be much better. Now in the textbooks the subject matter is repeated many times, and each time it is dealt with from the very beginning. The more difficult it is to attain the level, the more times the subject matter comes up for discussion. Now there is no more real compulsion to attain the level; if the pupil attains the level, he profits from it, for his task is much easier; but if not, he is not placed in an awkward position. This method of working is called "telescoped reteaching."

In 1955 we were convinced of the necessity of the higher levels to do exact sciences. This may be true for mathematics, although in some practical parts of this topic the higher levels are not so important. But in physics and chemistry, the higher levels of mathematics are not indispensable, unless somebody is studying the foundations of those sciences. However, in 1955 leading people were convinced of the formal value of mathematics: Learning mathematics meant learning to think, and to be able to think precisely you should have attained the highest possible level.

I continue the article of 1955 (pp. 295–297):

> The [fourth] level enables us to clarify how education can stimulate the attainment of a level. Among the pupils I have seen attaining the [fourth] level of late were a number who had changed from the classical section of the school to the modern section because of difficulties with classical languages. Let me say it better: Among these pupils there is a much higher percentage having attained the [fourth] level than among the other pupils. One would be inclined to conclude from this that a classical education surpasses the other—though it be a prematurely interrupted classical education—if not for some other striking examples that point in another direction. Another case is that of a girl who, having failed in the third form of a high school, afterward completed a program at a horticultural college and then, after a supplementary curriculum of a few months, attained the highest form of a modern college. This girl had clearly attained the [fourth] level. Other remarkable cases were found with pupils who, having had one or two years of secondary education and were later found in a [Japanese concentration camp], finally achieved, in one or two years in the Netherlands, their classical education. They also in general had no difficulties with the [fourth] level. It is not easy to accept that a horticultural college or a Jap-camp could give such excellent training of the mind. Much more acceptable is it to conclude that the girl at the horticultural college and the pupils who came from Indonesia realized that they basically had to succeed by their own energy; they were in the best condition to overcome a crisis of thinking.

> A teacher, beginning the teaching of geometry, should address himself to the pupils in a language they understand, he must not use the language of the [second] level, because the pupils have not yet attained that level. By doing so he inspires their confidence; the pupils will try to understand him. After some time he must speak to them about subject matter requiring the [second] level. If he realizes the need to postpone this moment for some time, not only will the pupils try to understand him, but they also will succeed. The crisis is overcome by the desire to keep up to date with the syllabus for the class and by the knowledge that in the beginning the pupils also succeeded in understanding the teacher. So it also goes on with the [third] level. But with the [fourth] level there are more difficulties. In the first place, the timing of the subject matter connected with the [fourth] level is most inconvenient, since it is just at the moment when the child has

to solve many other problems of life and consequently has little time for a thinking crisis in the domain of mathematics. But in the second place, most teachers do not have the courage to present the subject matter at a higher level. Instead they try to compromise: They indeed give the required subject matter, but reduced to the [third] level. We will give an example to see the consequences of this.

Pupils are asked to prove that the three bisectors of the angles of a triangle have one point in common. A pupil at the [fourth] level of thinking can give a proof as follows:

The statement: "a point equidistant to the sides *a* and *b* of triangle *ABC*" is equivalent to the statement "the point is situated on the bisector of the angle *C*."

Since this statement is sufficient and necessary, it follows that the intersection of the bisectors of the angles *B* and *C* is equidistant to the sides *a, b,* and *c*. (So now we are sure of the existence of a point inside a triangle equidistant to the three sides.) This intersection point is called *I*.

Since *I* is equidistant to the sides *b* and *c*, it follows that *I* is necessarily situated on the bisector of angle *A*.

I was defined as the intersection point of the bisectors of the angles *B* and *C*. So the three bisectors have a point *I* in common.

In the reduced form the proof can be given as follows:

A point is chosen on a bisector of an angle. With the help of congruence of triangles it can be proved that the distances of this point to the meeting lines are equal. Now draw an arbitrary triangle *ABC*. Look at the intersection of the bisectors of the angles *B* and *C*. Prove that this point is equidistant to the three sides of the triangle.

Now call the intersection point of the bisectors *I*. We have already seen that the distances of this point to the sides *AB* and *AC* are equal. Now prove with the help of congruence that *AI* bisects the angle *A*. *AI, BI,* and *CI,* being the bisectors of the angles of a triangle, we now know all have one point in common.

Mathematically the second proof does not differ from the first. But the language of the second proof is much easier for a pupil than that of the first. In the first proof, you will have to exert yourself more in order to get to the bottom of it. In the second proof, every step can be easily traced. Perhaps the pupil will make a mistake when proving the last congruence because he is distracted by the first congruence apparently being the same. But even if everything proceeded without difficulty, he, at the end, will be astonished that the proof is now finished: He has carried out the steps without understanding their meaning, the whole remained mysterious to him, the proof is a mousetrap.

A teacher who has to explain a proof of the first kind must take care not to make of it a proof of the second kind. His explanation must be focused on the points 'necessary and sufficient,' on the fact that in the first part of the proof the existence of a point equidistant to all three sides has been proved. On the other hand, the existence of such a point guarantees that all bisectors of the angles of the triangle go through it. The teacher will be happy if the pupils are able to reproduce the proof spontaneously; he will be much happier if they are able to give a similar proof in a similar situation. For a conscientious teacher, reproduction of a previous learning is worthless. And he is very afraid of the result of extra lessons outside the school where the pupil is given explanations of the subject matter with the help of a substitute approach at the lower level.

The above example sufficiently shows what must be taken care of in the first form. If the time has come to introduce congruence, we will have to do it; but then it has to really be congruence, that is, a relation between triangles (or other things). We must not try to reduce the matter to a lower level by a clever technique of writing it down with dashes and braces. If we cannot do without resorting to a lower level, we must not hesitate to postpone the matter until a more favorable moment.

To summarize: It is not certain whether all normal pupils will be able to attain [Level 3] in the lowest form. If not, we commit a great injustice by selecting the pupils at the end of the year by making use of norms that include the attainment of the [third] level. It is important not to lose sight of this, otherwise we might declare pupils unfit at the beginning of the summer holidays when at the end of the holidays the same pupils are indeed fit. But then the selection has already taken place.

This was the end of our first article about levels of thinking. You see that we did not try to describe levels higher than the fourth. Those higher levels are much more difficult to discern than Levels 2, 3, and 4. Moreover, it has turned out that such levels are easily too highly valued. And what are we going to do with such levels. In school we have to deal with Levels 2, 3, and 4. If our pupils do not understand us, it is at these levels, not when we are speaking on the fifth or perhaps still higher levels. Some people are now testing students to see if they have attained the fifth or higher levels. I think this is only of theoretical value. I think that for years and years very bad instruction has been given in mathematics. But that was because of neglect of Levels 2, 3, and 4—on the fifth and higher levels the mischief has already done its work. So I am unhappy if, on the ground of my levels of thinking, investigations are made to establish the existence of fifth and higher levels. This is a method to realize one's theoretical lusts, but I would much prefer that a beginning be made on the improvement of education with the aid of the levels of thinking.

9

The Consequences and a More Exact Analysis of the Theory of Levels of Thinking

The most distinctive property of the levels of thinking is their discontinuity, the lack of coherence between their networks of relations. For the last expression we might also use the phrase "their structures." In order to demonstrate the existence of levels of thinking we have to determine whether the discontinuities between the base and second levels and between the second and third levels really exist.

The transition from the base level to the second level is one from a level without a network of relations to a level that has such a network. It is true that at the base level there is a language, but the use of this language is limited to the indication of configurations that have been made clear by observation. At the first level you can say: "This is a rhombus."

It is an important phenomenon that without further explanation (how would such an explanation be possible!) another person can say: "And this also is one." But let us not mistakenly presume such phenomena are restricted to geometry. This is the kind of phenomena all human communication is built on. You show your baby a little hairy beast and you say: "This is a dog." Afterward the child sees a big Alsatian and he says: "Dog." Analysis of the phenomenon 'dog' in terms of characteristics is not relevant here. This is an application of one of the laws of *Gestalt* psychology: A class of notions can be recognized by only one significant specimen.

This phenomenon underlies a great part of human knowledge, and in the chapters on structure I have given many examples of it. It is one of the important principles of *Gestalt* (structured) psychology, but it seems to have been forgotten. When Skemp (1971) considers this phenomenon he speaks of abstraction and supposes that a child makes distinctions between various properties and thereby decides the application of names. This is an important issue: It is relevant to the origin of human thinking.

By exactly observing the fundamentals of human knowledge in many cases, even when advanced mathematics is concerned, we see this phenomenon. When there are differences of opinion at the base level there can follow an analysis leading to the second level: "This is not a rhombus, for the four sides are not equal"; "neither is this one, for it is a square."

Reasoning between the first and second levels can lead to results different from reasoning at a higher level. Before attaining the third level, one would maintain the proposition: "If a quadrangle is a square, it cannot be a rhombus." Afterward this opinion changes: "If a quadrangle is a square, it is a rhombus, for a square is a rhombus with some extra properties." It would be a great misconception to here conclude that this child has matured to the third level, and so has come to a better conclusion. The conclusion "Every square is a rhombus" is not a result of maturation, it is the result of a learning process. An intelligent person need not conclude that every square is a rhombus; this is only submission to a traditional choice. In some Greek philosophies, a square could not be a rhombus, for it had some properties a rhombus could not have. Even now there are people arguing that a parallelogram is not a trapezoid because a trapezoid can have only one pair of parallel sides. If it were natural to conclude that every square is a rhombus, it would be likewise natural to conclude that every parallelogram is a trapezoid.

The transition from one level to the following is not a natural process; it takes place under influence of a teaching–learning program. The transition is not possible without the learning of a new language. People of the first period reason rightly if they deny that a square is a rhombus. They are guided by a visual network of relations; their intuition shows them the way. Only if the usual network of relations of the third level has been accepted does the square have to be understood as belonging to the set of rhombuses. This acceptance must be voluntary; it is not possible to force a network of relations on someone. If you want to convince them, you can point out the difficulty of producing general statements about rhombuses that preclude squares. But if the pupils do not yield to this argument, there is little to be done.

Reasonings of the third level deal with the structure of the second level. Conclusions are no longer based on the existence or nonexistence of links in the network of relations of the second level, but on the connection that is supposed to exist between those links. This leads to a discontinuity of a quite different character from that existing between the base and second levels, but one no less real or far reaching. People who use a poorly developed network of second-level relations, or who use this network rather automatically, will have little view on the inner structure of this network and therefore will not be able to have third-level judgment. When two people differ on a question at the third level, they can only come to an agreement when they begin to construct a language in which they can express themselves about the structure of the network of relations of the second level. But such a language is just the language of the third level of thinking. About this network of relations they will have to agree, and afterward the point of difference can be resolved.

The question, for example, of whether the number 1 belongs to the set of prime numbers can be resolved in this way. Some reference books indicate that the first prime number is 1; others, that the first prime number is 2. It is easy to put an end to this difference by creating a definition. If you define *prime number* as any natural number that has exactly two divisors, then 2 is a prime number, for it has the divisors 1 and 2, and 1 is not a prime number for it has only the divisor 1. But such a definition is no real solution to the problem. By choosing a definition you can solve every quarrel as you wish. But other arguments are available. There is, for instance, the theorem that every natural number can only be written in one way as a product of powers of prime numbers. Then you will have to exclude 1, for 2 can be written as 2, but also as 2×1^3 and so on. But of course the opponent can start with quite another structure of the network of relations. After the explicitation of this structure there may be an agreement, but sometimes such agreement will not be reached because both parties have different interests.

The difference between the objects of the second and the third levels can also be demonstrated by different ways of writing. At the second level, calculation deals with relations between concrete numbers: $4 \times 3 = 12, 6 + 8 = 14$. At the third level of thinking it deals with generalization of results: $a \times (b + c) = (a \times b) + (a \times c)$. In these generalizations you do not return to the original objects of the second level, namely the concrete numbers.

The ways of thinking of the base level, the second level, and the third level have a hierarchic arrangement. Thinking at the second level is not possible without that of the base level; thinking at the third level is not possible without thinking at the second level. You may ask if it is possible to continue; if there exists thinking at a fourth, a fifth, or perhaps a still higher level. There are many circumstances seducing us to postulate such a build-up. Later I mention a number of them. But very obvious is the following reasoning: Different sciences like mathematics, physics, chemistry, biology, history, and linguistics have third levels each constructed in a different way. Perhaps it is just by this difference that we speak of different sciences. Well then, would it not be possible to construct a fourth level of thinking by the comparison of the different structures of the third levels? Would not this level just be the level of philosophy?

From the previous discussion you can conclude that a higher level is derived from the lower level by taking account of a certain point of view. You can call this second, higher level "descriptive," for at this new level the relations and elements are described. The descriptive level of algebra differs from that of geometry, for in algebra the attention is called to number, whereas in geometry, shape is prominent. But the third level (the theoretical level) of algebra is the same as that of geometry; in both cases deductive coherence is prominent. If we were to add to the descriptive level of geometry a theoretical level on a physical base, it would be quite different from the mathematical third level. When we want to demonstrate physically that the Pythagorean theorem is true, we have to draw a certain number of right triangles, measure their sides, and show that the square of the hypotenuse equals the sum of the squares of the other two sides each time. It is inconceivable that such a working method would be accepted in mathematics.

It is not necessarily the case that a comparison of the theoretical levels of different sciences leads to philosophy. It may be that another science will be developed only when another context for the comparison is chosen. And it is not necessary that such an analysis lead to a higher level of thinking, for sometimes different structures can be coordinated into one new structure, so that each of the original structures can be understood as parts of it.

That there are fewer levels than are sometimes supposed can be explained with *coordinated structures*. The following are simple examples:

1. We know that most quadratic equations have two roots, and that between those roots there are some relations. It is much easier to understand those relations if we know the relations existing between the roots of equations of a higher degree. But the study of such relations does not force us to think at a higher level: The new structure we use is a coordinated structure of the structure we at first studied.

2. It is possible to generate analytic geometry in the traditional way, starting with the two or more coordinates of a point. It is also possible to choose a modern method, using vectors. By doing so we may seem to attain a higher level: for now we have freed ourselves from the system of coordinates and the limitations of its dimension of space. Still, a higher level has not been attained; there is only a coordinated structure, which becomes clear with the possibility of understanding the old analytic geometry as a part of the new.

Sometimes in education such a coordinated structure can present itself in such a way that it appears to relate to a heightening of level. The learning process ceases to work, explanation seems to be impossible, again it appears as if we were working with two different languages. We can understand this, for the structure, very limited at the beginning, suddenly has a much greater extension. Still, the situation differs substantially from the heightening of level. An analysis shows there are not really two different networks of relations. And explanations are not necessarily refused. The pupil's inability stems from not seeing the links existing between the networks of relations. But the teacher can show the way around the obstacle by showing the relation between the new domain of study and the old. A good method is to show the original structure and the coordinated structure side by side and to note the similarities.

Another circumstance causing us to lose sight of the real relation between levels is *level-reduction*. It is possible to transform structures of the theoretical level with the help of a system of signs, by which they become visible. So algebra gives a transformation of structures of the theoretical level of arithmetic and formal logic gives a transformation of the theoretical level of algebra. If such a system of signs is used and if an evaluation has to be made, the second level would seem to be indicated. But for the interpretation of the results obtained by such a system of signs, thinking at the third level is often necessary. That is, if you have to judge the correctness of the results, a return to the higher level is necessary. A well-fashioned network of relations of the third level functions on itself as a primitive system of signs. Because judgment is more and more based on the network of relations, a continued study very often automatically results in a reduction of the level. In algebra and logic a new third level can be built on such reduced levels. When meeting such constructions, you can get the impression of a fourth or even a fifth level.

Perhaps you may think the reduction of the levels is of no importance. When a third level has been reduced to a second, and on this reduced second level there is built a new level, should we not say that four different levels exist, with the numbers one to four? In this way, in mathematics you could discern five levels, namely:

First level: the visual level
Second level: the descriptive level
*Third level:*the theoretical level; with logical relations, geometry generated
                 according to Euclid
Fourth level: formal logic; a study of the laws of logic
Fifth level: the nature of logical laws

The above classification is suitable to a structure of mathematics and perhaps mathematicians will be able to work with it. However, our aim was the improvement of thinking and, in view of that purpose, we characterize levels in a different manner.

There is another circumstance that gives us the impression that there are more than four levels of thinking. This is the course of the learning process by stages. In the learning process leading to a higher level you can discern five stages.

1. In the first stage, that of *information,* pupils get acquainted with the working domain.
2. In the second stage, that of *guided orientation,* they are guided by tasks

(given by the teacher, or made by themselves) with different relations of the network that has to be formed.

3. In the third stage, that of *explicitation,* they become conscious of the relations, they try to express them in words, they learn the technical language accompanying the subject matter.
4. In the fourth stage, that of *free orientation,* they learn by general tasks to find their own way in the network of relations.
5. In the fifth stage, that of *integration,* they build an overview of all they have learned of the subject, of the newly formed network of relations now at their disposal.

For example, consider the stages in the study of the rhombus.

1. First stage: A certain figure is demonstrated, it is called "rhombus." The pupils are shown other geometrical figures and are asked if they also are rhombuses.
2. Second stage: The rhombus is folded on its axes of symmetry. Something is noticed about the diagonals and the angles.
3. Third stage: The pupils exchange their ideas about the properties of a rhombus.
4. Fourth stage: Some vertices and sides of a rhombus are given by position. The whole rhombus has to be constructed.
5. Fifth stage: The properties of a rhombus are summed up and memorized.

This demonstrates the old-fashioned way of developing material. In the center of our attention we have placed the rhombus, a geometrical figure of some importance. But it would have been much better if we had centered our attention on a fundamental transformation, like 'reflection.' Then we would have the following first stage: a paper is folded, or one looks in a mirror. In Figure 9.1 it can be seen that point B is the reflection of point A on a given line l. On square grid paper one can see how the reflected point can be drawn when the original point is given. In the second stage pupils are given many geometrical figures and are asked to find their reflections in a given line. They can be asked to do it on square grid paper, but alternate approaches with mirrors or folded paper are available. It may be that the given figure and the reflected figure together form a rhombus. We can also reflect twice on two different perpendicular lines: The result is also a rhombus (Figure 9.2).

In the third stage the various ways of recognizing geometrical figures as reflections of each other can be discussed in class. In this way the language necessary for expression of the relations that have been seen is learned.

In the fourth stage, exercises are given on geometrical figures with axes of symmetry. Three of the vertices of an isosceles trapezoid are given and the pupil is asked to find the fourth. There are many ways to solve the problem; it is

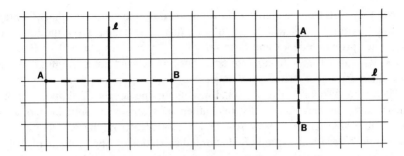

Figure 9.1

therefore an example of free orientation. In the fifth stage, the pupil is asked how symmetry in a line can be recognized. The characteristics of some geometrical figures having an axis of symmetry are summarized.

These five stages are of great importance for general didactics (general education). But that is not my subject in this chapter. In general didactics we should ask how a pupil can be supported in the five stages. In this chapter, I can deal neither with the fact that stages can coincide partially or totally, nor with the fact that a part of the stages leading from Level 1 to Level 2 coincide with a part of the stages leading from Level 2 to Level 3. This is all important for our guidance of the pupil, but I postpone this matter until later.

Of importance now is that pupils who have passed the third stage, and who are therefore acquainted with different relations of the new network, can base judgments on this network. They do not know how to find their way in the overwhelming quantity of facts, but they do know what they are about. They can follow a train of thought and reproduce it, but they cannot themselves set it up. In some cases the judgment will have to be intuitive, will have to belong to the lower level. This altered attitude, halfway through the learning-process, gives the impression of an interlinking extra level.

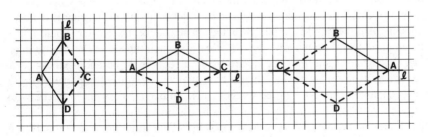

Figure 9.2

You may well have recognized the situation described above as Piaget's Stage II. But Piaget says that with most children this stage begins about the time they first enter primary school and lasts for about 2 years. So Stage II of Piaget is linked with age. It may be approximate, but it is age and not a learning process. This difference is of great importance.

There are frequent misunderstandings about the levels of thinking. Some people suppose they exist only in mathematics and even only in geometry. Others think the levels only borrow their importance from the part they play in education. After I had written my doctoral dissertation, "The Problem of Insight in Connection with School Children's Insight into the Subject Matter of Geometry," in 1957, a friend of mine, a university professor of algebra, wrote me that he was sorry—he had not encountered the problems I had discussed. I was really astonished, but afterward I heard the same thing many times from university professors: "In the university there are never problems with education and explanation. Such problems are impossible because in most universities it is supposed that teaching at a university need not to be learned. So, if there are some difficulties, it is always presumed to be the fault of the students."

Of course there are many advantages in using the levels of thinking when teaching some topic, for with the help of this theory you can find out where to begin with the topic you intend to teach. But also for your own knowledge of the topic the theory is important; you know there is a well-founded base to begin with—the visual-base level; you know the difficulties begin at the second level, for description depends on the context you have chosen; and you are aware of the instability of the following levels, for you have attained them by trying to understand the structure of the preceding levels in the way your teachers wanted you to. And if there were difficulties, have you, in your education, had the opportunity to fill the gaps? How many times in our teaching are we uncertain, do we have to explain things we ourselves have never understood clearly? The theory of levels can help us through: We know the trustworthiness of the third and higher levels is not certain; it is no longer necessary to hide our uncertainty from our pupils. On the contrary, we begin with it and perhaps by a good discussion with the class we will find better solutions.

Improvement of education is blocked by indoctrination (the teacher is to be all-knowing and the pupil is to be instructed). The task of the teacher should not be the impartation of knowledge. On the contrary, each time a teacher has to make ideas clear he or she must be aware of the necessity of defending these ideas again and again. The teacher should treat pupils as dignified opponents, opponents capable of introducing new arguments. To be able to bring in the network of relations of the second level, first a discussion on the structure of the visual level must be started. Afterward a discussion on the structure of the second level must be started, and again the pupils must be able to bring in their objections. In the fifth stage of the learning process, integration, the structure of the second level is described in words. This is a form of objectification and automatically leads to a reduction of the level. Shortly after the third level has been attained, material is presented to reduce it to a new second level.

This is the right way for a level-reduction to be brought about: The pupils have seen the structure of the third level, they have discussed it, they have themselves put the relations of the structure into words. When now they come to level-reduction by applying rules, they have made their own contributions to the reduction. If necessary, they can find their way back to the deserted third level.

To judge if logical laws have been correctly applied, one has to start from a generally accepted network of relations in which logical laws are implicitly present. Afterward, different persons must observe these logical laws of the network of relations in the same way. If this appears to be possible and if the descriptions afterward are in sufficient agreement, it seems probable that the words expressing the logical laws have the same meaning to all participants of the dialogue. Only then can an application of these laws on new cases be possible.

The above-mentioned working method is not usual in mathematics, nor in other sciences. It is customary to illustrate newly introduced technical language with a few examples, but these examples for the most part are too poor in structure to capture the point of the technical language. The error that is made is the supposition that the technical language itself is able to express our meaning; in reality the technical language only gets its meaning through the examples. If the examples are deficient, the technical language will be deficient too. With such poor language, all reasoning will be replaced by information *giving* in order to clarify what is being presented; instead, reasoning should *yield* information that follows from the given data: With such poor language, it is easy to come to an uncritical acceptance of assertions and systems. Too great a confidence about mathematical solving of problems is promoted by it. For by this method, one learns to give attention to the laws of systems of signs and not to their signification. The deductive presentation of subject matter generally neglects the importance of the third stage, the stage of explicitation. Research on the foundations of knowledge is highly obstructed by this circumstance.

10

A Psychological Approach
to Levels of Thinking

INTRODUCTION

In the preceding chapters I have discussed levels of thinking that are important
to the teaching of mathematics. My introduction to the levels was purely empirical; I noticed them because my students' learning processes got stuck at the
same places every year. Apparently the levels of thinking correspond with
plateaus of a very special character in the learning curve.

In this chapter I give a psychological explanation of the levels.

CONTEXT

To understand clearly a new subject, its context must be totally clear. In
geometry, for example, we first must establish that this subject concerns the
study of space. With this statement the context of geometry is by no means fixed;
the study of geometry, for instance, has very little to do with the way space is
experienced. Spatial conceptions like 'narrow', 'far', and 'ridgy' do not appear
in elementary geometry. We have a correct approach to geometry when we begin
to look at things geometrically, when we raise typical geometrical relations in
discussion. Still, what is 'geometrical'? Only after a phenomenal analysis can we
clarify the conditions under which a relation is typically geometrical. Only after
this can we know the contents of geometry, can we know when a context is
geometrical.

The lack of a clear exposition of the context of a given subject is nowadays one of the greatest shortages in teaching. An exposition of the context at the beginning of a study is seldom given. Sometimes there is an attempt to inform the pupils of the context by explanation, but this is useless: the pupils should learn by doing, not be informed by explanation.

It is easy to understand, however, why in geometry the exposition of the context is usually omitted. If we see geometry as a science, we have no concern for space, nor for geometric figures in space, but only for the relations between properties of those figures. At a high level of scientifically geometrical thinking, there is no thinking about spatial figures; the character of the relations between the properties of those figures is the only object of study. Therefore the context of a scientific study of geometry totally differs from the context at the introduction of the subject. The teacher feels a strong impulse to aim his instruction at the real objects of his topic, the relations between the properties of geometrical figures, and he is therefore inclined to speak to the pupils in a language based on a context that cannot exist for them. The objects of the context the teacher uses have no meaning for the children, and the teacher cannot give those objects sense by means of information.

But teachers themselves meet with a similar situation with didactics. For the teachers the real objects of didactics, the situations of learning and teaching, are also inaccessible as long as those objects have not been given a real content by means of a phenomenal analysis of the learning processes. Only after such an analysis has taken place is it possible to start with the real context.

SYMBOLS

The context of the visual level of a topic can become clear by an analysis of a representative subject of the topic. With such an analysis, symbols soon come into existence. With the conception of 'symbol' I think of the following passage from Meyerson:

> James, the Württemberg [group], Binet have observed in the course of their analyses that image sometimes has a tendency, a signification; that it can obtain the value of a sign, a symbol. What they did not sufficiently see is that it always has such a character. And they have not realized it because they have not clearly seen in general the symbolic nature of thought. By looking for a pure signification they have thrown the image out of thought, stripping it of all intellectual contents. By purifying thought, looking for unexpressed and unexpressable aspects, they withdrew from the concrete forms with which ideas and signs are constructed by us till they can be called things, and with fragments of those things, other things, and other ideas. This would led to the paradox of a pan-logicism, which, however, would leave out of the intellectual life facts which are inseparable from the course of intellectual operations.
>
> Is thought interwoven with images the most habitual form of thought? Is it the most adaptable form of the working of the mind? It seems not. It seems that beginning from a certain level, from a certain height, from a certain degree of generalization, thought needs less concrete signs, more detached from things, less adherent, more transparent, more flexible, more arbitrary and gratuitous, more conventional, less subjective, more

socialized, more logical. In such a way the image is left for the word, the word for a mathematical symbol; there are even physical laws that cannot be expressed by a verbal definition and undoubtedly there will be still more and more of them. (Meyerson, 1932, p. 582)

Many symbols begin their existence with an image in which the observed properties and relations are temporarily projected. However, after the explication of those properties and relations by an analysis or discussion, the symbol loses the character of image, acquires a verbal content, and thus becomes more useful for operations of thinking. By comparison of the symbols in the given context and the discovery of relations between them, their contents are enriched, their appearance is continuously differentiated.

Symbols are closely related to context. A symbol can belong to various contexts, and in general it will have a different content in each context. This may lead to mistakes: Sometimes properties are attributed to a symbol that are not applicable in the context involved. Often one is not conscious of the equivalence of symbols, but the same name can still point out the common origin. The relation is reciprocal: It is just as accurate to say that the symbols define the context as the reverse.

Duncker (1935) speaks of figure-to-ground relations in a perceptual field. It is possible to look at such a field in the context of ''red.'' Everything ''red'' jumps to the front and many objects are observed that were not seen before. Alternatively, paying attention to ''round'' totally alters the structure of space. A ball will be observed in the latter structure but not in the former, unless the ball happens to be red. In a similar way symbols appear in different contexts.

Before studying a phenomenon it is wise first to determine by analysis in what context the phenomenon appears as a symbol. I will call such an analysis a *phenomenal analysis,* but this has little to do with Husserl's phenomenology. It is clearly not sensible to expect maximum success in finding a ball by evoking the context 'red'. No more can you count on gaining the conception of 'insight' by evoking the context of 'testing', for we do not know if in that context 'insight' is an important symbol. And there is no more reason to expect to find the most suitable sequence of material for teaching about geometrical figures by evoking the context 'logical deductive system'!

The first aim in developing the didactics of a certain topic is the formation of symbols belonging to the context of the topic involved. Afterward, those symbols will have to be developed into the junctions of a network of relations that determines the second level of the topic.

SIGNALS

In the long run, symbols will determine a direction of thinking in a topic; after that, it will be possible to establish an *orientation in the topic.* We express this as follows: as soon as symbols influence an orientation in thinking, *the symbols act as signals*. Such a signalizing activity does not exist at the very beginning, not at the moment the symbols are formed. In the beginning, the symbol only acts as a totality of properties. The symbol becomes more and more filled with properties, but at the beginning those properties do not automatically anticipate the symbol; there is no automatic completion of the complex.

The symbols obtain their character as signals by a learning process, but in many cases this is incidental. Still, formation of the signals can be aided by teaching. In particular, this can happen if the intention of the pupils is directed at the orientation. The pupils must be conscious of the orientation; it must be an explicit goal in their study.

The expressions *anticipate* and *completion of the complex* are borrowed from the theories of Selz. This may prompt misunderstandings. For Selz (1913, p. 495) these expressions were strongly connected with posing of a problem and methods of solution. In our case, in which the point is the learning of an orientation in a certain field of thinking, no real problem is posed or solved. In our situation the pupil, at least, does not have the sense of being busy with a problem; he or she is fully busy with an exploration: The field of exploration has not yet presented problems.

Symbols are compared and, in the end, recognized by their properties. The appearance of problems is actually the indication that the pupil is about to leave the first level of thinking, and that the relations between the original objects of his thinking are about to become the new objects of study.

The ability of the pupil to orient himself in the field of study causes a change of character of the study. The addition of properties to symbols and of symbols to properties happens more automatically, the need to consult images occurs less often, and the junctions of the network of relations lose a part of their contents by transfering them to the connections between the symbols.

At the end of this learning process, the second level of thinking is attained. This implies, in the first place, that the context has changed. At the beginning of the study of geometry, the figures were totalities, on account of their global character. After being shown the figures, a young child is able to distinguish a rhombus from a square without being able to mention even one property of those figures. A pupil, after having attained the second level of thinking in geometry, again knows the rhombus and the square as totalities, but now as a collection of their properties and their relations with other figures; and those properties and relations have grown out of *characteristics* of the rhombus and the square. Now the figures are recognized by their properties, and with this the image has fallen into the background.

I must emphasize especially that the learning of an orientation in the first period and also later in the higher periods is a process that has to be done by the pupils themselves. The pupils have the intention to orient themselves, they have the need for mobility in the field of thinking, therefore *they* begin to compare the symbols; by *their* reflections the symbols get the character of a signal. The teacher can give guidance to the process of learning, for example, by giving the pupils the opportunity to discuss their orientations and by having them find their way in the field of thinking. But this guidance does not imply that the signals in the field of thinking of the pupils should come from the teacher's knowledge. It is not the teacher's task to have them learn which properties belong to given figures and how to act in a given situation. If the teacher attempts this, many of the pupils will have a network of relations at their disposal that is not sufficiently connected with the original global field of thinking. Such pupils, starting from a given concrete situation, will have difficulties returning to the corresponding signification in the developed network of relations. They will not succeed unless the concrete situation happens to be that of the teacher's original instruction.

There is a tendency to understand the above-mentioned concept of level as a special case of Lindworsky's theory of stratification. However, this would be a mistake. It is true that in geometry the first level is linked to visual and the second level to more schematic thinking, but we have already shown that thinking at the second level originates from thinking at the first level. It has been transformed by a learning process. After having attained the second level of thinking in geometry, a person will, when he sees a geometrical figure, always use the contents of the symbols of the second level. So even in visual thinking the newly formed structure of the second level is always at his disposal. There is only one exception: if he thinks in another context.

THE SECOND LEVEL OF THINKING

In the preceding discussion we have seen that the passage from Level 1 to Level 2 is a complicated process. It is also difficult to help a pupil with this learning process. Sometimes it may be useful to give a name to the period between Level 1 and Level 2; we will call it simply Period 1.

After the second level of thinking has been attained, and Period 1 is completed, we enter Period 2, which has its end in the third level of thinking. During the learning process of the second period of geometry, the *ordering* of properties of geometric figures is the object of study. With this ordering, old symbols get new contents, and at the end of the learning process the figures are understood as an ordered set of properties. But in this period new symbols are also born, like 'congruence', 'equality', 'parallelism', and 'following from.' These symbols can only be understood after the context of the first period has been changed. The new symbols are typical for the new context.

The sense of 'following from' may be discovered by an analysis of the intrinsic meaning of the properties of a geometric figure. To recognize a geometric figure, it is not necessary to trace all its properties; it can be recognized by only a few of its properties. Such a set of properties we will call 'characteristics.' For example, it is possible to recognize a parallelogram because it is a quadrilateral with diagonals bisecting each other. In consequence of this, other properties of parallelograms become certain: for instance, the property that opposite sides are parallel. From the first-mentioned properties of the figure (quadrilateral, diagonals bisecting each other) one can deduce the latter property (opposite sides are parallel).

It is out of the question that deduction be understood by pupils before they have surveyed such a range of properties, and this is only possible after the attaining of the second level of thinking. In Holland there has been some research work on syllogistic reasoning by Kohnstamm (1952, p. 67). He made use of the isomorphism existing between syllogistic deduction and topology. He transformed syllogistic problems into Venn diagram problems, and it turned out that children were able to find the right answer using the Venn diagrams. This experiment is irrelevant, however. The children were able to use the operation in the field of Venn diagrams, but this does not in the least guarantee that they understood anything about the essence of deduction. We can see these results as a reduction of the level, and because the reduction has been carried out by the teacher we may be sure that the children have understood nothing of it. We can be certain of this, for the children using this operation did not know that their answers had any relation to deduction.

There is no doubt that 'deduction' is a concept belonging to a high level of thinking, especially the intrinsic meaning of the concept. Teachers of mathematics, considered to be seasoned in their topic, still break elementary rules of logic, even the definition of 'deduction'. The errors I mean were surely not accidental; they were real errors of thought. Those who are well informed in the teaching of mathematics know how difficult it is for children to conceive of the logical coherence between the rules. Too often their work must be understood as the result of an action structure without any logical background. It takes nearly 2 years of continual education to have the pupils experience the intrinsic *value* of deduction, and still more time is necessary to understand the intrinsic meaning of this concept.

The above exposition brings us nearer to the concept of 'level'. The research guided by Kohnstamm was based on a reduction of an action to a lower level of thinking. In exact topics, such a reduction is usually possible because the operations in the field that has to be controlled can be disjoined from the context and practiced separately. By so doing, pupils are able to figure out all sort of things; they can name results of their calculations and various other data, but they do not really know what they have calculated or what the names they have mentioned really signify. In nonexact topics, such a reduction of level often develops verbal structures of thinking, borrowed from other sciences. Because the symbols that have to be ordered do not yet belong to the correct level of the proper topic, structures from other topics are used in which the symbol involved has a place. It is clear that in this way the proper topic cannot develop correctly. It is well known, for instance, that psychology for a long time borrowed structures from philosophy and later on structures from physics and biology. The difficulty of liberating pedagogy from wrongly introduced structures of psychology is also well known.

It is evident that the attainment of a level is the result of a learning process. This may be an unguided learning process, so that the level is exclusively attained by incidental learning. It would, however, be a deplorable error to suppose that a level is attained as the result of a biological maturation that the teacher is helpless to influence. We may be quite sure that a young child will not understand us if we speak in terminology that is usual in physics. And we may believe experiments that demonstrate that this situation improves in discussions repeated some years later. But if it is said that this is the result of a maturation of the child in the years that have passed, we must not conceive of this phenomenon as a biological maturation of childish thinking. The explanation must be sought in incidental learning processes that have meanwhile taken place. The child has lived among adults, has listened to their discussions, has participated in discussions, and has questioned phenomena. By association with adults, a child learns, but the learning processes were generally not guided—there was no didactic situation.

It is not necessary to bring in (biological) maturation in order to explain the development of logical thinking. The inability of children to think logically does not proceed from a deficit of maturation but from an ignorance of the rules of the game of logic. The child does not have at his disposal the structures from which the questions originate. He cannot understand the questions because he has not finished the learning process leading to the required level of thinking. The age of the children is important, in so far as they must have had sufficient time to go through the necessary learning processes. Especially if the environment of the children is not very favorable, such unguided learning processes may take much time.

The development of the concept of 'number' is often left to incidental learning processes. This is difficult to avoid: The first symbols, like 'three', 'more', 'as much as', are formed long before there is a question of teaching. Yet these are important symbols in the context of 'number'. Many more symbols constituting the concept of 'number', such as 'the same', 'belonging to each other', 'putting in a row', also belong to other contexts. At the moment formal education is introduced in the development of number, extensive network of relations has already been formed between those symbols. Many pupils have already attained the second level of thinking.

This appears clearly in the investigations of Piaget. In his experiments Piaget

fires series of questions at his youthful subjects, the answers to which require the
second or even third level of thinking. From the protocols it appears that some
children younger than six years are able to give reasonable answers. Piaget's
conclusions suggest biological maturation, especially since he pays no attention
to incidental learning processes (Piaget, 1941).

Instruction in arithmetic in the first grade of elementary school, as it is now
usually given, assumes the attainment of the second-level concept of number.
We may not call such instruction unjustified, because by far most of the pupils
will have attained that level. Still, there are children who have not attained it, and
therefore it is desirable to determine which children have and especially to
determine if all the signals necessary for the level have been formed. Many later
difficulties might be avoided by so doing.

We know that in the practice of education, not much attention is paid to the
levels of thinking. It is very usual, though always condemnable, to speak to
pupils about concepts belonging to a level that they have not at all attained. This
is the most important cause of bad results in the education of mathematics. The
result of such instruction is that the pupils are obliged to imitate the action
structure of the teacher. By doing so they usually succeed in mastering operations belonging to the level. But because the action structure does not result from
a real understanding (i.e., not by analysis of lower structures), it must result from
a global structure of acting. The success is seemingly complete: In the long run
the pupil is able to calculate almost as fast as the teacher.

The teacher does not use lower (visual) structures when he computes, neither
do his pupils. But whereas the teacher (as we suppose and hope) has obtained the
knowledge of computing by a transformation of the structures of a lower level,
with the pupils such a relation is absolutely absent. With the teacher, computing
will generally be connected with concrete material. He will, in a new concrete
situation, usually be able to apply his knowledge. In such cases, however, the
pupils will be powerless.

From the above, the functional character of the completion of a complex
becomes obvious. The transition from concrete material to knowledge of computing brings in an economy of thinking and it will, once the way has been
smoothed, usually pass without difficulty. Usually the return from calculations to
concrete material signifies an aggravation of a problem, and therefore we often
find the way in this direction blocked. Still, we must remark, in many cases the
teaching process has more favorable results than indicated in the preceding.
Intelligent and independent pupils are able to find for themselves relations between the given problem and well-known visual structures. Many deficits of the
guided learning processes are overcome by incidental learning processes.

The literature of psychology of thinking sometimes pronounces the theory that
human thinking passes through the steps (1) posing of a problem, (2) hypothesis,
and (3) testing of the result. Such thinking, however, is only possible after the

attainment of the second level of thinking, after a certain schematizing, a certain abstraction, has taken place. Thinking at the first level does not yet know problems, it is still in the stage of exploration; the person at this level is still free in his connections regarding the given material (tiles, squares, grids). Antitheses are not possible at this level, because in this insufficiently ordered subject matter there are no theses. Of course one who has himself attained the second level can suggest problems about the subject matter to the pupil, but these are not the pupil's problems. It may be that such an exercise will give the pupil some start in orientation, in development of signals, but still such a problem retains its imposed character. It is quite different if, at a higher level, the pupil meets with a contradiction between two abstract structures he or she has acquired. Then very often the solution will be found according to the above three steps, and the acquisition of the result *then* will be an important emotional experience.

Sometimes psychologists pretend that living is the same as problem solving: Even the child playing with blocks is in some degree busy with problem solving. It is not possible to contradict this thesis, but such "problem solving" is far from problem solving in the usual sense. I prefer to call such playing "exploration." If I am in a new town and I have no map, I begin to explore the environment of my hotel. There is no problem to be solved, for I have no specific purpose. After some time, when I have formed a scheme of a map in my head, the problems will come. Then, if I want to go to the post office and the cathedral, I can ask: what will be the best way to do it? It seems appropriate to say that first there are no problems; problems only appear after one has been busy orienting themself. But, of course, it is always possible to give "problem solving" such a definition that exploring also falls under it.

Only at the end of the learning process of geometry do real problems begin to be meaningful. Then they can serve to force the integration of structures that, in the thinking in geometry, have developed themselves more or less separately. After such an integration the pupil can experience geometry as a totality. But for this result the pupil finds the way himself. The integration is out of the question if the way has been carefully outlined. In this case problem solving is no longer a catalyst helping to prepare the pupils for the third level of thinking; it has become a chapter on itself, and as such it needs to be determined if the problems themselves are worth working on.

The development of schematized structures from (and not over, or next to) concrete visual structures is of great importance because of the special symbolic significance of language. The image is symbol for many things that are not expressed in words. A great part of it will still not be expressed in words after the schematization. If abstract structures are developed from visual structures in which images play an important part, a portion of the rich (and unexpressed) contents will probably be structured too. In such a way the new formed abstract structures have a much richer content than their verbal representatives.

TRANSSTRUCTURING AND RESTRUCTURING

In the initial education of mathematics, pupils need exercises promoting the formation of structures that lead to the development of symbols, inducing the pupils to orient themselves. We have already seen that such exercises are not problems. Rarely ever is there a question of a so-called restructuring. The original visual structures are gradually transformed into abstract structures, so it is better here to speak of a *transstructuring*. If a pupil see directly, as it were, to the solution of a problem about such a structure, there never was any problem.

Here is an example: A pupil educated with usual structures is given the following problem (see Figure 10.1): *AD* and *BC* are the equal sides of an isosceles trapezoid *ABCD*. The midpoint *E* of *AB* is joined with *D* and *C*. The midpoint *F* of *DE* is joined with *A*, the midpoint *G* of *EC* is joined with *B*. Prove that *AF* = *BG*.

The pupil reasons as follows: "Every isosceles trapezoid has an axis of symmetry, in this case it goes through *E* and is perpendicular to *AB*. *DE* and *CE* are corresponding line segments, *F* and *G* as well as *A* and *B* are corresponding points. So *AF* and *BG* are corresponding line segments; hence *AF* = *BG*." In this way the pupil argues from an extant total structure. He has nothing more to do than make explicit the links he can see. There was no restructuring involved.

Still, a restructuring of the field of observation sometimes can be very helpful. This could happen in the following sorts of cases:

1.   A number of actions not yet integrated into a single structure have to be executed. A restructuring of the field may lead to the integration. This takes place if structures of thinking have been developed independently of each other. Sometimes in geometry lengths of line segments can be found by first using the geometric structure to which the segments belong and afterward restructuring the problem to an algebraic structure for the calculation.

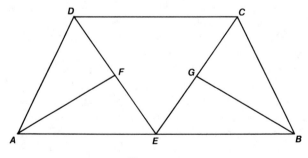

Figure 10.1

2. A number of actions without mutual connection have to be executed successively. Each new action requires a restructuring of the field. This can take place if man has to execute a series of actions which he has learned to execute in a certain sequence without the necessity to lose himself in the question if he might not be able to do so in another sequence. He might have had a better insight in what he was doing if he had tried to integrate the structures of the various actions in one more-inclusive structure. But because he has to execute a stereotyped series of actions, it suffices that he does them by constantly restructuring the field.

3. A number of actions have to be executed in a nonmeaningful sequence. This might be a specially designed test forcing the subject to experience the difficulties of restructuring. This case is often found in mathematical tests. A pupil is confronted with a test he cannot survey as a totality, but there are recognizable parts in it. He has to restructure the recognizable parts until he finds a total structure. In itself the thinking exercised by such tests may be very valuable; it is one of the tools for penetrating a new field of knowledge. Still, such problems are not designed to test whether insight in some domain of knowledge has been obtained. Besides, if many such problems are given, the integration of structure really belonging together is thwarted.

4. We have to solve an important problem but we do not know to which structure the solution of the problem belongs. We may try some structure. If we do not succeed, we try another, and so on. Everytime we transfer to another structure, we have a restructuring. The restructuring usually is very difficult, for the structures may be very different. This case involves the great problems mankind has had to solve. Many times centuries pass before the right structure has been found. The discovery of the structures of molecules and atoms to solve the problems of chemistry dates from the end of the eighteenth century, yet the ancient Greeks had already sought it.

SUMMARY

1. In the period leading from one level of thinking to the following, two important parts can be distinguished. In the first part we have the experience of the context and the forming of symbols for the context; in the second part an orientation will take place with the help of the formation of the signal character of the symbols.

2. Knowledge of the levels of thinking can prevent the teacher from appealing to pupils with concepts from a level they have not yet attained.

3. Knowledge of the levels of thinking can guard the psychologist from

attributing to (biological) development what really is the result of a learning process.

4. Restructuring the field of observation (thinking) may be very useful. Still, there are many different cases in which such a restructuring works, and we should not expect training in one of these cases to have much effect on the development of restructuring in other cases. Obviously, it is most difficult to find the appropriate structure for problems that have not been solved by anyone.

11

Intuition

In the *Grote Winkler Prins* encyclopedia you find the following paragraph by D. Wiersma:

> **intuition** (Latin *intuéri* = to contemplate, to consider) is in psychology generally considered to be the opposite of discursive thinking, attaining its conclusions step by step. A conviction attained through intuition appears more or less suddenly; the subject cannot give an explanation for it and usually supposes that there is none. Nevertheless, it is attended by an intensive notion of subjective sureness. Many laymen therefore think intuition objectively more reliable than discursive thinking, which is not at all always the case, however. About the essence of intuition, psychologists differ considerably. One group, with Jung as a typical representative, consider it as a separate capacity of man, totally different from discursive thinking. Jung calls intuition irrational; it directs to new insights but it is not infallible. It offers no reasons, and therefore sometimes discursive thinking may disprove a conviction obtained by intuition. Another group of psychologists, with Heymans a typical representative, do not see intuition as a special capacity: The only difference between intuitive and discursive thinking is that the latter happens consciously, the former unconsciously. Because in unconscious thinking one makes use of more data than in conscious thinking, intuitive insight is often more reliable than insight obtained discursively.

It is suggested here that it is possible to make a correct decision without thinking discursively. This idea we have come across before, namely, where one draws a conclusion on grounds of a visual structure he understands. For this conclusion, no discursive thinking is necessary, for the symbols of language that constitute such a discursive structure are developed later on, after the conclusion. We should now consider the relation between an intuitive decision and a conclusion based on a visual structure. The encyclopedia passage suggested "intuitive insight" as the opposite of "discursive thinking." If we take this seriously, a conclusion based on a visual structure must be part of intuitive thinking. If this is not the case, there must be an omission in the passage, an omission of other contrasts to discursive thinking.

Heymans is characterized as suggesting that intuitive thinking goes on unconsciously, that in unconscious thinking there should be more data at one's disposal. This is in complete accordance with a reading of a visual structure. Nevertheless, intuition is not unconscious; the reading of a visual structure happens in full consciousness.

I take it that something in this passage is confused. In psychology and even more in philosophy one often distinguishes only two methods of reaching conclusions: those that are derived from discursive thinking and the others, which are brought about unconsciously. This distinction blocks the way to seeing things as they really are. It throws everything that differs from discursive thinking, including reading visual structures and drawing conclusions on prejudicial grounds, into one pile and gives it the name 'intuition'. The difference between these two ways of coming to a conclusion is enormous: The decision on the grounds of a visual structure may be just as reliable as a decision on the grounds of discursive thinking; in both cases one comes to a correct decision as long as no surprises occur. A decision on the grounds of prejudices is simply a decision for which one has no structure at his disposal and only the guidance of misunderstood sympathies and antipathies.

One who acts from a "faultless intuition" probably concludes on the grounds of visual structures. Because often it is difficult to express these structures in words, conclusions sometimes seem mere guesses. A physician who regularly, intuitively makes the right diagnosis has visual structures at his disposal. Fortunately, the accuracy of his judgment can often be confirmed by discursive thinking afterward. Then the physician is liberated from the hocus pocus and stands again on the firm ground of scientific thinking.

The continuation of a structure without intervention of discursive thinking I will describe as 'on the grounds of an intuition'. In doing so I join Mallinckrodt (1959), who translates *intueri* as 'looking at something, viewing closely'. In this way I withdraw from the usage that gives 'intuition' a negative connotation.

A decision based on an intuition, that is on a "close consideration" without the aid of discursive thinking, may be correct. If we have access to a strong structure, the sureness of the decision may be quite justified. In such a case, one has seen a very clear structure from which the solution of the problem can be easily read.

It may be true that in chess, strategies pass through the mind of the players before every move. But in checkers, on the other hand, it seems that often a player sees directly that a certain arrangement is unfavorable. And it is clear that a pedestrian passing through heavy traffic does not decide, on the grounds of discursive thinking, "now the moment to walk has come."

Whether teaching methods are based on the Socratic method, class conversation, or lectures with question periods, they all depend on discursive thinking. This is so even in methods in which children themselves have to invent the theorems. Only in classes for infants do we find opportunities for exploration without engagement with the material. And even when material is used, it is not used for free, exploratory play. Some teachers of the Montessori method, for instance, do not allow their pupils to use materials for purposes other than those for which they were designed. Obviously I do not agree with such an approach. Children, and adults as well, need the opportunity to play with material, under some condition, in order to get acquainted with its structure. Of course teachers can gain instruction time by directing children's play with material in order to guide them in learning its structure. Still, if the structure of the material is to demonstrate itself to the children, a certain freedom is desirable.

In one of Piaget's experiments (1941) six dolls widely separated and six others shoved together were shown to a child. Earlier, the same dolls had been placed in two rows, with each doll of one row just opposite one doll of the other row. At this time the child had seen and expressed that there were just as many dolls in one row as in the other. In the new situation, the child decided that there were more dolls in the widely spaced row than in the bunched row. Questions demanding discursive thinking were then posed: "How is it possible that there are more dolls in that row now? Where did they come from?" It is easy to understand why a child could not answer such questions: It had at its disposal a feeble structure in which 'more' and 'less' were linked with 'wide' and 'narrow'; the question "Where did the dolls come from?" had not found a place in this structure. The child's structure was for the most part visual, intuitive; the structure Piaget appealed to was discursive.

If someone in botany takes a teasel for a Compositae, we know that their conclusion is founded not on discursive thinking, but on a visual structure that is not strong enough. We may advise that person to use a textbook, from which discursive thinking is added that may help to reinforce the visual structure.

If someone makes the conversion

$$\frac{a + b}{a + c} \rightarrow \frac{b}{c},$$

they will be reproached for not having thought enough about the problem. There will be no reproach, however, if they make either of the following conversions:

$$\frac{a \times b}{a \times c} \rightarrow \frac{b}{c};$$
$$a + b = a + c \rightarrow b = c.$$

All three conversions could have been made on the grounds of a similar visual structure, but such a structure is not strong enough to cover all three cases.

Action on grounds of visual thinking is essential for development of thinking. If the analysis of 'conclusion' is restricted to discursive thinking, a good view of the development of thinking will not result. The possibility of thinking at the visual level is important for understanding: (1) the psychology of discussions, (2) teaching–learning processes, and (3) the development of sciences.

In *The Psychology of Learning Mathematics* Skemp writes:

> At a lower level, we classify every time we recognize an object as one which we have seen before. On no two occasions are the incoming sense data likely to be exactly the same, since we see objects at different distances and angles, and also in varying lights. From these various inputs we abstract certain *in*variant properties, and these properties persist in memory longer than the memory of any particular presentation of the object. In the diagram, $C_1, C_2 \ldots$ [such as Figure 11.1] represent successive past experiences of the same object; say a particular chair. From these we abstract certain common properties, represented in the diagram by C. Once this abstraction is formed, any further experience C_n evokes C, and the chair is *recognized*: that is, the new experience is classified with C_1, C_2, etc. C_n and C are now experienced together; and from their combination, we experience both the *similarity* (C) of C_n to our previous experiences of seeing this chair, and also the particular distance, angle, etc., on this occasion (C_n). Awareness of the *differences* between C_n and C_1, C_2, C_3 is (according to this diagram) a more indirect process: and this accords with experimental data—children find it easier to give similarities between, say, an orange and an apple, than differences.
>
> We progress rapidly to further abstractions. From particular chairs C, C', C'', we abstract further invariant properties, by which we recognize C^h (a new object seen for the first time, say in a shop window) as a member of this class. (1971, p. 20)

And analysis of this passage may bring us somewhat closer to the understanding of intuition and discursive thinking. The successive experiences $C_1, C_2,$ . . . belong to very early experiences of children recognizing an object. These

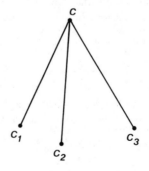

Figure 11.1

experiences happen when children cannot yet speak, so no discursive thinking is involved. At the moment a child learns to call something a chair, the gestalt C of 'chair' has already been formed. Experiments show that it is not necessary for a child to have seen more than one chair to be able to say of a new chair: "this is a chair." If a child has seen a dog and knows it is called "dog," then usually that child is able to recognize a dog of a quite different kind and size without having seen other types of dog. And even when a child has understood the gestalt of 'dog', he is generally not able to mention any property of 'dog' except for such properties as 'four legs' and 'a head,' which do not enter into the definition of 'dog.'

So if we speak of an abstraction in this case (and of course we can), we must realize that such an abstraction differs very much from abstractions in which people have defined a thing by choosing from its many properties and *can mention them*. Recognizing an isosceles triangle by its property 'two sides equal' is quite another thing than recognizing an isosceles triangle because of its gestalt. The construction of the gestalt C out of the views $C_1, C_2, \ldots$ happens without thinking; it is therefore a very low-level abstraction. If a child sees a chair, he sees the gestalt C, and if you ask him to draw a chair he will try to represent the properties that belong to the gestalt. This is easy to demonstrate: Ask a child to draw a round table; though he has always seen the top of the table as an ellipse, he will try to draw a circle.

Why do I give so much attention to this passage from Skemp, if, in the end, I do not quite disagree with him? Because this passage is found in a chapter called "The Formation of Mathematical Concepts." But the medium in which mathematical concepts are formed is the medium of discursive thinking. So, though I do not disagree with Skemp, the context of his comments is inappropriate. The abstraction that leads to a mathematical concept is of quite another quality than the above-mentioned abstraction. Confusing these two, a decision based on an unconscious reaction and a discursive decision, is more serious than confusing an intuitive decision with a discursive decision.

If we define intuition as 'concluding on the grounds of direct observation,' we to some degree conflict with normal usage. Many people will object to speaking of intuition in a case in which someone continues a tiled floor on grounds of direct observation. Here is another example. In a photography shop a customer complains that the developer he has prepared failed because the sodium sulfite (Na_2SO_3) was no good. Before adding the Na_2SO_3, the developer worked normally; afterward it did not. The customer suggests that the shopkeeper has given him fixer ($Na_2S_2O_3$). A chemist who happens to be in the shop offers to analyze the substance. He puts some of the substance in his mouth, is first satisfied that it is sulfite, but then suddenly says: "No, sulfur!" He has ascertained that there is fixer in the substance.

In this case we cannot speak of intuition, for the chemist's conclusion is based on discursive thinking. Still, there is also direct observation involved. Were the customer to remark that the chemist had taken a great risk—there could have been mercuric chloride or some other strong poison in the substance—he might answer: "Oh no, I would have seen that directly; I knew for sure that it was a sulfite or something of the sort." Still, this way of acting does not differ so much from the working method of the chemist in a laboratory. There he puts the substance in a test tube, pours some hydrochloric acid over it, smells the liberated sulfuric acid, and sees in the liquid the troublesome sulfur.

This train of thought consisted of discursive thinking, but it was preceded by a direct observation. We often lose sight of this because the observation is so simple. "This is a sulfite, you can smell it; that is sulfur, everybody can see it!"

Intuition has an unfavorable reputation; this is included in the concept. If everyone can see what I see, my action is not on account of an intuition; if someone else can learn to see the structure on which I have based my judgment, I did not act intuitively. But if I see the solution to a problem directly, but without being able to tell how the structure I have seen was arranged, then there is the tendency to speak of an intuition. And if the structure is so feeble that I am not able to identify its elements, then surely it must be an intuition. The unfavorable connotation is related to jealousy. "This man was right, but he failed to give an explanation for his judgment. We, on the contrary, had an explanation for our judgment. Though, after the fact, we appear to be incorrect, still we are more intelligent than he." And with this statement the "intuiter" is classified with the gamblers, although statistics may prove that his judgment cannot be based on chance.

If we speak of an intuitive introduction to geometry, we allude to a start in which observation gets the place it has a right to. There is no question of an unfavorable connotation. The word "intuitive" is then simply used in connection with 'observation.'

12

Reality, Individual, and Language

Language may be instrumental in the interaction between the individual and reality—in our recognition of understructures and superstructures. The structure in Figure 12.1a may be described as "a structure of triangles." In this structure one can observe the understructure 'saw'. On square-grid paper one can use these saws as a means to draw a structure of quadrangles (Figure 12.1b). The words "saw" and "structure of triangles," which belong to an understructure of the structure of quadrangles, enable us to "understand" the latter structure.

It is possible to indicate the vectors of which a saw is constructed. The saw in Figure 12.2 is built with the vectors $(1, 2)$ and $(1, -1)$. We are able to understand this structure by analyzing and giving names.

Language is imbued with a notion of time—we see it, for instance, in the conjugation of verbs—and without exaggerations we may say that time for the greater part is constituted by language.

Language helps us with the communication of structures. The designations of leaves, 'kidney-shaped', 'heart-shaped', and so on, are easy to understand. These designations help when observed forms are analyzed; they make it possible to single them out.

Structures are extended by making use of language. We can immediately understand expressions like a "curtain of water," a "rain of decorations." Sometimes an element of a structure is created by some event. Everyone knows what a boycott is; everyone understands expressions like a "sadistic action" or a "Don Juan." Many people are not familiar with the origins of these expressions; often they learn them through new, more recent stories.

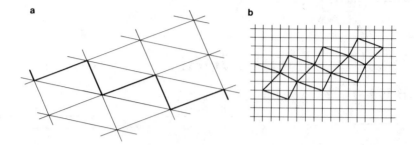

Figure 12.1

This introduces an important way of understanding the meaning of a word. To be able to understand "intuition" we need to trace the situations in which the word may be used. To understand "sadistic action" we must be acquainted with a description of De Sade's actions or of other actions of the same quality. This we will call *semantic analysis*. In such an analysis, sentences are advanced in which the word involved has a place. In discussion, we must settle in which sentences the word is used correctly and in which sentences it is not. Such a semantic analysis looks much like phenomenal analysis, but there is an important difference. In physics, for instance, we use a phenomenal analysis if we want to know the meaning of "magnetism." We order phenomena that are related to magnetism, we experiment, and after that 'magnetism' has new shape. The concept of 'magnetism' is deepened by a description of the situations in which the word "magnetism" is used.

With intuition we have another situation. We know that many people already use the word "intuition," but often in different ways. Without hearing these other people, we have no right to say "This is intuition and that is not." Therefore we begin with a semantic analysis, to determine the meaning of the word for these others. After the semantic analysis, we often have to make a

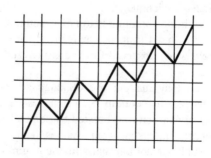

Figure 12.2

choice. We may have to say: "Many people use the word 'intuition' in another sense than I now intend to do. They are free to hold to their own opinion, but if they want to understand me, they must know how I will use the word in my article."

If in a learning process an individual has learned to understand a structure by direct contact with reality, he has to learn the language for it, giving him the ability to exchange views about it with other people. This is a phase of the learning process that I call *explicitation*. Before the explicitation the involved structure is controlled implicitly—one has understood the structure and knows how to work with it. After explicitation the structure becomes explicit; it becomes possible to talk with other people about it. If we have to deal with a learning process starting from visual structures, such an explicitation is quite necessary for discursive judgments. In the beginning of the explicitation, related structures of daily life, in which a primitive language has usually already been developed, are used. By analyzing the structure with the help of that language, gradually the words of the technical language come under discussion.

With the language that makes it possible to speak about the structures comes the possibility of describing the superstructures by reproducing the links between the given structures. After this, one can attain a higher level of thinking.

It is easy to cite words that designate concepts of a higher level of thinking. An example is "isomorphism." Here there is no question of a directly observable reality. The word "isomorphism" refers to a superstructure that becomes observable only after abstract reflection and explicitation about observable visual structures.

The concept of 'abstraction' here is quite another than that concept of 'abstraction' we have mentioned earlier from Skemp. An extensive analysis of 'abstraction' is given by Van Parreren. Van Parreren (1981, p. 99) describes six levels of abstraction. It is useful to ascertain the place of those levels with respect to the levels of thinking of my theory. Van Parreren's lowest level is Level 0: the perceptive level. At this level, experimental subjects show the ability to sort according to color or shape.

The following level, Level 1, is called *selective accentuation*. This level is attained if the experimental subject is able to switch in the field from one accentuation to another. A room takes on quite different relief if, after being seen in the context 'red', it has to be seen in the context 'round'. Van Parreren remarks that, though the classification happens on the grounds of an abstracted characteristic, this switching may happen totally in the visual field. Van Parreren (p. 103) adds to this: "In this connection it still is important that . . . verbal qualifications may support certain perceptive accentuations, by which they may be more easily retained and also generally become more intentionally available." Obviously we are here concerned with information and explicitation at the visual level of thinking.

Level 2 is the level of rules.

> At this level it is possible to act on the basis of an internally retained, *explicit rule,* and orderings become possible that are not supported by a field of observation. A child, after having attained this level, no longer must directly see what belongs together, that is, on grounds of accentuation striking resemblances. He acts in accordance with a rule. (Van Parreren, 1981, p. 103)

Level 3, the level of generalization of rules, becomes clear when Van Parreren (1981, p. 108) gives an example from Vest: "Vest shows that to be able to know what multiplication is, the pupils will on one hand have to recognize different models, and on the other hand will have to be able to recognize that all these models embody the same principle." The concept of 'multiplication' is only understood by the pupils, according to Vest, if when asked the question, "What is multiplication?" they are able to explain how the principle of multiplication is used in various models, such as those of Figure 12.3. Here we have a clear example how "telescoped reteaching" may work. The actions may be very well performed on the visual level, as well as the determination of the result: $2 \times 4 = 8$. But the explanation is totally of the descriptive level of thinking. Thus it is possible to have pupils work at different levels of thinking.

Level 4, the abstract–symbolic level, may best be understood in the following passage:

> At this level for the first time in explicit form another characteristic moment of human thinking appears. Because now with thought, which also means activity with not-given, perhaps even not-existing objects, a need comes into existence to make these more seizable. For this man uses symbols. Each object, whatever status this object might have—real given, represented, or only thought, is denoted by a sign, a word, or, for instance, a letter. (Van Parreren, 1981, p. 109)

Here we see, as I have expressed it before, that the concept has become a junction of a new network of relations. So here we are in the middle of the second level—the descriptive level.

At Level 5, the level of relativity,

> abstractions are built upon abstractions: a class that has come into existence by a general application of a rule of action may itself act as object of the application of a "higher"

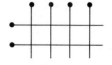   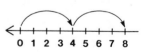

Figure 12.3

rule. An example of this is the determination of whether a class includes another class. (p. 112)

The core of the difference [between the structures of action of Levels 0 and 1] is that at the higher level many *mental* actions have become possible, by which an ordering has been brought about, whereas at the lowest level only *perceptive* actions function. (Van Parreren, 1981, 113)

I get the impression that at Level 5 many things have been thrown into one pile. To this fifth level belong things like axioms, converses of a proposition, but also properties of parallelograms and parallel lines. The conception of the first-mentioned is much more difficult than the understanding of the following. Between them there is quite a difference in levels of thinking.

In Chapter 9 I mentioned Skemp's use of 'abstraction'. He used it in the context of visual structures, so we may say that it was an abstraction of Van Parreren's Level 0. As an example he suggests a 12-month old infant, who, having finished sucking his bottle, crawls across the floor of the living room to where two empty wine bottles are standing and puts his own empty bottle neatly alongside them. It is clear that the feeding bottle, for the child, belonged to the same structure as the two wine bottles. But does this imply that there has been a selection of properties by constituting such a structure? We cannot say that Skemp has confused different types of abstraction, but we can simply say that he has not distinguished between various types.

There have been investigations in which children and adults were asked if a square (given in a picture) was a rectangle or a rhombus. Many of them said, no, it wasn't. So a square is not seen as a particular quadrangle with some extra properties; a square is recognized as itself, as a whole. And so, I am sure, many other symbols have a life of their own, without the intermediary of a superset. The formation of representations and symbols at the visual level is something quite different from the formation of concepts by making use of language, and contrary to Piaget, I describe such formation of concepts quite differently from the formation of representations and symbols at the visual level.

"Abstraction" refers to something that does not belong to World 1: It is a mental construction. After it has been brought into discussion, it has become part of World 3. Van Parreren's analysis shows that the concept of 'abstraction' belongs to many different contexts, and that in each of those contexts it has a different significance. We have seen that such an analysis can guard us from using a certain meaning in the wrong context.

In the above we see how important such analyses of seemingly well-known concepts can be. If we want complete security about the correct use of such concepts, the analysis ought to be followed by ample discussion. This would be more important than developing many new theories with laboriously defined concepts that still cannot really clarify problems.

13

Structures at Different Levels

At the visual level, the first level, language in the beginning only serves to make communication about structures that can be observed by all people possible—and also to support accurate thinking about these structures. The second level, the descriptive level, allows thinking about the nature of the structures of the first level. To make such thinking possible, the symbols of the first level are associated with properties; discussions in the first period have aided visualization of those properties. In learning geometry at the first level, children see in the structure of congruent triangles new figures, like saws, parallel lines, and equal angles. Observation of structures has been improved by the use of words indicating those figures. So, whereas in the beginning of the first period language is introduced to describe figures that are observed, gradually this language develops to form the background of a new structure: the structure of the second level, the descriptive structure.

After the forming of this language, now at the second level, the relation between parallel lines and equal angles can be discussed. In the structure of the congruent triangles, as in Figure 13.1, you can see similar triangles. Now, at this level, the pupils can be asked how similar triangles can be recognized and what they need to know before they can establish that two triangles are similar. They can be asked about the *characteristics* of similar triangles. This is a level of thinking quite different from that of the first level. At the visual level, it is possible to see similar triangles, but it is senseless to ask why they are similar: There is no why, one just sees it. The discussion, but also the understanding, of

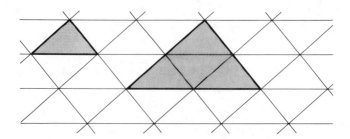

Figure 13.1

such questions needs the language that belongs to the descriptive level, and this language has been developed in the first period.

Still, at the second level it is not yet possible to prove that two triangles are similar. For this you need the language of the third level: the theoretical level. At the second level you are able to construct a square, the diagonal of which has a given length. You can because you know that diagonals of a square are equal, bisect each other, and meet at right angles; so it is easy. But you are not able to give a proof. You see that it fits: The quadrangle you have constructed has four equal sides and right angles, so it is a square.

If you are asked to give a proof that you have constructed a square and that this square has a diagonal of the given length, you are first obliged to give a definition of a square. However, 'definition' is a concept of the vocabulary of the third level. Let us say that a square is a quadrangle that has four equal sides and one right angle. Then after the construction we may say that the four sides of the quadrangle are equal, because the quadrangle has two axes of symmetry: the diagonals. Because of the equality of the diagonals, the quadrangle is divided by its diagonals in four congruent isosceles triangles, each with a right angle. Therefore all the angles of the quadrangle are right angles. We have begun with a diagonal of the right length, so our quadrangle turns out to be a square.

This seems all very easy, but to give such a proof, one must be able to argue at the third level. One must have learned the language of this theoretical level. To be able to understand such a language, one must have made a study of arguments at the descriptive level and have understood that it is possible to arrange such arguments in an order in which each statement, except those at the beginning, is the outcome of previous statements.

For most people who use mathematics it is not necessary to give arguments at the third level. Just as in physics, where one only has to be able to solve, usually easy, problems, proof afterward is not usually necessary. It is usually sufficient to "see" the solution.

I will give still another example of the three levels of thinking. In Figure 13.2a you see two hexagons. They are similar. You may see it—first level.

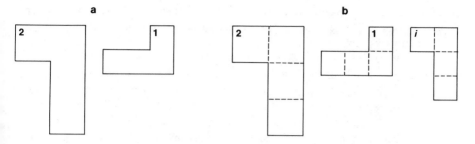

Figure 13.2

Perhaps you do not see it. Then I will give an explanation. Each hexagon can be divided in four squares Figure 13.2b. Give hexagon 1 a rotation of 90° counterclockwise, then you get the intermediary hexagon *i*. This is still the "same" as the hexagon 1. You see now that hexagon 2 is an enlargement of the intermediary hexagon *i*.

Here we have used a statement of the descriptive level: two figures, (1 and 2) are called similar if there is a third figure (*i*) that is congruent with one of the figures (1) and an enlargement or diminuition of the other figure (2).

Still, this is not a proof. If a proof is wanted, the pictures must be put aside. To begin with, the hexagons must be described (Figure 13.3): given hexagon $ABCDEF$ with $AB = 3$, $BC = 2$, $CD = 1$, $DE = 1$, $EF = 2$, $FA = 1$; $\angle A = 90°$, $\angle B = 90°$, $\angle C = 90°$, $\angle D = 90°$, $\angle E = 270°$, $\angle F = 90°$; given hexagon $A_1B_1D_1D_1E_1F_1$ with $A_1B_1 = 4.5$, $B_1C_1 = 3$, $C_1C_1 = 1.5$, $D_1E_1 = 1.5$, $E_1F_1 = 3$, $F_1A_1 = 1.5$; $\angle A_1 = 90°$, $\angle B_1 = 90°$, $\angle C_1 = 90°$, $\angle D_1 = 90°$, $\angle E_1 = 270°$, $\angle F_1 = 90°$. In the proof you can give hexagon $ABCDEF$ a rotation in such a way that the transformed hexagon and hexagon $A_1B_1C_1D_1E_1F_1$ have parallel

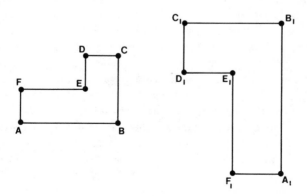

Figure 13.3

sides. The proof is not very difficult but it requires many words. It is much easier to describe everything at the second level than to prove it at the third.

In textbooks such proofs are never given. Why not? Because from such examples everyone can see how silly proofs may be.

Of course, levels of thinking are not limited to geometry. We find them in every science. We have seen it in the teaching of mathematics. At the first level we see a pupil learning his lessons. The result of this learning is tested by the marks he gets. This is a conclusion of the first level of thinking in teaching. The result is a visible thing. But the teacher can ask himself: Why did I give that lesson? What are the purposes of my teaching? Reflection on such questions may bring him to the second level of thinking: the descriptive level. Perhaps this reflection will occupy him so much that he begins to study about "the real meaning of "learning.' " At this point he tries to think at the theoretical level.

Let us review the three levels and their language, with examples.

The language at the first level makes it possible to speak of visual observations. This language is not necessary for a reaction to an observation. But still the language is useful, because by the mention of a word parts of a structure can be called up. The language increases the power of reaction.

The causal, logical, or other relations that are included in the observed structure are a part of the language of the second level of thinking. By using this language new structures are born. These structures were unthinkable before the language of the second level was developed. Discursive thinking, and thus explanation, for the most part use the language of the second level.

The language of the third level has the same relation to the language of the second level as the language of the second level has to the language of the first level. The language of the theoretical level has a much more abstract character than that of the descriptive level because it is engaged with causal, logical, and other relations of a structure, which, at the second level, is not visual. Reasoning about logical relations between theorems in geometry takes place with the language of the third level. If someone has difficulty understanding at this level, you cannot help him by showing him a visual geometrical structure. Still, it is possible to give a visual representation of a connection of theorems, but this is a scheme that functions to support memory. The *understanding* of the connection is not brought about with the help of a visual representation.

The statement "the sum of two integers is an integer" belongs to the third level. It is a statement about structures that belong to the second level. In contrast with 'one', 'two', and 'three', 'integer' is not a symbol of a visual structure. To build the concept of 'integer' you must become acquainted with nonintegers, after which you can see integers as their contraries. So first of all it must be clear to you that it is meaningful to speak of numbers that are not integers. This occurs at the second level.

The statement "in addition, two and one is three" is a statement of the second level. To make the statement clear you can refer to visual structures, and with the statement you say something general about such structures. If you put two objects and one object together and afterward state by counting that there are three objects, you have done this at the first (visual) level. But if you speak in general, saying that every time you do such an act you will find three, you have left the visual level and have formed a conclusion at the second level. But here you use another language; you say "Two and one is three," but the objects do not appear.

The statement "$\frac{2}{3} + \frac{5}{3} = \frac{7}{3}$" is a statement of the second level; visual structures can help. Much more complicated is the statement "$\frac{2}{7} + \frac{5}{13} = \frac{26}{91} + \frac{35}{91} = \frac{61}{91}$". But even in this case it is possible to make the statement visual (see Figure 13.4). Still, such visual structures can only be understood after you have become acquainted with some structures of the second level. You have to know something about area and you must be acquainted with the multiplication tables.

The rule "If you want to add two fractions not having the same denominator, you will first have to give them the same denominator" does not deal with visual structures, and so, because it is a statement about nonvisual structures of the second level, it belongs to the third level. Children who do not speak the language of the third level make the problem visual as in Figure 13.5. In this way they reduce the structure of the third level to a structure of the second level. We may say that they have not understood anything of the real problem.

I do not like to teach with such reductions of level. If you teach things that are not really understood, you are teaching bad habits. Why should we teach young children to add such fractions? They will never need it! Sometimes you can see

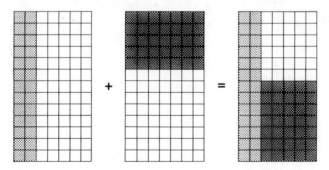

Figure 13.4

$$\frac{2}{7} + \frac{5}{13} = \frac{2 \times 13 + 7 \times 5}{7 \times 13}$$

Figure 13.5

fractions in visual structures. This is a fine opportunity to teach children something about fractions. Most operations with fractions, however, occur at the third
level, and without long preparation these are too difficult for children to understand. But they do not need knowledge of such operations before further education. Stop teaching such superfluous things; there are many better things to teach.

Mathematicians also make use of reduced structures when they do routine
work. But, when by doing so they meet unexpected obstacles, *they* are usually
able to return to the structure of the third level. I must say "usually," not
always, for mathematicians do not always notice that they have gone beyond the
bounds.

14

Consequences of the Languages at Different Levels

As I have remarked before, there is a tendency to suppose that every conclusion has been preceded by discursive thinking. It is considered meaningful to ask: "Why did you solve it in such a way?" It may be that you simply saw what you had to do, but still you are expected to give a discursive answer. But you must think about your solution in order to be able to give that answer, so the question does not necessarily presuppose that there has been discursive thinking in the solution; it leaves open the possibility that the reasoning can be given afterward. So you see, a conclusion may at first be given at the first level, but sometimes afterward it may be brought up to the second level.

If a teacher tells pupils that mathematics is too difficult for them, that they should not go on with it, then the pupils will not be content if the teacher only explains with "This is how I see it." Such a first-level answer will not be very convincing. But if the teacher says, "You have answered your test questions rather poorly, and all the pupils who have succeeded have answered their test questions in a much better way," then perhaps the pupil will believe him. Then the teacher has given a reason based on a structure of the second level, and it is possible to talk it over. Of course it may be that the pupils are still not convinced; it may be that they interpret the structure of the second level in their own way, taking account of their own circumstances and their desire to go on in mathematics. But now, at the second level, reasoning has become possible: The pupils are not condemned to accept the verdict of the teacher without protest.

After a conclusion based on a visual structure, it is not always necessary to ask for an explanation. If a weaving mistake is pointed out in a carpet, or if it is said that somebody has an affected speech, usually an explanation will not be asked.

If somebody has given a wrong continuation of a visual structure, the language of the second level will usually be used to convince him that he was wrong. But if he does not know the structure sufficiently, it will be necessary to show him the structure, to teach him the language symbols that belong to the structure and give it shape. In such a way his language can be brought from the first to the second level. It may be that he immediately sees the continuation of the structure; it is also possible that this will happen after reasoning at the second level.

There is clearly a question of human gifts here. Some people are endowed with very good visual insight; they easily see structures at the first level. But other people have much more trouble with such structures; they much prefer to develop structures at the second level, especially if simple structures of the second level can replace difficult (for them) structures of the first level. Some people have well-developed spatial insight; they see most solutions to solid geometry problems very easily. Other people never see those solutions; they prefer to use analytic geometry for problems of solid geometry.

There are also conclusions that can only be drawn after the language of the third level is learned. Those who have not been able to think at a level higher than the second cannot take a part in such discussions. Here is an example. In history there may be some doubt about the possibility of objectivity. Is it possible to practice history in such a way that it may be called an objective science? Or is it impossible for a historian to be objective because he has his own meanings. Even if he restricts himself to giving the pure facts, the order in which he gives those facts, the language he uses, all tell us his view on the events in question. So it may seem that objectivity in history is quite impossible. To discuss resolutions of this problem it is necessary to be clear about the signification of ''objectivity,'' ''history,'' and many other words. They all belong to the third level of thinking, so only at that level is a true discussion possible.

When professionals of different sciences discuss common problems, they often are not aware of the existence of a third level. Each person uses the third level of his own branch, which was attained by a learning process that is peculiar to the branch in which it has been developed. Those others that this person communicates with are only able to understand at the second level, because their third levels have been developed in other contexts. In such a way there may be many misunderstandings; each professional translates the facts he has heard into his own third level.

In education, teachers often give their students unsolvable problems. They use the language of the third level and the pupils often are not even able to use the language of the second level. Sometimes the pupils have not even formed a language of the first level that accompanies the visual structures.

A typical introduction to an algebra text book might read as follows:

LETTERS USED AS UNIVERSAL NUMBERS: Just as in stenography we have marks in order to write letters, syllables, and words faster, in mathematics letters are introduced to make calculation faster and clearer.

IN ONE AND THE SAME EXERCISE A LETTER ALWAYS REPRESENTS THE SAME NUMBER. IN SUCH A CASE IT IS CALLED A GENERAL NUMBER. With general numbers, one can describe the mathematical operations in the following way:

1. $a + b + c = d$ 　2. $e - f = g$ 　1. and 2. $u + v - w = t$

3. $k \times l = m$ 　　4. $p^q \quad = r$ 　　5. $x \div y = z$

Before the pupils were given this exposition they were taught to perform operations with given numbers. It is clear that this exposition does not give them information about the real meaning of the introduction of letters. "In one and the same exercise a letter always represents the same number" is remarkable: It seems that the only purpose for introducing letters is to be able to do exercises.

In most textbooks the beginning of a topic is given on too high a level. Just open a textbook on a topic with which you are not very well acquainted, and you will see for yourself.

15

The Development of Number

METHODS OF RESEARCH

One rightly objects to recent attempts to explain the development of children's thinking in terms of the thinking of an adult. The arguments against such an endeavor are well known: The attempts of adults to remember the difficulties in learning they themselves had in their youth must fail because the later insight has superseded all former thinking. It is impossible return oneself to a position in which one still has to collect one's knowledge.

It would be a mistake, however, to try to determine a notion of the thinking of a child without any use of adult thinking. Such an attempt is doomed to fail, because the description of the process still requires the help of terms of adult thinking. But the situation is not hopeless. It is possible to put adults in a situation in which their thinking and acting may in some ways be compared with that of a young child who still has to discover the world. We have such a situation if we introduce the adult to a learning process that is totally new to him.

The learning process of an adult and that of a child, of course, only resemble each other to some degree. In a totally new learning process an adult still relies on experiences that a child has not had. Certainly of great significance is the fact that an adult knows that he is learning and knows how one learns. In comparing the learning processes of children and adults, one must guard against perhaps only superficial resemblances. On the other hand, there would be no means to explain the learning of a child if the learning processes of adults were totally ignored: We would be faced with an absolutely unknown world in which the things a child says and does would be completely uninterpretable, for such interpretation would always lead to a comparison with the thinking of an adult.

Those who want to understand thinking and learning of a child must start from the thinking of adults; this is certainly not a superfluous point. One must examine closely research which claims to interpret children's thinking and learning without recourse to adult thinking. The adult thinking, indispensable for the interpretations, is likely to be smuggled in by a back door.

In this chapter I hope to demonstrate that Piaget (1941) repeatedly interprets from an adult perspective, and that his interpretations—if one pays attention to the well-controlled learning processes—are unacceptable in many respects. I also demonstrate that Piaget's results may lead to important conclusions if they are regarded in connection with the general progress of a controllable learning process.

THE COURSE OF A LEARNING PROCESS STRETCHING ITSELF OVER SEVERAL LEVELS

Examples of controllable and well-known learning processes should not be sought among young children. Better results can be expected if we examine the learning of geometry. For children do not begin to learn geometry until they are about 12 years of age. At this age they can express themselves pretty well. They are thus able to speak with their teacher of the difficulties they meet in their learning. Especially beginning geometry instruction holds great significance for pedagogy, which is why there is already an extensive literature on this topic. Moreover, it is evident that a certain connection exists between the learning process and the logical structure of geometry. Our knowledge of this structure, therefore, may help us better comprehend the learning processes. (We must immediately add that many teachers presume much too great a resemblance between the beginning of geometry and pure mathematics and in this way imagine that they can use the structure of mathematics in beginning geometry.)

The first and most important fact we have to point out with this learning process concerns the great difference between the object of study at the beginning of the teaching and 5 months later. Moreover, the character of this object of study changes more than once. An isosceles triangle originally presents itself to the children as a figure recognized by its clear shape. The properties of the triangle do not play a demonstrable part—at any rate they are not explicitly recognized by the children. The seeing and recognition here may be compared with the recognition of an oak or a mouse. At a later stage, when the pupils have attained the second level of thinking, the visual form has already fallen into the background. Now the isosceles triangle is just recognized by its properties: two equal sides or two equal angles. If the pupils are sure of those properties, they have no doubt that a given triangle is isoceles, even if the figure is indistinct or if there is an optical illusion. At the third level of thinking, these properties are no longer the object of study: Now the connection between properties is involved. The equality of the sides of a triangle now implies the equality of two of the angles, and the converse of this theorem holds as well. At the fourth level of thinking, the nature of the relations between certain theorems has become the object of study. What, for example, is meant by "The equality of two sides of a triangle implies the equality of two of the angles"? What is meant when one speaks of the "converse of a theorem"? A child, not yet having attained the second level of thinking, is not able to recognize an isosceles triangle by the equality of two sides or two angles; for he has not yet learned to see figures as totalities of properties. For such a recognition the child must have built up a network of relations in which the figures are interconnected on the basis of their properties. He must have become acquainted with this network in such a manner that he combines the properties automatically without any need of a pictorial representation.

Those who have not yet learned to see the theorems of geometry as independent entities cannot understand in what ways they can be brought into a mutual logical connection. They cannot understand that a theorem signifies a connection between a premise and a conclusion. If one wants pupils who have not yet attained the third level to prove a theorem, then one would have to lead them to believe that proving it means pointing out that it is true. The pupils then get the impression that the teacher has a doubt about the truth of the theorem and that they have the task of convincing the teacher by giving a proof. If, however, one in this way introduces a mathematical demonstration into the learning process too early, this will cause pupils to doubt the usefulness of mathematics: Very often they will also be convinced without proof that the conclusion is true. Moreover, they will in this manner get a wrong impression of the essence of a deductive system.

The heart of the concept of level of thinking is that an object within one science at each level signifies something different; this results in the fact that people speaking to one another at different levels are very often not able to understand each other. These people are speaking in different contexts. With this we are on a pretty familiar ground. That word symbols in one context may have a quite different significance in another we already know from many discussions in which partners are at cross-purposes.

We may see the ways in which levels within a science are connected if again we pay attention to the learning process of geometry. At the first level, geometrical figures are recognized by their shape. At the second level they are considered as bearers of properties. At this level, one is occupied with objects belonging to an internal ordering of the first level, the intuitive stage. It is the properties of the figures that determine their external form; at the first level a pupil is perfectly familiar with the external form, but not with the properties. At the third level a pupil is engaged with the connections between the properties of figures, with the manner in which one property may be deduced from another. These connections, however, allowed one to compare and distinguish figures; for this, the internal ordering of the second level must be determined. *At each level one is explicitly busy with the internal ordering of the previous level.* In geometry this may be clarified in a striking way by naming the levels.

At the first level, space is regarded as it presents itself; so we here speak of *spatial thinking*. At the second level we have *geometric spatial thinking*. At the third level there is *mathematical geometric thinking;* at this level the meaning of "geometrical thinking" is investigated. At the next level *logical mathematical thinking* is studied; here the object is to know why geometric ways of thinking may belong to mathematics.

Many people are of the opinion that pupils first have to know the internal ordering of a field before they are able to begin with the study of the subjects of this field. But this is one of the most serious mistakes one can make. It would be much better to reverse the order; one has to know the subjects of a field, before one is able to study the internal connection. What is the sense of speaking about the connection between properties of geometric figures if these figures themselves have no visual shape? It is not true that one first has to be able to think logically in order to apply logic to mathematics; on the contrary one first must have been busy in some way with mathematics in order to develop by careful analysis the logical structure of the internal connections of mathematics.

Such context transformations also happen in many other sciences. It is clear for example that "cat," "rose," and "egg" may be found at the first level of biology, but that "heredity," "instinct," and "metabolism" belong to a network of relations of a higher level. At what levels and with what significance various topics appear can only be answered by didacticians after thorough study. And it is rather sure that determination of the levels will not be easy, for their arrangement in related topics like arithmetic and algebra is exposed to mutual influence, and their outline will be much less distinct.

THE PHASES OF A LEARNING PROCESS
AIMED AT THE ATTAINMENT OF A LEVEL
OF THINKING

The science to be studied is defined by the context in which the language symbols will have to be developed. The teacher must try to help the child with the development of those language symbols and he must do this just in the context belonging to the science he wants to introduce. So the first phase of the learning process never happens in another way than through *information*: The teacher holds a conversation with the pupils, in well-known language symbols, in which the context he wants to use becomes clear.

The second phase we call *bound orientation* or *exploration*. In this phase the guidance of the teacher is again of great importance. Though now the pupils are able to read themselves the relations between the language symbols—or between forms out of which those symbols will be developed—of the total structure, the teacher helps them trace those relations. For now it is important that the relations belonging to the context are spoken of. The best means to this goal is the presentation of efficient material or assignment of efficient tasks. Without exaggeration we may say that the activities, provided they are carefully chosen, form the proper basis of thinking on the higher level. In the learning processes of geometry, folding figures is the basis of symmetry, filling a box with 1-cm^3 cubes the basis of the concept of volume, and folding of a piece of paper twice in succession the basis of the right angle.

The third phase is directed at the *explicitation,* that is, making explicit the structures involved in the activity. This explicitation is brought about in a class discussion. Under the guidance of the teacher, pupils give their opinions about the regularities they have found. The teacher takes care that the correct technical language is developed. At this time it becomes clear how important it is that the pupils exchange views about the new things they have discovered during the orientation. And because the technical language plays such an important role in this exchange, it is learned very easily.

The fourth phase consists of a *free orientation*. The pupils now know what their subject is about, they have read relations from concrete situations, they now know the relevant language symbols. The domain of their study is distinctly marked out. The moment has come at which the children will have to feel at home in this domain. From a number of tasks, which may be executed in different ways, they have to find their way into the indicated field, in order to get acquainted with it from all directions. In this way signals, precursors to symbols, are developed. The symbols gradually lose part of their visual content and develop into junctions of the network of relations that has been formed. Through free orientation the pupils become so acquainted with the field of thought that the symbols are anticipated. In this way the pupils in the long run are enabled to choose from various possibilities and eventually, if the learning process lasts long enough, to perceive the whole field of thought.

If the learning process advances this far, the next level of thinking is attained. Here the language symbols express quite different things than they did at the first level. They no longer relate to visual structures, but to certain relations with other language symbols. A geometric figure is called ''rectangle'' because it has right angles and not because the pupil recognizes it directly by shape. We will not deny that there is another way of learning, one in which the pupils are informed directly of the relations of every level and must learn them by heart. In this way, too, a network of relations is formed, and it is possible to teach the pupils to orient themselves in the field, for example, by having them perform many exercises. This network of relations is also formed by activity, though it may be on paper. The foundation of the concept of congruence in this case is formed by having the pupils write the three equal elements of two triangles, by placing a bracket ({}) around them, and by noting which congruence characteristic (S S S, etc.) they have to use. The network of relations in which this 'congruence' is included has a great resemblance to the network originating from activities, explicitation, and abstraction on the foundation of the first level. Still, we would not expect that these pupils could further apply the relations they have found to concrete situations. And even if they were taught the application to some concrete situations, we would still not expect that they could apply them in quite new concrete situations. And still less would we expect that they were conscious of the connection between their world of observation and the deductive system. In short, though the teacher had given the pupils a network of relations, they could not make use of it.

THE LEVELS AND THE DEVELOPMENT OF NUMBER

It is more difficult to understand the learning process in arithmetic than in geometry, because a great part of the former takes place in the period before school age. If we draw a parallel with the learning process in geometry, we may expect that the second level in arithmetic is attained after the child has learned to see numbers as abstract symbols—after the child is free from the visual form of the things he has been counting. Whereas at the first level 'four' is linked with figures, for instance the vertices of a square, or is used in the sequence one, two, three, four, five, . . . , at the second level 'four'' is a junction in a network of relations. Here it is 'two and two', or perhaps 'two times two,' or perhaps 'five minus one.' In any case it has loosened itself from the concrete material. Most children have already attained the second level of thinking in arithmetic before they enter elementary school, and teaching has probably adjusted itself to this fact. With an educational system based on an average development of a child it would be very difficult to proceed in any other way.

The third level distinguishes itself from the second by the fact that the relations between numbers have become objects of thinking. Three times eight is found by a child adding eight and eight and again eight. The child is able to construct the multiplication tables, or to find the sum of eight and five by first adding eight and two and then adding three to the result. At this level, the relations are still linked with given numbers. It is improbable that a child can see subtraction as the inverse of addition or division as the inverse of multiplication; for this presupposes that the child has developed a network of relations in which the operations of arithmetic have become joined. In such a case, the numbers themselves would have disappeared, or would at most act as a model to be generalized.

The fractional numbers present a special difficulty. They too are developed with the help of concrete material; for instance, the partitioning of suitable objects into congruent parts. Here too we deal with a new subject matter that at first has to be developed at the first level. At the second level, the fractions will have certain properties and in the network of relations will have loosened themselves from the concrete material. Then, in the network of relations, one encounters some symbols belonging to the context of the calculation with integers. But only at the third level will a complete connection—a common calculation—come into being. Here an extension of the context, brought about adding a new field— fractions—to the third level of thinking, has been attained.

SIMILARITIES BETWEEN PIAGET'S ANALYSES AND THE THEORY OF LEVELS OF THOUGHT

Let us begin with the concept Piaget considers central to thinking: the *operation*. An operation is characterized by three properties: (1) it springs from an activity, (2) it is reversible, and (3) it is associative.

The first point needs no further explanation. In the above we have already emphasized that pupils can only understand symmetry after they have worked with it; when, for example, they have folded paper or handled a mirror. The whole second phase of the learning process, the exploration, is aimed at these activities.

The operation is reversible. From Piaget's investigations, it appears that a child sees a situation well when he is able to find to logically reverse an action ,that is, negate it. Together with the third property, the associativity of the operation, that is, the capacity to think of a series of actions as a whole, the second point reduces itself to determining when such reversible relations become possible.

It is therefore no wonder that criticism of usual teaching methods by didacticians who support Piaget's theories agrees with ours in broad outline. A great part of *The Child's Conception of Number* is devoted to the proof that it is not possible to impart to young children insight into operations with numbers if they have not yet "matured" to it. Indeed it is senseless, even harmful, to have children add and subtract numbers before they have attained the level at which abstract numbers originate.

The three stages Piaget speaks of have a certain resemblance to our phases of the learning process. At the first stage, children think that a quantity of pearls changes as soon as they are poured into a cylinder of different dimensions. We should observe that the relations among the concepts of 'quantity', 'pouring into', and 'counting' are so little understood by these children that they are not yet able to operate with them; they have not worked enough with the material.

At the second stage, the children are uncertain about their conclusions. They are inclined to accept that the quantities are equal, but still they can again and again be deceived by appearances. We would say here that many simple relations have already been constituted, but the children are not yet sufficiently oriented in the field. They are not yet able to see the field of thought as a whole.

At the third stage, children come to the right conclusions immediately. Practically without thinking, they can say that the quantity has remained the same, that they are just the same pearls. If one asks them why the level in one cylinder is higher than in the other, they need only think for a moment: "Because the first cylinder is thinner." Now the field of thought has become a totality. The children are able to find many ways to the goal; they know the coherence of the phenomena.

OBJECTIONS AGAINST PIAGET'S METHOD
OF INVESTIGATION

Although a theory of levels of thinking appears to have been developed by Piaget, there are important differences from our theory that are more than terminological. Piaget's investigations are related to psychology of development, whereas we have discussed the progress of a learning process of intelligence. (I will emphasize here that there is a great difference between the psychology of learning skills and the psychology of developing intelligence.) The stages of Piaget all belong to one period, leading from one level of thinking to the next. From the following discussion it emerges that Piaget, just because he was not aware of the existence of more than two levels of thinking, sometimes came to wrong conclusions. We can understand why, in this way, he more than once uses a terminology that creates confusion.

One of the first theses of Piaget in *The Child's Conception of Number* is that the constitution of the concept of number keeps step with a logical development. To this thesis Piaget attaches uncommon value, as is indicated by the frequency with which he uses the word "logical" when he analyzes the answers of the children. Still, "logic" must here be understood in a somewhat different way than in mathematics, which appears most distinctly by the fact that Piaget almost always speaks of logic in a context of actions and experiences. One might think it reasonable to pass by this difference with the remark that it is only a question of terminology, but this would be a mistake. The deviating signification of the word "logic" originates from Piaget's striving to place all thinking in one period, a period in which he tried to deduce mathematical and logical thinking directly from action and experience.

According to our theory of levels, however, one does not in this manner come any farther than the second level of thinking. To go higher, one must pay attention to the relations of the network of the second level, examine the nature and coherence of those relations in a certain context in bound orientation, take part in an explicitation of the observed internal ordering on that level, and finally find one's way in the new field of thought by free orientation. In this way the network of relations will develop into a totality. Such thinking, too, has been developed by activity, but by quite a different one from that of the first level. In arithmetic, for example, the new activity consists of addition, subtraction, multiplication, and division of abstract numbers.

Piaget's deviating use of the term "logic" is also connected with his view that a theory of number might be founded by tracing a child's discovery of the concept of number. According to the theory of levels, however, this is impossible—the ordering of the relations leading to a deductive system can only take place at the fourth level of thinking. The language symbols with which a system of logic are constructed have abstract contents. They may appear the same as those the child uses, but they belong to another network of relations and are in general linked with each other in other ways. So it is not possible to build a deductive system with the language symbols of the child without giving a totally different content to those symbols; in other words, without conforming their contents to thinking of the higher level. But then one has quite another way of thinking from that of young children.

Still, it is quite possible to come to new insights by following the train of thought of children. Although they reason in another way than we do, they sometimes make connections that are productive and that an adult does not expect. But it is adults who see their full significance, because they are able to interpret the connections within their own network of relations. Children often have productive thoughts, they often contribute to the simplification of long discussions, but in most of the cases they are not aware of the importance of their thoughts. Often they do not remember that they have contributed to the discussion. If we want to interpret actions of children, this experience must caution us. Of course, for the adults who know the internal ordering of the actions, it is easy to indicate, at their own level, why the children have acted correctly. But this does not imply that the children have acted from the same understanding.

There are children who immediately see that the number of pearls does not alter when they are poured from one cylinder into another. They are not confused by the different shapes of the cylinders. Piaget concludes from this that the children have seen the relations of the dimensions of the cylinders and have perceived that the cylinder diameters and levels are inversely proportional. Indeed, answers of children in the third stage might affirm this opinion. At least, by pointing to the difference in diameter after the event, they can give an explanation for the difference of the levels. But just this explanation, after the event, makes it probable that initially the children were convinced of the constant volume for other reasons and that only after the event were they forced to an explanation. Naturally it remains difficult to determine what actually brought the children to the insight that volume does not alter. A comparison with natural sciences shows that often it is not simple to determine the reasons for a conclusion concerning constant magnitudes. Sometimes there is a whole network of relations within which the constancy of a magnitude leads to important simplifications. How long was it before the law of the conservation of energy was discovered? Certainly is it not easy to explain why energy is thought of as constant. Of one thing, however, we may be sure; namely, that insight about constants of volume develops from an action—for instance, the pouring of bottles with lemonade into glasses of different shapes. Does not the utterance "It still is the same amount of lemonade" show a familiarity with the material, a familiarity arising from action? The pouring of the lemonade may, in the end, produce the notion that there exists something—let us call it *quantity*—that does not alter with the action.

The question of which grounds a child uses to conclude a constant volume still has not been answered. The solution proposed by Piaget is unacceptable because in some sense it imputes the higher-level thinking of an adult to the child. We have no reason to presume that children are capable of such thinking. Piaget concludes such thinking only because he can not imagine another conclusion: The child has reasoned correctly because he came to a conclusion in accordance with the adult thinking; the conclusion must have been reached as an adult reaches a conclusion, because the correct answer was found. Piaget remarks regularly that such results are peculiar. But apparently he has failed to notice that the character of his questions and the way in which his experiments are set up determine this conclusion; every possibility of finding something else is precluded. Characteristic of his working method is this example from *The Child's Conception of Space* (1956). Piaget asks children what the result would be if a line was divided in more and more (unlimited) even parts. In the first stage, they say that there will be ever more, smaller parts. But in the third stage, they come to the conclusion that finally one would have points as a result of the division. Most teachers of mathematics will be less content with the latter answer than with the former. Syswerda (1955) discussed an experiment in which he gives pupils of a secondary school the same questions. We have repeated the experiment. Our pupils answered practically unanimously, to our relief, that the parts never could become points, however great their number might be, because points have no dimension whereas little parts have. So in some way the answers are influenced by the method of asking. Because Piaget had an unusual representation of a point, he also found with his experimental subjects an unusual development of the concept of point.

Number is constituted by one-to-one mapping: Two sets are equal if every member of the first set can be placed opposite one and only one element of the second set. This definition, however, does not belong to the second level of thinking; it is possible to acquire a concept of number at the second level, without visual aid, without realizing that the above definition implicitly determines the possibility of introducing abstract numbers. So if Piaget establishes that many children are not able to conclude, with the help of a one-to-one mapping, the equivalence of numbers, this does not yet imply that it is not possible to teach those children arithmetic. This would even be possible if the mapping did belong to the second level.

The difficulties originating from Piaget's failure to take into account levels of thinking are most distinct in his experiments concerning insight in the develop-- ment of the concept of multiplication. Here he uses objects that belong together naturally, like vases and flowers. A number of vases are put side by side and the child must put a flower into each vase. Afterward, the flowers are placed in a pile. Next, the child must put a new flower in each vase, and these flowers, too, are placed in a pile. First the child must see that the two heaps are equal, and next he must understand that when all the flowers are put back into the vases, with a equal number in each vase, one would find two flowers in each vase.

From the experiments, it appeared that young children made wrong conclusions. They seemed generally to conclude on grounds of (from an adult point of view) disorderly attempts. The result of this experiment does not astonish us. Such relations between sets, which by most of the children cannot even be counted, belong to the third level of thinking. Many teachers have assured us that many children will never see such relations. So it might have been worth while to investigate whether children who succeeded with the experiment had not calculated with certain numbers for themselves, for example like this: "The first time I had ten flowers; the next time ten again; so now I have ten times two flowers." But that would not have been the same task as was given to the young children. Those children were expected to conclude: $a \times 1 + a \times 1 = a \times 2$. Such a task is a generalization of the concrete example and therefore belongs to a higher level.

In one of his protocols Piaget describes how a child, after having first seen that two sets of pearls were equal, afterward thought that one set contained more pearls than the other. When asked where the new pearls came from, the child answered "from there" and pointed to the cylinder from which the pearls were poured. For a child who has not yet seen 'quantity' and 'constant' linked, the question has no sense. For such a child the extra pearls need not come from anywhere. In the same way, a juggler has little success with young children—not because children simply accept juggling, but because they do not appreciate how extraordinary it is. It is also said that children observing the pouring of a liquid from one cylinder into another think that liquid can arbitrarily expand or contract. But again, this explanation belongs to adult thought. Children do not believe that liquids expand or contract, because in the network of relations at their disposal there is no place for the concepts of expansion or contraction. 'Expansion' and 'contraction' are language symbols dependent on the belief of a constant volume; after this belief has been undermined, concepts like 'expansion' and 'contraction' come into existence. One ought to keep this well in view if one is inclined to think of "magical" thinking by children. What one calls magic is often concluded on the basis of a poor network of relations.

PIAGET'S DEVELOPMENTAL PSYCHOLOGY
AND THE NEEDS OF THE DIDACTICIAN

Once again we will draw up a balance sheet. From Piaget's investigations it appears that young children are not able to operate with structures of thought of too high a level. It is true that they know the language symbols, but not in such a manner that they fit into the network of relations of the higher level. This is an affirmation of the theory of levels, but it does not induce us to accept Piaget's theory. Our first objection concerns his use of the word "logical"; with this word Piaget suggests that thinking goes on in only one period. And this objection is also leveled against Piaget's way of asking questions, which is no better tuned to the level of children's thinking. Piaget's train of thought suggests the thesis that one must know (a priori?) the implicit structure of a field of thought before one can conceive of this field. This, however, is completely contrary to our conception of a structure issuing from an action (and being implicit in this action) and, by means of an analysis and an explicitation, leading to the higher level of thinking.

There is a second objection. Piaget studied the development of children, whereas we observed learning processes. These are by no means the same. Human development takes place in the following ways:

1. biological maturation
2. confrontation with the cultural environment
3. exploration
4. guided learning processes

Biological maturation refers to the phenomenon in which man, by growing in body and mind during a certain period of his or her life, is capable of ever more and better performances. Biological factors can limit performance. Perhaps young children cannot be expected to sit still for long periods, because at their age they need much bodily exercise. But it is difficult to judge how far mental maturation is determined by biological factors, because such maturation is also always brought about by a confrontation with the environment. Lack of mental progress should not quickly be attributed to defective biological maturation if the influence of the cultural environment on development is unknown.

The confrontation with the environment is complicated because it takes place in different ways. In the first place, there is language. The development of a child is in a large measure dependent on the language environment. Language— its structure—plays a role in the discovery of new and special relations. The word "maturation" leads one to think automatically in the direction of biology, because one first learned the word in a biological context. If the connection with biology is not intended, then is it better not to use the word "maturation." In the second place, confrontation with the environment is also shaped by the behavior of people in the direct environment of the child. On one hand, the child wants to imitate that behavior; on the other, he wants to be different. In either case, however, his development is influenced. In the third place, the influence of the environment is determined by culture. A child growing up in the country develops quite differently from a child growing up in a city. The child of a physicist might be exposed to quite different things than the child of a poet.

In *exploration,* the individuality of children expresses itself. They do not develop exclusively on the basis of intelligence; the development is also strongly influenced by the cultural environment. But children develop each in their own way, exploring their unique environments and directing themselves to that which fits the unfolding of their personalities. The exploration leads to a development that may be understood as an interaction of intelligence and environment, and something quite new comes into existence: the personality of the child.

Guided learning processes are established by adults with a special pedagogical aim in mind. A child must learn to eat decently, to dress, to behave respectably in society, and so on. At school the guided learning processes are clearly directed at intellectual performances, where the child must be able to express himself well and learn reading, writing, and arithmetic.

Usually all forms of development not falling under guided learning processes are attributed to maturation. That is understandable, for it is very difficult to distinguish between biological maturation, confrontation with the cultural environment, and exploration. Still, the choice of the word "maturation" for all these different factors is somewhat unfortunate; it has too strong a tie with a biological context. An added reason to deplore this is the fact that the development of language and arithmetic, as far as the lower levels are concerned, occurs for the most part in the period in which the child does not yet go to school. So this development nearly entirely takes place through unguided learning processes and is therefore called "maturation." A child is said to be not yet mature for reading, writing, or arithmetic. But if this sort of maturing were really a matter of confrontation with the cultural environment or exploration, then it would be possible to make the child mature by leaving less of the development to chance and by arranging the guided learning processes in ways other than school education. This might be done in various ways. School children who have not "matured" might be helped by giving them more apt material. At any rate, waiting till "maturation" has taken place is not the right solution.

We have seen that the experiments of Piaget concerned maturation. But because he has not distinguished the various forms of maturation, he gives the impression that only biological maturation is relevant. The parallels, however, between his results and the stages of a learning process makes it very improbable that this maturation is importantly biological. Piaget's results principally give us information about the development of young children as it appears with incidental learning processes—learning processes connected with a confrontation with the environment and with exploration. What he has shown us is not the development of the child in general, but a development that often takes place with children of the West European cultural environment in the middle of the twentieth century.

For a didactician, it would have been interesting if Piaget had been able to present reliable material about the progress of the incidental learning processes, if he had been able to tell in which ways children help themselves from one phase to another. Piaget, it is true, gives his opinion about this, but this is only a debatable hypothesis. Rather than drawing conclusions about the formation of ideas from the actions of the children, he projects his own adult thinking into the actions of the child.

With an example I will suggest another possibility. In a variation of an experiment of Piaget, I set before my daughter (4 years, 3 months), who was able to count up to ten, a series of seven widely spaced squares. Opposite these I set a new series of seven squares, but these I set close together. I asked her which series was greater, and as in Piaget's experiments she said that the first was, although she knew that in each series there were seven squares. I repeated the experiment with two rows of four squares, with the same result. After this I repeated the experiment, but now with a row of three widely spaced squares opposite a row of four squares lying close together. This time, my daugher said with great assurance that in the second row there were more squares: "Four is surely more than three!" I repeated the experiment with two rows of four squares, and this time she thought the rows were equal. And she continued to arrive at this result as long as the experiment was repeated with numbers she was able to count. My elder daughter (5 years, 8 months), just coming home from the kindergarten, first also thought that seven squares lying side by side were less than seven squares with space between. When the younger girl heard this, she said: "But don't you see that there are just as many of them, they are in each way seven," at which the elder daughter, after a long reflecting, said: "Oh yes, now I see, you have pushed them together."

The younger child originally ordered the sets by their length and density. But she was also convinced that four is more than three. The initial unanalyzed ordering left the possibility of two different quantities of four. But the dilemma caused by the conviction that four is more than three was solved by changing her mind. This, however, had important results: From this point on, her judgment was based on the well-known ordering of natural numbers. To this argument the elder sister had to give way, but she felt forced to seek an explanation for the contradiction she had stated.

This experiment can be repeated. The results are not always the same; sometimes a child may say that four objects put together are more than three with space between but may also remain positive that the two rows of four are different. This is not surprising: The result depends on the understanding of the symbol "four." More important than the result is the fact that a child may learn in and by the situation, that it is possible that a child, with the help of the presented material, may change from one of Piaget's stages to another. Piaget generally arranged his experiments in such a way that a child could not learn by the situation. Such an arrangement is quite correct if one takes the view that developmental psychology has the task of investigating what a child of a certain age in an average cultural environment in western Europe has on the average made himself familiar with. But this approach does not answer questions about which are influences of cultural environment and which of exploration, or of how it is possible to give guidance to the learning processes.

What a didactician would like to know is not so much how far a child of a certain age has advanced by his incidental learning processes (or ought to have advanced), but how a child learns—in what ways it becomes evident to a child that four is more than three or that a quantity of liquid is not altered by pouring, or that trees are moved by the wind and not the reverse. It is not so much with what children and at what age it may be possible to begin with stereotyped teaching processes, but how education must be arranged to allow children to complete efficient learning processes.

With such experiments the developmental psychologist might get important support from didacticians; for the latter know how, in general, such learning processes occur and so what a developmental psychologist might find. Such cooperation is particularly desirable. Especially when learning processes in elementary school are concerned, a didactician will not be able to attain his goal without a considerable knowledge of the manner in which unguided learning processes occur. He also needs to know what children have learned before they go to school and how they have learned it. However, when an explanation of the observed phenomena is at stake, the developmental psychologist cannot succeed without the help of the didactician.

It still remains for us to explain why Piaget supposes stages in the development of children, whereas we have found phases in a learning process. How is it possible that with children of a certain age one comes upon the same stage of development in different domains? On reflection this is not astonishing. In every domain, the children begin at the first level; with their learning processes they begin in the first phase. In their first years of life they attain a higher level of thinking in hardly any domain, and therefore their development may be read from the phase they have attained in the first period leading to the next level of thinking.

Many people have assured me that Piaget did not distinguish between maturation and learning. From many of his papers, one can conclude the same. This makes application of his results difficult. For if learning were concerned, a comparative study of the learning of children and of adults would be appropriate. Moreover, a statement from him on the relation between maturation and learning would have clarified his intentions. Then we would know that Piaget had not presumed biological maturation. But if he really intended only to investigate learning processes, we have to object to his serious restriction of such processes to only one period.

SUMMARY

1. Piaget's thesis that insight very often arises from an action is true.
2. Piaget gives convincing proof that children's thinking is different from adults', and that children's thinking cannot be understood from the study of adult thinking.
3. Piaget rightly distinguishes a number of phases in concept development, but they have to be understood as phases of a learning process.
4. Piaget overlooks the fact that a learning process repeats itself at a higher level, that there is a new action from which a new insight is born, and that at the higher level the same phases are repeated.
5. Piaget's failure to distinguish between the higher levels of thinking has the consequence that he values too highly the thinking of his experimental subjects who are at the end of the three stages.
6. Piaget's experiments are not efficiently arranged to investigate the course of learning processes of young children.
7. Piaget has not clearly distinguished between development by biological maturation, by confrontation with the cultural environment, and by exploration. For a didactician, however, such distinctions are necessary.

16

Levels of Structure in Argument

The term "level of thinking" naturally implies emphasis on psychological aspects. Certainly the levels are significant for the psychology of man, but in education special attention must be paid to communication. There the most important thing is not the way of thinking, but the results of thinking, results that are fixed in speaking and writing. This is not only important for mathematics instruction, still they also have an important implication for mathematics itself.

Let me begin with a simple statement: "This figure is a rhombus." What is meant by this sentence depends on the speaker. If he is a naive beginner in mathematics, he probably does not mean any more than: "This figure has the shape I have learned to call 'rhomb'." Frequently this designation is connected with the position the figure has with regard to the observer. We also know that such a speaker is inclined to exclude squares from the rhombuses. I refer, for instance, to the experiments of Cattegno in this domain. If someone has already studied mathematics for some time, he means by the statement "This figure is a rhombus" something different. The figure he refers to is a collection of properties, properties he has learned to call "rhombus." A square has all these properties and therefore is rightly considered to be a rhomb. In a later stage, these properties are ordered, and the person will know that a figure is a rhombus if it satisfies the definition of quadrangle with four equal sides. Still, the meaning of his statement has not changed: He still wants to express the fact that in the given figure all the properties of a rhombus are collected.

In the case of the first speaker, the judgment was based on an observation; in that of the second, it resulted from a network of relations that was at the disposal of the speaker. In such a network of relations, the words "rhombus," "side," "angle," "square" are junctions; each of these word symbols represents a collection of properties. They are linked with each other by different relations. We do not, of course, suggest that the thinking of the second speaker must take place without any observation. Perhaps the second speaker, when speaking about a rhombus, always sees it distinctly before him. But this is not of interest to us here, for it is not our intention to enter the domain of psychology. Our investigation is into the basis of judgments, and for the second speaker that is the network of relations. Even if a figure were drawn the sides of which were not exactly equal, this would not change the judgment if the second speaker was assured that it was the intention of the one drawing the figure to make the sides equal.

Without the existence of a network of relations, reasoning is impossible. The first speaker did not arrive at his judgment by means of reasoning. He saw the rhomb and that was sufficient. Nor would it be possible to have his judgment withdrawn by means of reasoning. To do this, he would have to acquire a network of relations. One never has the recognition of a network of relations from the beginning. By our definition, a person not having a network of relations of a certain subject at his disposal is at the first level of thinking about this subject. Whoever does possess this network of relations is at the second level of thinking.

In education, the difference of level between the teacher and the pupil can sometimes be clearly observed:

1. The pupil cannot follow the reasoning of the teacher. He understands nothing of it. He actually does not know what the teacher is speaking about. When he is asked to reproduce the reasoning, it appears clearly that he is lacking every insight.

2. The teacher feels powerless; all arguments he advances turn out to be useless. It seems he is speaking another language than the pupil, which indeed is the case. If one uses the method of 'telescoped reteaching', this short-circuiting between teacher and pupil does not occur. For, at the moment the difficulty threatens to arise, the teaching process for this subject is interrupted for some months. When the teaching process is taken up again, the pupil has come nearer the higher level. Then the knowledge that was earlier presented to him has had time to settle.

3. When once the pupil has attained a level in his development, backsliding rarely occurs.

The development of the network of relations has resulted in the rhombus becoming a collection of properties. Now the relation of the rhombus to other figures is defined by these properties. If pupils have made certain progress, they will answer the question "What is a rhombus?" with "A rhombus is a quadrangle with four equal sides, in which the diagonals intersect each other perpendicularly, in which the diagonals bisect the angles, and in which opposite angles are equal." On the basis of this statement, a square is a rhombus. A technical language has been developed that makes it possible for people to interchange thoughts. The acceptance of this advantage also involves obligations: One has to stick to the network of relations. While on the grounds of observation a diagonal of a quadrangle is inside the figure, one must admit on the grounds of the network of relations that diagonals also occur outside the quadrangle. The transition from the field of perception to the network of relations can also be an impoverishment: Often more is included in the observation than can be embodied in a network of relations. It is much more difficult to recognize a plant with the help of a classification table than with the help of a good picture or a similar specimen. In mathematics such an impoverishment is, as it were, the target: One tries to build up the network of relations in such a fashion that only the essential parts remain.

Only after the rhombus has become a totality of properties is an ordering of these properties, perhaps a logical ordering, possible. Only then, for instance, can one say that the property 'a rhomb has a diagonal for an axis of symmetry' implies that two opposite angles of the rhomb are equal and that the diagonal bisects the other two angles. In instruction, one must delay the logical ordering, the proving of properties, until the pupil has been sufficiently acquainted with the properties. (This is just as true in the university as in the secondary school.) Even when the pupil already has a notion of what a logical deductive system is, it still makes no sense to begin his acquaintance with the measurement of solids with axioms. And this is the case for every new domain of mathematics.

What it means to say that some property "follows" from another cannot be explained. One can seek analogies, like a genealogical tree. One can say that it is necessary to use "following" when one wants to convince somebody of a certain fact. However, this is no guarantee that a pupil has understood. For the statement "From A follows B" does not prove that B is true; it only shows that the possible truth of B depends on the truth of A. The links of a genealogical tree are of a different character than are those of logic. There is a much better chance that a pupil will understand the use of logical links if in some situation that pupil draws a logical conclusion. Then it is possible to point out that just this is the "following from."

In this matter the field of observation can only disturb. Here it does not matter if the diagonal really is an axis of symmetry, or if the opposite angles really are equal; it is not even necessary to suppose that they are equal. The only thing of importance for the following of assertion B from assertion A is that the simultaneous truth of A and falsity of B is impossible.

The above reasoning forms a part of another network of relations. In this network the contents of *A* and *B* are of no importance. The only things of importance for the further train of thought are the links existing between *A* and *B*. With these links the new network of relations is constructed. So the new network of relations is just as detached from the former (the second) as the second network of relations was from the first. Therefore we speak of the third level of thinking. In instruction, this demonstrates itself just as clearly as the second level of thinking.

The network of relations of the third level can only come about sensibly after the second level of thinking has been sufficiently built up. When this second network of relations is present in so perfect a form that its structure can, as it were, be read from it, when the pupil is able to speak with others about this structure, then the building blocks are present for the network of the third level. Put another way, the second network of relations must be present in such a perfect form that a process of analysis and a process of objectivization can take place: Analysis makes distinguishable and recognizable the different qualities of the network, objectivization supplies word symbols to those qualities and thus makes them possible objects of discussion. This course of events does not always or even generally take place. It is possible to build networks of relations piece-meal, and this often happens. It happens when methods of calculation are learned verbally, are memorized without the effort of determining why something is calculated in one way and not in another.

It is important to distinguish different cases. When someone wants to study group theory, he can begin by studying the conditions that the elements of groups have to satisfy. Next he can study the theorems dealing with groups and he can trace their proofs. Such an approach is suitable for those who are acquainted with elementary mathematics. For, in that case, the approach is at least familiar: It is a variation and a generalization of rules and methods that are already sufficiently known and of which the sense has been understood. It would be totally unsuitable, however, for one to get acquainted in this way with elementary mathematics or fractions. Then it would not be easy to put known algorithms into practice, and one could not expect pupils to be able to manage with new problems.

There is much more at stake here than some improvement of methods for teaching in secondary education. The greater part of our knowledge is obtained by learning, and how far we can rely on this knowledge depends on the nature of this learning. Most mathematical knowledge, presented to us in the usual form for mathematics, is not sufficiently reliable since we were not sufficiently pre-pared for it, not knowing the aim; thus we were only able to criticize after the completion of the argument. When a curriculum begins with axioms, a criticism of those axioms is impossible because the pupil does not know their purpose. A criticism of methods is also difficult when only after frequent use does one begin to understand how these methods actually work. When the teacher has not explained his purposes beforehand and the development differs from that which the pupil has supposed, the pupil first will think that she has misunderstood the teacher. Instead of a pupil, you might also consider a reader of a journal article in the same circumstance: Only if the reader, at the end of the argument, has time and perseverance to reread the whole matter, when he can link the material with that which he already knows, is there a possibility for criticism. Those who know the overloaded programs of the present day will understand that such quiet reconsideration often does not happen.

If one expects of a pupil something more than the ability to slavishly repeat that which the teacher has asserted, if on the contrary one hopes the pupil will take a critical position with respect to assertions and will be willing to help with their improvement, one will have to teach with a new, unusual approach: One will have to investigate what the pupil knows about the subject; point out as soon as possible that which one wants to demonstrate; continually invite the pupil to make objections—not only because in this way it is sure that he can understand the argument, but also because in this way there is more chance that mistakes, occurring in nearly every argument, will be found.

Reasoning from a logical deductive system belongs to the third level of thinking. The network of relations based on the fixing in words of facts of observation belongs to the second level of thinking. These levels have networks that do not change from one to the other: Reasoning takes place either in the second or in the third network of relations. We now trace by an example how this actually takes place (see Figure 16.1).

Two triangles are congruent if they agree in two sides and the included angle. In rectangle *ABCD*, triangles *ABC* and *BAD* agree in two sides and the included angle. So triangles *ABC* and *BAD* are congruent. In congruent triangles corresponding sides are equal. *AC* and *BD* are corresponding sides of congruent triangles, so *AC* and *BD* are equal.

This type of reasoning is totally given over to the truth of the propositions. Questions of coherence are forced into the background. For the teacher, the exactness of the argument is determined by the connection of the deductions to the contents of the statements. When he has to defend this exactness with colleagues, he will do it by making this structure explicit by means of word symbols

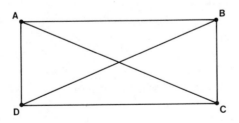

Figure 16.1

or mathematical signs. Therefore his judgment is based on a network of relations of the third level of thinking.

For the pupils, two triangles are involved of which they know they agree in two sides and the included angle. Next they know that the corresponding sides of two triangles are equal, from which it follows that the diagonals of the rectangle are equal. About this they are sure. Still there remains an unsatisfactory feeling for them, because they had already known that in all rectangles the diagonals are equal, perhaps by seeing the symmetrical shapes of the rectangle. They did not need the reasoning to be sure. In the most favorable case, the pupils sometimes intuitively appreciate the transition to the third level of thinking. If this intuition deserts them, they feel uncomfortable. Their uncertainty is demonstrated by incorrect linkings or by a falling back to visual aids. In the latter case, they refer to coincidences in the figures they have drawn.

This example shows us that a judgment can be based on a structure of the third level, but that this structure often is not made explicit. Perhaps it may be that in many cases a few explorers make the structures of the third level explicit, but a great majority of the pupils do not go any farther than a verbal or algorithmic assimilation of those structures. And in this way they move farther from the real content of the theorems.

17

The Intuitive Foundations
Of Mathematics

WHERE DOES THINKING BEGIN?

Recall the question posed by my two daughters (Chapter 2): Does a person think at all times other than when asleep? One daughter thought it quite ordinary to take a walk through the woods without thinking at all; the other thought that if one knew she was walking in the woods, she must be thinking.

At that time I was inclined to grant that the second child was right; at present I sympathize with the point of view of the first. The starling that flies continually around my cherry tree in order to choose the ripest cherry definitely perceives the tree with the cherries and also notices which cherry is the ripest, but I have the greatest doubt that thinking is coupled with this perceiving and choosing. Thinking can only be observed when it is followed by a statement. In other words: *Thinking is only ascertained at the moment there has been a pronouncement*—or to speak in more general terms—*when there has been a symbolization*.

The question of where and how thinking begins is more important than one would at first suppose. A child who has already sailed in a little boat is not astonished by the fact that a boat does not sink. Nor is that child surprised that a stone does sink. But this does not establish that the child has an explanation for the boat's floating and the stone's sinking. With little experience with boats, a boy of 12 years can calmly pull a plug out of the bottom of a boat and afterward experience shock at the sinking of the boat. A floating bridge can awaken for a child great feelings of terror: A floating bridge is a bridge having the greatest difficulty keeping itself above water. But these words of mine give a poor image of the situation: The child has a wordless judgment of the alarming image of the floating bridge, but a judgment that maintains the critical nature of the situation.

It is well known that Piaget does not much value the wordless judgment. He asks questions like "Why does the stone sink and why does the boat not sink?" Such questions only have sense when the child has learned to put the situation into words and, moreover, has come to an analysis of different situations.

Piaget starts from the idea that a child will independently come to such an analysis; the possibility that such an analysis will be brought about with the help of a teacher is not included in his views. Especially with the problem of sinking and floating, this point of view seems to me very extreme: I imagine that many adults cannot solve the problem of sinking and floating.

Thinking is preceded by a viewing of the situation, a phase in which one "undergoes" the situation. In this phase that precedes thinking, insight is already possible: one can assimilate structures in such a way that appropriate action in new situations is possible. It is easy to accept this statement by remembering that there can be talk of insight with animals. If man acts in such a way, one speaks of *an intuitive choosing of the right means*.

THE RATIONAL APPROACH TO A SITUATION

Thinking about a situation requires symbols. These may be language symbols or signs. They also may be images with the character of signs. With the use of language symbols and signs it is possible to exchange one's insight into a situation with other people. Sometimes, for example when hieroglyphics are used, the signs maintain the character of the previous images. With the help of symbols a language can be formed; with the help of this language a theory can be constructed.

If one wants to test a teaching–learning process, one can investigate how far the pupils have progressed in their knowledge of a theory. If intuitive insight is present, the way is open for the learning of a theory. The investigation into the readiness of a pupil for a teaching–learning process must therefore not be aimed at the knowledge of the theory but at the accessibility of the pupil to intuitive insight. Piaget's experiments aimed at children's knowledge of a theory about sinking and floating have created much confusion. The teacher is not interested in the part of a theory a child incidentally picks up; he is interested in intuitive knowledge that has to be acquired, the ways in which such knowledge has to be acquired, and finally how the child, with the help of such knowledge, can be brought to a theory. Primitive builders of canoes probably have little theoretical knowledge of upward force and specific gravity, but they presumably have more insight into the stability of a canoe than many of us. *Whoever wants to investigate whether a child has insight into something or has the capability to acquire such insight rapidly must avoid deductive approaches as much as possible.*

HIGHER LEVELS OF THINKING

One might object that there are types of insight that come into existence only *after* a rational approach to a problem. This is surely true: In such a case, we have *insight at a higher level of thinking*. When a situation has been made clear with the help of symbols, it is very often possible to discover a new structure between these symbols. New statements are possible on the grounds of this new structure. This structure is also at first "undergone"; only after the introduction of new symbols is thinking about the structure possible. In earlier chapters I have discussed this phenomenon in terms of the use of language at a higher level of thinking. For thinking at a higher level it is necessary to have learned to argue at the previous level of thinking, and in this way to have obtained control of the symbols.

I long supposed that psychologists applied tests with a too strongly verbal character because they did not realize the levels of thinking. Now I have reason to suppose that they do this while insufficiently conscious of the fact that action from insight is possible in situations for which the actor has no thinking structure. *Not only with animals but also with man, action on the grounds of a structure need not be joined with the possession of a thinking structure.*

THE INTUITIVE APPROACH TO A TOPIC

In topics like geometry, physics, or geography, which do not make use of the framework of another topic, it is incorrect to start with a deductive approach. If this were done, language symbols that had been developed in incidental learning processes (learning processes outside of the teaching process) would be appealed to. In such a case, the teacher would run a great risk of not being understood by his pupils.

The intuitive approach begins with the presentation of a structure. It is necessary that this structure appeal to the pupils. The teacher can have actions performed that are evoked by the structure in consequence of the task. Then the teacher can put the results into discussion, thereby developing language symbols. In short, the learning process enters the phase of explicitation.

An efficient beginning structure in geometry is square-grid paper. You can choose a point on the paper. From this point, a line segment can be drawn "two to the right and one upward." From the beginning, it becomes clear that it does not matter which side of the paper is placed horizontally at the bottom: There are four directions on the square-grid paper, which cannot be distinguished from each other without additional expedients. When one has drawn such a series of segments, a recognizable figure can be constructed. With an interchange of right and left, similar but usually not identical figures are obtained. In this way the conception of reflected image is born. With the interchange of upward and downward, another reflected image comes into existence.

The properties of the structure of square-grid paper are so many-sided and so easy to read that pupils who have been acquainted with geometry in this way have difficulty believing that formerly geometry was a difficult topic. My experiences with the former difficulty of teaching geometry led to the observations on the levels of thinking. It is still a question whether these observations would have been possible with the new geometry. On the other hand, the new geometry is inspired by the discovery of the levels of thinking.

The importance of the square-grid paper is principally that observed properties can be expressed with the help of numbers or pairs of numbers. With this a great number of obstacles to elementary education can be removed.

THE INTUITIVE BEGINNING OF COUNTING

If one goes from A to B by means of the vector $(4, 1)$ (notation for "first four to the right, then one upward"), and afterward from B to C by means of the vector $(2, 5)$, then one can also go directly from A to C by means of the vector $(6, 6)$ (Figure 17.1). The pupils, then, must see that "first four to the right and then two to the right" directly agrees with "four plus two to the right." This is an addition, and every addition originates in counting. What is the intuitive foundation of counting?

It would carry us too far afield if I tried in this context to give a complete account of this intuitive beginning. Indeed, there are still many uncertain points. Still, I make a brief suggestion.

Once I witnessed a young child being given a doll as a present. This doll had a likeness to a doll she already had in her arms. It was interesting to see how the look of the child was directed now upon the new doll, now upon the doll she already possessed. With the similarity her face expressed extreme astonishment. Without any doubt the principal contents of the concept 'two' was born with this child at that moment. It contained 'the one and the other', with which 'the one' and 'the other' without any difficulty could be interchanged. He who objects that for the constitution of 'two' it is not necessary that the objects resemble each other overlooks that without resemblance there has already been a certain abstraction: The possibility of adding two totally different objects supposes a "universal set" of which these objects or conceptions are elements.

For the concept 'three' it is necessary that first 'two' has been fully thought out; this will probably be very difficult before a symbol, language symbol or other symbol, is known for 'two'. 'Three' means 'two and another one', but with the particularity that every element of the trio can act as 'one'. In thinking of 'three' as the corners of an equilateral triangle, the equivalence of the three

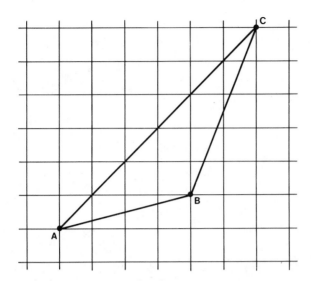

Figure 17.1

elements is included, but also included is the possibility of splitting up three in three different ways into 'two' and 'one'. A more difficult symbol is 'three on a row'. With this symbol the middle element has a separate position; the child must play with this symbol to understand that the other elements can also take the place of the middle element.

'Four' is probably the last cardinal number that is accesible to an intuitive approach. If the symbol of the corners of a square is used, the equivalence of the elements will strike us at first, and directly afterward the possibility of splitting into two pairs (in three different ways). The splitting of 'four' into 'three' and 'one' is more difficult, because seeing 'three' is very difficult in itself (see Figure 17.2).

With the above I have tried to indicate how the numbers 'one', 'two', 'three', and 'four' can be experienced. The creation of the following cardinal numbers takes place abstractly. A teaching–learning process can help with this abstraction. Memorizing the series of cardinal numbers may help; mapping may also help: By adding one element to a set, we go one step farther in the series of cardinal numbers.

It is clear that teachers of mathematics in elementary education that attempt to approach the concept of number by the presenting numbers of objects without any ordering—that is, in an amorphous grouping, start with the wrong point of view. They reject the intuitive structures that should form the foundation of the concept of number. The subject matter they want to begin with is the end of a

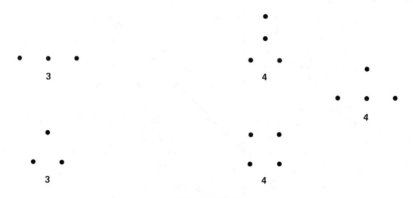

Figure 17.2

process of abstraction; they approach the children with too high a level of thinking.

The number 'one' indeed is intuitively knowable, but it appears at first in contrast to 'two', and afterward as part of 'three'. Of course the number 'five' can be known as a structure. But in Figure 17.3, for example, you see that this structure is founded on a 'four' that already has obtained some abstraction. As long as the child does not recognize a "law of conservation of number," he does not necessarily see that 4 + 1 is the same as 2 + 3.

In this guided learning process, leading from intuition to first abstraction, the concept of 'set' is of no use. 'Set' is the terminal point of an abstraction: It is the loosest link facilitating "counting." It is easy to see that 'set' has no intuitive contents by consulting the textbooks that introduce sets. Some speak of "elements with a common property." Indeed, the only real common property is that they all are elements of the same set. Other textbooks start with a set of stamps or a set of boulders. This also creates confusion, for "collecting" does not play a part in a mathematical set. The identity of the elements of such sets is often problematic, as well. A concept is likely to be element of a set if it is defined in such a way that it can be recognized. This condition is necessary and sufficient. But sets used as examples in textbooks almost always have elements that are very difficult to recognize.

With counting, sets play a very temporal part. If a number of marbles are counted, the marbles that have been counted have already lost their identity: they are elements of the set of the counted marbles without being distinguishable one from another. The same holds for the marbles that still have to be counted. Only the marble that is immediately being counted has at that moment an identity; it is the only marble with a definite associated numeral. So such counting only is possible after an abstraction has taken place.

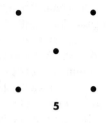

5

Figure 17.3

The rods of Cuisenaire are symbols and therefore abstract. It is possible to change a rod of five for a rod of two and a rod of three (Figure 17.4). This is a symbolic description of the joining of 'two' (intuitively knowable) and 'three' (also intuitively knowable) with the result 'five in a row' (no longer intuitively knowable). If the use of such material is to be recommended, it should be explained why these symbols are more understandable than number symbols. It must also be demonstrated how these symbols will finally be replaced by the number symbols; otherwise one must defend the view that visual recognition of 'five in a row' and 'six in a row' is itself worth the trouble.

SYMBOLS OF LANGUAGE ACCOMPANYING THE CONCEPT OF NUMBER

The preceding exposition may be easily misunderstood. To give the exposition, I was forced to use language symbols. When I write that 'four' can intuitively be experienced as a decomposition of two pairs, "intuitively" means that a child does not yet have a symbol for 'pair'. When the child gains the symbols for 'pair' or for 'two', he becomes capable of recognizing 'four' in a more abstract way. Then 'four' can be exchanged abstractly for 'two plus two' or for

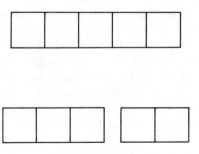

Figure 17.4

'three plus one'. With the help of language symbols, the intuitive knowledge of 'four' can be replaced by an abstract knowledge. Then, for instance, the child knows that the cardinal number 'four' and no other cardinal number is linked with a certain set. In this way, also, abstract knowledge of 'five' is possible: as successor of 'four' and as the combination of 'two' and 'three'.

The knowledge that a set of blocks linked with the cardinal number 'five' cannot at the same time be linked with the cardinal number 'six' is not obtained by biological growth, nor is it self-evident. It is a law discovered by experience. It is just as correct to speak of a "law of conservation of number" as it is to speak of a "law of conservation of energy." For all such laws, a development of symbols is necessary, and the validity of all such laws is limited to a system the conditions of which are too often tacitly presupposed.

The recognition of two principles, (1) that the construction of a concept begins with an intuition, and (2) that a concept becomes exchangeable with others by means of symbols, is of great importance for philosophy as well as didactics. Objectivity about a certain concept cannot be obtained if different people do not have the same intuitive starting point. Didactics must aim for (1) a correct choice of the intuitive starting point, and (2) the development of the correct language symbols for this intuitive knowledge. Whether a pupil is already ready for a certain subject depends on whether he can know the subject intuitively. If he has a deficiency of vocabulary or verbal conception, then at first a teaching–learning process must overcome the deficiency. But before this, one must be sure about the correct intuitive foundation. Perhaps a pupil is not capable of such intuitive knowledge: An investigation into this is easy.

THE INTUITIVE INTRODUCTION TO GEOMETRY

As I remarked earlier, square-grid paper is known intuitively. Many of its properties can be made explicit with the help of number pairs: vectors and coordinates. Concepts like angle, parallel, distance, enlargment and diminution, or perpendicular can be developed at the intuitive stage with the help of vectors. This is why I pay so much attention to the intuitive knowledge of the concept of number. With the help of square-grid paper, the difficulty of intuitive knowledge is for the most part removed to a much earlier period in the life of the student. This is not the case when vectors are not introduced early. Instead, an intuitive introduction begins with symmetry. With tiled floors laid with the use of congruent triangles pupils discover parallelism, translation, and the properties of the sum of the angles of a triangle. Here it is the pattern of triangles that is known intuitively. When square-grid paper is used it is much more difficult to establish the existence of an intuitive structure. If in 1955 we had begun with square-grid paper, the discovery of levels of thinking would have been much more difficult.

Van Hiele-Geldof (1957) records the following protocol, which gives a clear example of the intuitive knowledge of the concept 'congruent' and illustrates a method for evolving a definition.

Pl (Leader of the experiment):   Do we know the word "congruent?" (Nobody appeared to have heard this word before, as I expected. I tried to approach the word in the following way:)

Pl: When I look at the chairs on which you sit, I can see that they are congruent. (Several pupils thought they knew it now: "the same tiles, equal tiles.")

Pp (experimental subject) 17:   When you stack two tiles, they have to fit. (We then started looking at the phrase "the same.")

Pl: If I say, Tomorrow you will sit on the same chair again, I do not mean the chair of your neighbor. So the phrase "the same" is not clear enough. Now the word "equal"; what then is equal?

Pps: The area.

Pl: Let us try. Area is measured in . . .

Pps: Square centimeters.

Pl: Now imagine two tiles, each of whose area is 12 cm². They are thus equal. Are those tiles really congruent?

Pp 8:   No, because they can differ in length and width.

Pl: Could you show that on the blackboard? (Pp 8 Draws two rectangles, 2 × 6 and 3 × 4 cm².)

Pl: Indeed they are not congruent—the word "equal" is also not such a good choice.

Pp 17:   They do not fit on each other either. (We conclude that Pp 17 has given the best answer so far.)

Pl: When you sat down at the breakfast table this morning, were there any congruent objects on it?

Pps: Yes; plates, knives, forks, mugs.

Pp 11:   At our house the mugs are not congruent. (My conclusion that she came from a large family was correct.)

Pp 11:   Each of us has a different mug. Then we know which one is ours.

Pl: But in the afternoon, when you have company at home, do you drink out of congruent teacups?

Pp 11:   Yes, but we have different teaspoons.

Pl: When I look carefully at your chairs, they are not congruent. (The pupils understood immediately. I made reference to the little labels with a number at the back of each chair.)

Pl: What are those numbers for?

Pp 10:   To tell them apart.

Pl: Correct; in order to be able to make a distinction, to be able to distinguish them. The teaspoons of [Pp 11] serve the same purpose. You can thereby distinguish congruent teacups. Who can now finish the following sentence: Congruent objects are . . .

Pp 17:   They are objects that fit onto each other.

Pl: I believe that congruent teacups do not entirely fit onto each other; the handle is in the way. With tiles it works beautifully.

Pp: Objects that have the same volume.

Pp 8:   No, because then it can still be high or low.

Pp 2:   Congruent objects are objects that cannot be distinguished from each other. (This was accepted with general agreement—that was well said.)

Many conclusions can be drawn from this protocol. In the first place, "congruent" is known intuitively. The word is a designation of something that has been observed much earlier. Next, how difficult it is to describe such a concept is evident. The "fitting on each other" mentioned in some geometry textbooks appears to be a means that often does not suffice. By the end the class—through carefully checking in a guided discussion what the concept does and what it does not express—we come to the statement: "congruent objects cannot be distinguished from each other." With this, the relativity of "congruent" is also established. Indistinguishable objects can in many cases be distinguished from each other with expedients.

Did the leader of the experiment know from the beginning what definition would evolve from the discussion? It may well have occurred to her only in the course of the interchange of thoughts. In any case, you can be sure that at the end she aimed for this definition. But it is possible to work for years with a concept without knowing its definition: Often an intuitive knowledge suffices.

INTUITION ON A HIGHER LEVEL

A great conformity exists in the set of integers for addition, the set of rational numbers (without 0) ($\mathbb{Q}/\{0\}$) for multiplication, and the set of vectors for addition. This conformity makes the "group" concept useful. Therefore, in the set of integers $\mathbb{Z}$, for the operation 'addition', the four following properties apply:

1. Addition is possible for all elements of $\mathbb{Z}$.
2. There exists a neutral element for addition.
3. For every element of $\mathbb{Z}$ there exists an inverse element for addition.
4. Addition in $\mathbb{Z}$ is associative.

One can also notice that a similar structure exists in the set $\mathbb{Q}$ for the operation 'multiplication'. A similar structure also exists in the set of vectors for the operation 'addition'.

A comparison of these data may lead one to set up the concept of 'group'. The constitution of this concept is achieved after summarizing its rules. We know what they have to be, because we know them intuitively. This intuitive knowledge has become possible because of the recognition of an extensive field of language symbols between which many links exist. The words *neutral element, operator, inverse element* have already been introduced to facilitate the concept of 'group'; they lead from the intuitive concept of 'group' to the rational one. Here again it is difficult to discover the intuitive character of a beginning stage if the teacher (or the textbook) has used the languages symbols so early that the concept of 'group' is anticipated.

Somewhat clearer is the intuitive foundation of 'proof'. It begins with a pupil's statement that belief in the truth of some assertion is connected with belief in the truth of other assertions. The notion of this connection is intuitive: The laws of such a connection can only be learned by analysis. By analyzing and expliciting these laws, logic is created, forming the rational foundation for 'proof'.

THE SENSE OF AN EXAMPLE

Let us suppose that the teacher introduces 'group' by immediately stating the axioms of a group. Next she says: "To clarify the matter, I will now give you an example." The example given is the group $(\mathbb{Z}, +)$. Here the order of teaching is just the reverse of that above: First a rational foundation is given, and afterward the intuitive knowledge is to come. This development is not necessarily objectionable. One may defend it by asserting that if the definition is given first, the purpose of the argument will be clear; with a clear purpose, the means will follow. If the pupils already are familiar with this sort of structure, the argument will not fall into a vacuum.

Without the example the pupil will have many difficulties. When he reads of a set of elements in which a rule of composing is defined, he will have an empty feeling. He already knows that a set of elements can mean anything, and the words "rule of composing" means nothing to him without an example. Because of the absence of an example, he has no well-known structure to fall back on. Only if he is a serious, budding mathematician will he try to find additional information by himself and apply the rules of logic to it. With a discussion of his mistakes, he will find the information he should have had much earlier.

He who wants to build up a science, of course, has the liberty to choose the definitions himself. In this way the intentions of the author become clear. But it would be better to begin with examples and from them to develop the definition. Especially in cases like this, where the purpose for everyone need not be the same, it would be better first to discuss the phenomena, then to point out its structure, and finally to investigate what definition in the given case is the most efficient.

GAPS IN REASONING

All rational knowledge begins with intuitive knowledge. Relative objectivity can be obtained when the participants of a discussion try to develop language symbols for this intuitive knowledge. Then first the discussion ought to be about the relations between the chosen symbols of language. If this discussion introduces no problems, objectivity relative to the discussion group is reached.

It is desirable to render an account of the relativity of such objectivity. It is tied to a time, for the image of the world may change in such a way that the intuitive knowledge of situations is also altered. The objectivity, however, is to a large extent tied to the discussion group: The starting points of the members of one group may differ importantly from the starting points of equally competent members of other groups. If such differences lead to a certain group arrogance, forming a hindrance to communication with the other groups, then within such a group a technical language can develope with the character of technical jargon. In this way the objectivity that comes into existence is limited to the members of the group and is doomed to disappear with the dispersal of the group. In this extreme form, such a phenomenon would be easily recognized. In a much more weakened form, it can be found when a professional language is used as a smokescreen behind which one tries to protect self-conceit.

A much better objectivity is obtained if it is possible to extend the discussion to many more people. The insight developed by this can be applied in new situations. Language is an important means; it provides us with the ability to use symbols for similar objects in similar situations. The word "similar" shows the intuitive factor in the use of language. Only a discussion among many people can make it probable that similar situations and similar objects can be experienced by others as such. A complete guarantee, however, is impossible: Every argument, even if it is given with the help of well-defined mathematical symbols, has gaps based on not yet objective intuition. One must realize that no argument, no matter how accurately it may be built up, gives the security that the hearer receives it just as the speaker meant it. It is therefore objectionable to declare, after making a judgment, "the case is so clear that I have nothing to add to it." It is still more objectionable if a problem is given in such a form that it is clear that it will be interpreted in another way than is necessary for the solution. Such problems, in which disruptions to communication are built in beforehand, are more frequent than one might initially expect. Even examinations in mathematics are not free of them.

18

Direct Reactions to Visual Structures

Man is able to react directly—without the intermediary of a language—to visual structures. As is usual in psychology, I include here with visual perception everything that can be perceived with the sense organs. We know that such direct reaction is possible, because we see the adequate responses of animals. But even after a language is learned, when language is used in reactions to visual perceptions, one still can see, by studying his own acts, that in many cases visual perceptions are reacted to without the intermediary of language.

To avoid misunderstandings, we must distinguish two very different cases. There is, in the first place, a direct reaction to visual structures in which language never plays an important part. But there is also a direct reaction to visual structures in which language was at first necessary but in which discursive thinking has been omitted afterward.

A driver of a car can react directly, without reflecting on road signs, but their meaning has been made clear to him by earlier discursive thinking. A mathematician performing an algebraic conversion does the greater part his work automatically, without thinking, because he has learned to do so from prior experiences and understanding. (Such understanding is of various kinds, but this is not under discussion now.)

Many actions are performed after a direct relation has been formed between a given reality and an action structure. The action structure is not understood by the performer, for he is not able to make the structure of action explicit. An example—one out of a great number—is typing. A person who is busy typing pays no attention to his fingers; the action goes on very well without thinking. Still, visual structure is relevant, for if the keys have been covered by caps, he may not be able to go on. However, the visual structure is no more than a confirmation of the structure in his mind, for the fingers react much faster to the text in his mind than they would if he was obliged to look for every key. If he moves to a typewriter on which some keys have different positions, he will make mistakes. In this case we do not have a reaction to a visual structure with the intermediary of discursive thinking. Some who teach typing introduce discursive thinking, but I am not sure this is the right way. I prefer the constitution of an action structure through a routine in which every element of the structure is fixed by trial and error. An action structure obtained in such a way is just the opposite of a structure developed through insight.

Let us better analyze typing. In preparing the manuscript for this volume, I had to type "An action structure . . ." Before I could do so, I had to think about what I was going to write: I had to construct the sentence. This is thinking at the third level. Afterward I had to determine the spelling of the words: This is given to me by a structure of the first level. It is a structure of the first level because I *see* the spelling in my mind before I begin typing. The typing itself happens without thinking, the letters come of themselves, mostly in pairs or threes. So you see, typing an essay is a complicated affair. It consists of thinking at the third level (composing the essay), thinking at the first level (seeing the spelling), and at last an action without thinking, a stimulus–response reaction (typing the words). The action structure corresponds to the spelling structure directly, without thinking.

I wrote above about "action structure," but is it correct to suppose action has a structure? For structure involves insight, and in the above, where structure is not seen, I denied insight. However, psychologists who study actions use the word *structure* in such cases. Are they right or wrong? I think I must defend their point of view. For although I cannot see the action structures and I do not understand them, although I do not know how they are put together, I can act with such structures in new situations—I can type any word I can spell, even if I have never typed it before. So I should call this insight, though it be insight at the first level. To express the narrowness of the structure, I prefer to speak here of action structure without insight.

Of course, it is possible to give simpler examples. A man who is stung by a wasp reacts directly to the visual (perceptual) situation without thinking. But if I had introduced this chapter with such examples, you might think that the direct correspondence between action and perceptual structures only happens in extraordinary circumstances.

19

Direct Interactions between Reality and Common Human Knowledge

Usually common human knowledge (World 3) will be built up by the individual knowledge of one or more people, that is, by World 2. However, this is not always the case. The result of a computer calculation is displayed before any individual has taken part. Some tables can be composed without human intervention. Tables of logarithms were long ago composed by individuals; now they are handled by computers. Such computers can also construct the tables, and the time they take is no more than the time taken for writing the results. If we need to know some logarithm, we can look it up in a table or we can use the calculator, which is much easier, but the information stored in those tables or in the calculator could not likely be determined immediately by any individual.

By the above a riddle is solved. At first you might think that it is quite impossible to transfer structures of World 1 to higher structures of World 3 without the intervention of human thinking. We have shown earlier that World 3 is a construction of the human mind, so how might it be possible to transfer anything from World 1 to World 3 without human thinking? But in this example human thinking has already done its work: Human thinking has constructed the computer and the calculator, and the interpretation of the result is also made by human thinking.

More information is stored in common human knowledge through photographs. The starry sky is registered through photographs. Changes in the sky can be observed before the changed objects have been seen by an individual. Technology has made it possible to observe numberless new structures, but it has also enabled man to refine structures. Printing has enabled man to disperse structures between many people, the techniques of reproduction have made it possible to observe structures at any moment, film enables us to observe movements exactly (for example the movement of a jumping horse.) The tape recorder enables the soloist to hear his own playing objectively and critically; television enables man to observe events around the world.

There are innumerable structures man can recognize because of their place in the depot of common human knowledge. If the intelligences of two persons have to be compared, how far those persons have advanced into this depot should be taken into account. We must also realize that, though man has admission to the accumulation of human knowledge, a person can possess directly only a small fraction of it. So, to be able to act effectively in a given situation, it is necessary that one use more and more refined systems. This is an important observation for education: It is better to learn how information can be obtained quickly from the depots of common human knowledge than to learn many results by heart.

Teachers must help their pupils if they teach them to work with insight. For this insight the pupils must recognize many structures. The higher structures they must have in their minds, but the lower structures can be found by instruments (calculators) or textbooks. It is important to investigate how far it is useful to teach the lower structures themselves and how far it is useful to teach the pupils to look them up.

20

Switching Over from One Structure to Another

Psychologists know of the phenomenon of transstructuring. We meet it as follows: To solve a certain problem a structure is chosen; this does not work, the solution cannot be found with it. Therefore another structure must be chosen. I will give a famous example.

A square is given, and a subject is asked to draw another square with an area twice as large. To solve this problem the subject begins by drawing a square with sides twice as long as the sides of the original square (Figure 20.1). It is easy to see that now the area of the new square is four times as large as that of the original square. So this cannot be the right solution. But if perhaps the sides could be made one and a half times as long; would that give the solution? The idea is not bad, but, as in Figure 20.2, we see that there is a little square too much: The new square is $2\frac{1}{4}$ times as large as the original square. Now the subject remembers that a square can be split into two equal halves by a diagonal. This is a quite new structure. With four of these halves a new square can be formed, and in so doing the solution of the problem is found (Figure 20.3).

The change from one structure to another more suitable structure is not very easy. The first structure is chosen because of its inviting character, because of the knowledge that this structure is appropriate for solving many problems. The necessity of the switch can only be understood after a conviction that the first-chosen structure does not contain the solution.

There are structures that force themselves so strongly on us that we incorrectly

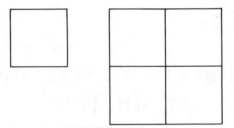

Figure 20.1

think to be tied to them. In Figure 20.4 one is asked to draw four lines, one after the other and going through all nine points, without taking the pencil from the paper. Hardly anyone succeeds, yet the solution is simple. The difficulty consists in the nine points forming a square and the taboo against leaving that square. If we can ignore this taboo, we find the solution, as in Figure 20.5.

Living conditions can force us to use other structures than we are accustomed to. In the winter of 1944–1945 in the west Netherlands, a tree was a supplier of wood with which you could fuel your auxiliary stove and thus remain alive. Every tree you saw that winter was valued by the amount of wood it could supply and its potential for being cut down and brought home unseen. After the liberation, this structure had to be totally restructured: A tree was again a feast for the eyes, and above all could be cut down only sparingly. For this restructuring some time was necessary.

The ability to think and act with a given structure guarantees a certain safety. In action structures, a given action automatically evokes another action; the composed action happens of itself in a fixed pattern. Often the structure is so strong that an incidental but necessary change may spoil it. If one has a fixed action structure belonging to leaving his house, he may forget to shut the back door if during the actions the telephone rings, forcing an interruption of the series. I have already mentioned that the changing from one typewriter to another

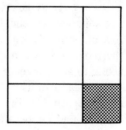

Figure 20.2

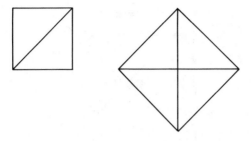

Figure 20.3

with some keys changed may cause mistakes to be made as long as the place of the keys is not known by heart.

The existence of thinking structures is of enormous importance, and the need to progress now and then and to change to other thinking structures may bring mental distress. We must realize that in many cases not such simple structures as those above are involved; structures that have been studied for years are extended, refined, taken up as a part of a more inclusive structure, brought to a higher level, and so forth. The substitution of such a structure by another can be compared to an emigration to another country.

I give here some examples of such changes of structure:

1. It is possible to introduce vectors in mathematics at a very early time. In this manner a strong structure comes into existence and pupils can easily assimilate it. The acquisition of such a structure does not require their invention and does not depend very much on memory. Still it is very difficult to convince teachers of the utility of introducing vectors in mathematics early. The structure of mathematics the teachers are familiar with is so different from the structure of mathematics built on vectors that the teachers consider the switch as a leap in the dark. They have invested so much time and energy in the original structure that they consider it unjustified to give it up.

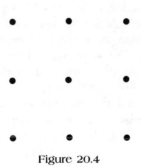

Figure 20.4

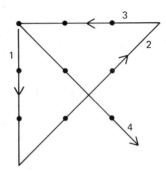

Figure 20.5

2.   A spelling reform usually provokes passionate resistance. The arguments most often used show clearly what the issue is. The image of the word one is used to disappears, newly spelled words look odd; in short, there is a complaint that the structure one has made oneself familiar with has to be given up for a simpler structure. The complicated trustworthy structure would become senseless? That cannot be.

3.   It would be convenient if all over the whole world it was established that traffic keeps to the right. Still, the transition from the structure 'keeping to the left' to the structure 'keeping to the right' would be difficult. Not only would people have to change their conduct in traffic, cars also would have to be changed, as well as the roads and parking facilities. Here we have a very strong structure that has penetrated everywhere.

Often with restructuring it is not realized that existing structures must not be destroyed before the new structure has had time to develop. In 1967 in the Netherlands a law was accepted controlling all secondary education. This law brought about a totally new structure of that education. Teachers were unhappy for years because they had to act in a mostly unknown structure; even the drafters of the new law did not know the structure. Still, the new law was necessary: The laws that it replaced were very old and did not fit the circumstances of the time. The fault of the government was that the new law came too suddenly. It would have been better if a transition period had been created in which the two structures had existed together. The advantages of the new structure would have manifested themselves so clearly that after a short time most of the teachers would have been convinced of its efficiency.

In the above I have outlined the least risky method of introducing new structures: Allow people to fall back to the old structure as long as it is not yet clear how the new structure is to be used. In that case the making of a resolution will not imply new adventures. Of course this brings the disadvantage that the two structures will coexist only with difficulty. This, however, is compensated for by the possibility of agreement to come and the smoother adjustment of the participants.

An example of such a gradual change is found in the history of chemistry. Originally, in the nineteenth century, compounds were written in the notation of equivalent weights. In that time water was written as HO. Afterward atomic weights were introduced and then water was written H_2O. In a transitional period of some 10 years, both notations were used side by side. Here a strong structure was replaced by another which in the end proved to be stronger.

Some people take a conservative position in a progressive environment and a progressive position in a conservative environment. There is much to say in favor of such a strategy: In a progressive environment you may expect that there will be no concern for the safety the existing structure warrants, for the difficulties the transition to the new structure brings with it, or for the possibility that new elements will be brought in without any structure. In a conservative environment too much attention is often paid to the difficulties the transition to the new structure brings about; the security gained from the existing structure is valued so highly that there is no willingness to think of a new structure.

21

The Relations among
the Media of Structure

THE POSSIBILITY OF ONLY ONE MEDIUM

Do the media of structures I mentioned in Chapter 7 really exist? Is it not possible that by deeper examination it will become clear that they all originate in your own brain? As I suggested earlier, it is possible to maintain that nothing exists except your own brain. The world you see, the people you speak to, the forms and the warmth you have felt, the melodies and the noise you have heard, they all are there because your brain has told you so. So, if your brain is telling you tales without any reality, as it does when you are dreaming, there is no method to discover it. If you pretend that there is no real world and I myself do not exist, there is no method to prove you wrong. When you speak to me, when you read this book, it is not a real person and a real book you deal with; in reality you are speaking to yourself, another self presented by another person or a book. In order to demonstrate that you really understand the absence of a real world and other real persons, you could change your speech a little. In stead of speaking to me, you could speak to the other part of yourself as if it were another person. And, in a similar way, you could speak of the world. It would be very tedious, not only for yourself, but also for the other part of yourself acting as ''the other person.''

DIFFERENT POINTS OF VIEW EXPRESSED IN ONE LANGUAGE

If you are convinced there is only one medium of structure, settled in your own brain, you can make it easy on yourself by pretending there are also other media; henceforth you will speak as if they were real. You may say that you know for sure they do not exist—they are all made in your brain—but you will speak as if they do exist. Some 400 years ago we had a similar case. At that time it had been found that it would be very easy to describe the movements of planets, sun, and stars by representing the sun in the center of a planetary system with the earth turning around its axis. But it was forbidden by the pope to think in such a manner. Still, there was a possibility of getting around this difficulty by saying "Of course we all know that the earth stands still and everything turns around it. But to give an easier description, we act as if the sun was the center and the earth was turning around its axis." Since the time of Einstein we have known that what we choose to consider as "still"—earth, sun, galaxy, or something else—depends on our interests. In our descriptions, we now take as center what best fits our special case. People 400 years ago had reasons to risk a conflict with the pope and to maintain that it was the earth that moved—and not just as an easy description. And those reasons were not inspired by astronomy (see Pukies, 1979).

As in the above, it does not make any difference if we accept that there is only one medium or if we accept the existence of five. It is only a question of terminology. Two people, one thinking in terms of a single medium—his own brain, and the other, thinking in terms of more media, may understand each other well by each speaking their own language. They should not meet any difficulty; it does not make any difference what their starting points are; one medium or more, you cannot hear it by the language they speak. So there need not be any point in disputing about the number of media. If I speak of five, it is because I think it better to express my ideas. So if you ask me if the world in which we live really exists, I have no answer: In this discussion this question has no sense; "really existing" is something I do not understand.

REALITY: WORLD 1

The world in which we live is experienced as a reality because we see and hear that other persons have the same experiences we have. This is what they *say*, but we are not sure of it. Is the red we see the same as the red other people see? We know that what we call red is also called so by other people, but we do not know what they have experienced when they say something is red. We can teach young people to call a thing red that we ourselves also call red. Sometimes it may be primary red and sometimes a mixed color. This is a phenomenon that always succeeds, unless the other person is color blind. If this phenomenon did not occur, color photographs would not exist. We can agree about the success of color combinations, still we do not know what the other has really seen. We might say we do not know what "really" is.

There is no possibility of comparing experiences of pain between different people; still, my experience of pain has a place in an objective world: The dentist makes use of it when he is working on my teeth.

WORLD 1 AND LANGUAGE

A child not yet able to speak experiences a reality; he reacts to the world in which he lives. Because he sometimes imitates us, he makes an impression of understanding us to some degree. He strengthens this impression when he coordinates his actions to our actions. So we know that speaking is not an essential medium between our brain and the world in which we live. We can extend this idea to the world of animals: They also react to World 1 and they also have the ability to imitate. So in animal psychology, also, two media may be spoken of: the brain and the world in which the animal lives.

I have shown above that it is sensible to speak of World 1, even if one wants to deny its existence. I have shown that language is not necessary for the constitution of World 1. Still, language may be used to point out parts of this world. We can do this with children before they are able to speak, we can also do it with animals. You can say to a dog that he will be taken out, you can say to a cat that she will have some fish; in both cases the animal reacts appropriately to the speech. We do not know anything about what representations of such sayings the animals have—an important point for the discussions that follow.

LANGUAGE CONSTITUTING WORLD 3

At first language is directed only toward World 1; with this language nothing is added to this world. But with indications like "red" and "round," when speaking of a red or a round ball, a classification with far-reaching consequences takes place. For after the addition of the adjectives, things are seen as having properties; the red ball and the red book have something in common, however different those things may be. With the mention of properties, World 1 has been left; it is no longer possible to say that it is still the same world. But even if we are inclined to say that it is still World 1, with the introduction of the adjectives we have begun to build up a new medium: the medium of common human knowledge, World 3. Round, red, and other properties determine structures;

many of those structures can be observed by animals and reacted to appropriately. To this degree, those properties belong to World 1. But still we are not sure if the animals are likely to disjoin the properties from the objects they belong to. We know man can, but we know that because man can speak.

DIFFERENT ASPECTS OF LANGUAGE

When we speak of a round, red ball, it is spoken of as more than a part of World 1, the world observed only by our sense organs. Something is added that has been obtained by experience and by things other people have told us. Round can be seen in relation to rolling, red can be sorted. If a ball does not roll, something is wrong with its roundness; if a ball is red we can ask how the paint has been applied to it. Parallel with reality, the new medium, World 3, is built up. It is difficult to give a proper name to World 3. Of course, common human knowledge is also a kind of reality, and we are accustomed to calling it so. But so too is World 1 defined by common human knowledge. So to know the difference between the two media meant in this chapter, we first have to give an example by which the difference becomes clear. The apple I have eaten is a part of reality, of World 1. If I consider an apple as a fruit of a tree belonging to the family Pomacae, it is a part of World 3. But it is also a part of that medium if I consider it as an article sold by a grocer. We can say that the apple ceases to be a part of World 1 as soon as it ceases to be an object of thinking with a visual base. Selling apples, of course, has a visual aspect; you see it when children are pretending to sell apples. However, this clearly differs from really selling them.

Here we see the varying significance of language. Language is a medium enabling us to make World 1 objective. In discussion, language also constitutes World 3. So we see that language is a new medium, one that does not belong to the other three media: It is an intermedium. But now we also see why it is so difficult to discern World 1 from World 3: The same language symbols are used for both worlds. If we see the grocer, he may be part of World 1, for he may be the man whom from childhood we have called "grocer." But he is also a part of World 3, for we know he is a merchant with an important function in society.

In the above I have spoken of World 1 and World 3, and in this way avoided speaking of "real" and "common human knowledge." It is no longer adequate to speak of "real" and "existing." Are molecules and atoms "real" or are they not? In daily life we do not meet them, in chemistry they have a clear meaning, and in wave mechanics they no longer exist. They have a distinct place in certain contexts, but to speak of "existing" is very confusing.

Language is not a part of the medium called "our brain," World 2, for it has come to us from outside. We have learned the principles of language in connection with the Worlds 1 and 3. When we talk to ourselves it is an attempt by our minds to make contact with World 2.

LEVELS OF THINKING AND WORLDS 1 AND 3

When we speak of a joiner having made a table, this is a piece of language related to World 3. There is still some relation with World 1, for we may have visual representations of tables and joiners, but this relation is very indirect. It is even more indirect with a statement like "the Council of State has nullified a decree." Here reality is very far removed. So it is clear that ideas belonging to the second and third levels of thinking are part of World 3. However, would it be a mistake to pretend that the partition between World 1 and World 3 is given by the difference between Level 1 and Level 2. In this chapter I have already shown that an important part of Level 1 belongs to World 3. Already in the beginning of the first period, the period leading from Level 1 to Level 2, language is at work moving its objects from World 1 to World 3. At the second level, World 1 has vanished, but it may still be brought in. At the third level, it is no longer possible to use visual structures to clarify ideas.

Our knowledge of World 3 is determined by the language with which others address us. If we have picked up many things accidentally, there is a great chance that our concept of World 3 differs very much from that of other people. If we want pupils to have a good concept of subjects of World 3, we will have to introduce those subjects in extensive discussion.

THE EXISTENCE OF SCIENTIFIC CONCEPTS

Scientific concepts are constructions of the mind. They belong to World 3. They have been made to explain World 1. If the results found in World 3 are not in harmony with the experiences of World 1, we have to make alterations in World 3. The modern theory of particles is a creation of our mind that is in many respects an excellent model to elucidate many phenomena. Sometimes, however, a theory does not quite fit, and then it has to be amplified or changed. Sometimes we maintain the unchanged theory in simple cases and use the new theory in more complicated cases. Sometimes, in a fairly small domain, we can act as if the surface of the earth is flat; on the other hand, if we have to measure in a rather large field, we have to use spherical trigonometry. The atomic model of Bohr has been used for a long time, even after it was clear that the model had become untenable. So it is not meaningful to simply speak of the reality of such a construction.

Once I showed a colleague of mine an experiment set up in a physics laboratory. There she could see how cosmic rays came in and could follow their trace by the condensation of a vapor. She was impressed by the continual passing of the rays. It was a revelation to her that such things could be seen with the naked eye. The following day she told me that I had deceived her. She had spoken with her husband, a professor of theology, and he had convinced her that she had not seen the particles themselves: The only thing she had seen was condensation of vapor. Then I told her that she did not know the meaning of "seeing." "Do you see this window pane?" I asked her. "Yes," she said, "of course I see it." "But the only thing you see is the dirt on the window pane and a reflection of the things in the room." I cannot say that with this I convinced her. Still, it is remarkable that a professor of theology argued in this way. What are the visual foundations of his theories?

Of course, when you see cosmic rays, you only see a condensation of vapor. You have not seen the cosmic rays in World 1, you have seen them in World 3. But it is the same with the window pane. You can verify the seeing by touching it, but what you feel is resistance, not a window pane. A window pane is a construction of our mind—animals have much difficulty with it.

Black holes—do they exist? You can see what a misleading thing "existing" is. You cannot trace blackholes by any of your sense organs; they are only in the world because of a brilliant theory designed to explain cosmic events. There are many ways to affirm their "existence." The theory of particles together with Einstein's work predicted their existence. It is possible to investigate their position by the movement of matter in their neighborhood or by the deflection of light passing them. The theory is strong enough to work with black holes, but as long as no light can escape from the black holes it makes little sense to ask what happens inside them. Only after a theory has established the possibility of such escape, or of the destruction of black holes, can the inside of them hold any real interest for us.

The theory of particles keeps open the possibility of the existence of neutrinos. There are experimental phenomena that can only be reasonably explained with the help of neutrinos. So it is good to use them in theory. But since the trace of a neutrino cannot be observed in any way, it is not meaningful to ask what the trace of a neutrino in a certain case would really be. Here, in this question, we imagine a reality belonging to World 3, not to World 1 or World 2. But what do we ask for if we speak of a reality in World 3? With such a supposition we are back to the "Ding on sich" of Kant, a thing you can never meet in your life, neither in your visual world nor in the theories and concepts you have built.

RATIONAL AND IRRATIONAL NUMBERS

In the theory of numbers there is a difference between rational and irrational numbers. The set of real numbers is split into those two sets: They have no elements in common. But does this difference also "exist" in physics? Is it meaningful in physics to talk of a square the diagonal of which has exactly the length of $\sqrt{2}$ cm? If in physics we say that the length of the side of a square is exact 1 cm and that therefore the length of its diagonal is exactly $\sqrt{2}$ cm, there is always leeway in those measures. So, although $\sqrt{2}$ is definitely an irrational number, one cannot insist that the length of a diagonal is an irrational number. If one must carry out calculations with the length of a diagonal, it may be quite useful to calculate with $\sqrt{2}$, but one does not mention that this length is really an irrational number.

In physics the difference between rational and irrational numbers does not exist. In physics (and technology) all calculations are done with a calculator or a computer. The numbers there are used in a sufficient approximation; the instrument reduces all numbers to rational numbers. So if we are sure that all our pupils will continue their study at a technical school or will use mathematics only in lessons of physics or chemistry, we may omit teaching the difference between rational and irrational numbers. I repeat—in the context of physics, chemistry, and technology, this difference is not of any importance. It does not exist there.

In mathematics the difference between rational and irrational numbers exists, but even there we must determine which situations we will have to use it. Practically everywhere we have to work with numbers in mathematics, this difference can be omitted; only in the theory of numbers can beautiful theorems and proofs concerning irrational numbers be found.

THE REALITY OF MOLECULES AND ATOMS

Sometimes the reality of a thing can be suddenly changed. In chemistry, at the beginning of the nineteenth century, molecules and atoms were very easy to use in the description of chemical reactions. One could understand some of what happened by writing $2H_2 + O_2 \rightarrow 2H_2O$. But how these atoms were situated in the molecules was at that time not a sensible concern. You can still find it back in old chemistry books, in those using equivalent rather than atomic weights. Therefore, in the beginning, the above equation was written $H + O = HO$.

In 1874 van 't Hoff gave an explanation for optical activity by supposing that molecules in organic chemistry had a three-dimensional shape. With this the foundation of stereochemistry was laid. It was a brilliant idea, very comprehensible if you believed in the reality of molecules and atoms—but at that time most chemists did not. They thought molecules and atoms were helpful for describing reactions, but this did not mean that they really existed, so attributing shape to them was going too far. Now, in the second half of the twentieth century, we would not be able to understand the composition of a protein molecule without using a three-dimensional representation. And now, too, atoms and molecules are used in so many contexts that it would be absurd for anyone to want to eliminate them.

MUST WE REJECT VERBAL REFERENCES?

Dreams are very difficult things. We have seen that your whole life may be a dream without you ever being aware of it. If you never awake, it does not make any difference to you if you are dreaming or not. Sometimes it is difficult to decide if you are dreaming or not. A dream may have such a realistic character that other people have to tell you that the events you have gone through were not real. On the other hand, reality may at times be so remarkable that it is difficult to believe that it was not a dream. But what must we say about dreams of other people. We may say that they have no reality for us, for the only way we know about them is by the hearing other people telling us their dreams. How can we ever know that they do not lie? We can imagine many reasons for people not telling us the truth—because they are ashamed of their dreams, or because they want to get our attention. So we might say that the contents of a dream can never have any objective value, and therefore that Freud's studies about dreams cannot have any scientific worth.

With such a statement we would make a serious mistake. A great part of our conception of life has been built up by the interpretation of assertions of other people. It must be admitted that in many cases the assertions are not true or are very subjective: for instance, if a war report is concerned. But if we rejected all this information as worthless, we would never know anything about the subject that was spoken of. Let us begin to put things in order. In the first place, we know that we sometimes dream, so we may suppose other people also dream. In the second place, from reports of other people we can discern dream symbols— repeating themselves if we hear more people. The likelihood of these symbols increases when we recognize these symbols in our own dreams. Evidently there is only a difference of degree between the understanding of dream symbols and our conception of the world we see. With sensitive equipment we can test if a person is dreaming, but our understanding of dreaming would be improved very little if this test was the end of it.

We have the same situation with the psychology of thought established by Otto Selz (1913; 1924). His theory is based totally on reports of thought people have given after having been instructed in a certain way. Of course the subject may deceive the researcher, and one is quite right to doubt the information, but if one wants to know something about the process of thinking, Selz's results will illuminate one's understanding. It is very important to go on with such explorations, for if people after instruction have found a right answer, we usually suppose that they have reasoned, whereas in many cases such reasoning has not taken place. Many times the result has been obtained by seeing and not by reasoning, although the result may be confirmed by reasoning afterward. Still, the fact remains that the result was not found by reasoning. Often people's thoughts are tested on the basis of written results and the reasoning carried on in this writing, but by doing so an erroneous notion of the way of thinking is reached. But I confess that if you want quantitative results, it is tempting to study thinking in this manner. If you accept the method of Selz, it will be difficult to cope with the results statistically. It is regretable, but there are more things that must be done without statistics.

THE DIFFICULTY OF DISTINGUISHING WORLDS
1 AND 3

Modern physics give us a model for reality—for World 1. Still, the model belongs to World 3. Because I intend to place the concepts 'reality' and 'model' face to face, I analyze them further here. The tree I see belongs to World 1. I see the leaves, the stem, and the branches. These are all parts of World 1, but I borrow the names from World 3. I also know that the tree sucks water from bottom to top, but this knowledge is of World 3; I cannot know it directly with my sense organs. To demonstrate that this is surely no reality (World 1), but a model, I remind you of the fact that there are different explanations for the movement upward of water through the stem, and that the designation "sucking" is not adequate for all of them. Even if an experiment made the movement upward of the water visible, we still would not know if "sucking" was the right word. So even if I am a very common man, the nature I live with belongs in a certain part to World 3. I cannot help it that many things I have learned about trees occur to me when I see a tree. We have seen a similar circumstance in the earlier discussion of the levels of thinking: When I speak of a square, it may be that I mean a figure drawn somewhere (World 1), but it is also possible that I mean a figure with axes of symmetry, right angles, and so on. "Square" can refer to an object of the first or of the second level. In these descriptions I was careful. It is better to be so, but if I maintain this position now, I cannot enter a discussion of whether molecules and atoms are real or not. You know I have some difficulty with "real," "reality," and "existing," but sometimes a discussion of these is inevitable.

Teachers of mathematics sometimes say pure squares do not exist. I will agree with them, if they reason in the following way: A square belongs to World 3, only things of World 1 can be said to exist, so a pure square does not exist. In this reasoning it would be better to skip the word "pure." But I do not agree with them if they say this: "You can draw whatever quadrangle you want; you will never succeed in making one that, after measuring, turns out to have all sides equal and all right angles." For now they are confusing things of World 1 with things of World 3. In World 1 a quadrangle is a square if it is sufficiently square; in World 3 squares are things that are thought of but not drawn.

We can say that an attempt has been made in mathematics to create an ideal world that in many aspects resembles the real world and has laws that are approximately true for the real world. Mathematicians try to make a model of the real world and they know they are doing so. For physicists the task seems quite different. Sometimes they say (or have said) that they are solving the riddle of the universe. So it would seem as if they were seeking a real world for the world they daily see. With this meaning of "real" the confusion of the tongues is complete. Even if we are sure that they intend to be building a model, they speak of a discovery of new particles, an unraveling of the atomic model. This all points to the view that a structure of nature exists—having been there all the time, waiting for mankind to describe it in detail. And this has its consequences for the teaching of physics. If the teacher is telling a truth that others have discovered, the only thing he has to do is be understood by his pupils. But if he is explaining a marvelous model, he has to make clear why just this model was chosen and what phenomena made the theorists set up this model. And the pupils must have the opportunity to propose changes to the model or even to advance a better model.

In a physics lesson I once spoke of the lowering of the freezing point of water by pressure. I showed the pupils a beautiful experiment with a block of ice over which was draped a steel wire with a large weight on each end. They saw how the wire went through the block without splitting it, for after the pressure had been removed the undercooled water refroze. I also told them that by this principle skating was possible. I had read this example in many physics textbooks for secondary schools. A pupil asked me if I could give him a table of the freezing points of water at various pressures. I was glad I could give him one and also of his demonstration of interest. The following day he told me: "There is something wrong with your example of skating. According to this table, you have to weigh more than 100 kg if you want to skate at $-2°C$. It was easy to see that he was right. In a next session of a group of physics teachers I asked if someone could help me, and fortunately someone had met this problem before and could give me a better explanation for skating—one based on heat of friction. So you see it is wise to listen to the pupils and to have them raise their objections. For they may be right, even if the subject matter is in the textbooks and is therefore objective.

THE THIRD LEVEL OF THINKING

Pukies (1979) critizes education in the sciences that tries to make the great theories (the principle of inertia, the law of conservation of energy, the atomic model) clear by deriving them from experiments. With the help of original texts he clearly shows that those theories were not found by experiments, they were speculations that experiments afterward confirmed. It is worth remarking that though a theory may be confirmed if the experiments do not contradict it, it always is possible that a better theory will later be found.

When I read Pukies, I remembered that I was never satisfied in my attempts in physics lessons to derive the principle of inertia from experiments. I always had the idea that I was deceiving my pupils somehow, though I did not know what the mistake was. Now I know: It is not possible to derive the principle of inertia from experiments; it is a creation of the mind. But it is silly that I had to read Pukies to come to this conclusion, for if one accepts the theory of the levels of thinking, one also has to admit that all theories, because they belong to the third, theoretical, level, are constructions of the mind and for that reason cannot be derived from experiments.

To some degree, statements of Level 2 can be derived from experiments: They are descriptions of the things that have been seen in the visual world. The language at the Level 2 to some extent gives a transcription of things that have been seen at Level 1, and the language at Level 1 directly refers to World 1. Still, we must be careful if we say that the descriptions of Level 2 are the result of the experiments, for even at Level 2 the descriptions are given in a certain context. We know that two different people may give totally different descriptions of the same thing without lying. But at Level 3 a theory is built up from descriptions of Level 2—the visual world and the experiments have disappeared into the background. So we are sure: Theories are constructions of the mind, they do not follow from experiments.

We now see how careful we must be in accepting the theories of nonnatural sciences such as economics and psychology. These have in common with the natural sciences, such as mathematics, physics, and chemistry, that their theoretical level belongs to World 3. But today the third level of natural sciences is always based on a second level that has a very narrow relation to a first level connected with World 1. In the nonnatural sciences, this second level is often absent. Sometimes even a third level (theory) is brought in to constitute a second level. It is clear that I think such an approach totally absurd.

From the above we can conclude that the distinction between the different structures has practical consequences. If we are aware that World 3 is a construction of the mind, we also know that a child must have freedom to choose his own solutions. Of course society poses its limits, but a sufficient scope must be given. I have been present at an assembly trying to found a training college for teachers of Montessori education. Most of those present insisted that the ideas of Montessori should be explained over and over again until the pupils needed only to swallow them. You can understand that I could not continue my collaboration with this group.

DIFFERENCE OF CONTEXT DOES NOT IMPLY DIFFERENCE OF LEVEL

If by conversation the thinking on a subject has been brought from Level 1 to Level 2, the subject is also transferred from World 1 to World 3. We know how careful I must be in stating this: At the moment that language is brought in, World 3 begins to be created. But still, at Level 1 we are always in contact with World 1. The subject of Level 2 acts in another context than the subject of Level 1. When two lovers are enjoying the moon, it would be misguided for one of them to speak of the moon as a satellite of the earth going around it in some 27 days. The moon we enjoy when we are in love is another thing than the moon some astronomers are so fond of. If a landing on the moon happens to occur at just this moment, the lovers' joy may be increased by thoughts of the space travelers; in this case their subject of thinking is transferred a little to World 3, but it connects well with their moon of World 1.

The space travelers also have a place in the thinking of the astronomers— some of them having given information to render this voyage possible. Their thinking is also of World 3 and of the second level, but in a quite different context. So you see that transferring from one level to another also means transferring to another context; but in one and the same level—here the second— you may have very different contexts.

Animals, about which we only know that they live in World 1, can also act in different contexts. There once was a young seal left by its parents. It was brought up by a woman, who, after some time, gave it dead fish. Because this was its natural food, it liked the fish. But although it swam in a pool in the midst of many live fish, it had no idea that such fish also represented food. Those fish belonged to quite another context. A punctual process of education was necessary to make the seal understand that swimming fishes also represented food.

REDUCTION OF THE LEVEL

There are many rules for driving automobiles. If you have to take an examination for a license, you will have to show some insight into those rules, and therefore you must understand them at Level 2. But when you are driving your car and you must obey the rules, thinking about the necessity of the rules is undesirable and even dangerous. When driving your car you are living in a visible world, that is to say World 1. The symbols of Level 2 have been reduced to Level 1, and with this you are in close contact with World 1. Such a reduction of level happens often. When you are converting expressions in algebra like $(a + b)^2$, you do not reflect on commutative, associative, or distributive laws; you know you have to do certain things with the letters and you do them. The advice of the teacher to always think before you act does not work in this case, for it makes you operate much too slowly. So in the interest of the results of your work, you have reduced your thinking from Level 2 to Level 1. The chemist does the same in working out chemical equations or making models of complicated organic molecules. With these models many things may become clear: We see that some atoms are very near to each other, we also see how new parts can be attached. This gives some indication of how some chemists think that molecules and atoms are so concrete that they belong to World 1.

THE FIFTH MEDIUM OF STRUCTURE:
HUMAN ACTION

Someone once suggested that we speak no longer of levels of thinking, but of levels of acting. At the base of this suggestion is a seductive idea. Actions you can codify, you can construct a scale of appreciation for them, in short, you can make them what some people call objective. Thoughts, on the contrary, can only be known by interpretation or by being told by the person who has been thinking. In the preceding discussion we saw how people who had to act on the basis of laws of the second level reduced the level and by this acted on the basis of the first level. Is it not much easier to say that they first acted at the second level and afterward at the first?

I am not happy with this suggestion. When you see a person converting expressions in algebra, it may seem that he is thinking at Level 2, for his operations are guided by commutative, associative, and distributive laws, which surely belong to Level 2 of thinking. But we know he is not thinking at this level at all. He does not make use of the notions of Level 2, he is acting in a visible world, working at Level 1. We know it because he says he is removing parentheses, he is bringing factors out of parentheses, perhaps he even will say he is taking a minus sign out of the parentheses. We are not surprised by these descriptions, nor are we alarmed. Reduction of level is a necessity in this world of complicated structures of thought. Instead of making use of laws of the second level of thinking, we do innocent things like removing parentheses. Such actions are useful, but there is a condition. If we teach pupils algebra, we may allow them to skip factors, and so on, but it is necessary that they know what they are doing and why. If they are questioned, they should be able to explain their actions by pointing to the commutative, associative, and distributive laws. They must know that from $\log(x + y) = \log z$ one may not simply conclude that $x + y = z$ (canceling out "log"), for they must know that the domain of the function $x \rightarrow \log x$ is the set of positive numbers and not the set of real numbers. So reduction of level is allowed, is very often necessary, but when using this trick you must be able to go back to the higher level with your thinking. If you do not have the ability to go back to this level, you will not be able to act in new situations, and in practice most situations are new. Only the flexibility to go back to the higher level guarantees insight.

From the above you can understand my resistance against the idea that levels are situated in action. If we use the actions of the pupils to test the level they have attained, we may overrate them. It may be that they work at a reduced level and are not able to think at the higher level. It may seem that they attain sufficient results, but later, when the subject matter becomes more difficult, they may fail.

So defining the levels in the action is a dangerous affair; it may promote bad study habits.

The question may become somewhat clearer if we again consider animals. With animals, no levels of thinking are possible. But could we perhaps speak of levels of action? No. It is quite impossible to speak of a descriptive level of action with animals, for this level can only be attained with the help of descriptions, and for such, language is necessary. So we see that no description of levels of action can be given without calling in the thinking that is necessary in passing through the phases of the first period beginning at Level 1 and terminating at Level 2. We may say with a clear conscience that introducing levels of action obscures practically everything and explains nothing.

22

Is It Possible to Test Insight?

HOW DO WE CHARACTERIZE INSIGHT?

Before we try to answer whether it is possible to test insight, we must first try to characterize it. We can do this by imagining a number of situations in which insight plays a part.

1. A cat is locked up in a cage and tries to escape. She makes a great number of motions in order to get free and eventually her tail touches the button by which the door of the cage is opened: The cat escapes. The cat is again put in the cage, and this time she immediately touches the button with her tail. Another cat, brought into the same situation, puts the mechanism into action with her right hindleg. In following cases, this cat regularly liberates herself with her right hindleg. The stereotyped actions of these cats inclines us to not speak of insight in this case.

2. A chimpanzee finds himself in a cage. Somebody puts a tube in the cage and in the middle of it a banana. The tube is placed horizontally in a fixed position. The chimpanzee has seen the banana and tries to get it out of the tube. However the tube is too long; neither from one side nor from the other can the chimpanzee reach it. After a few fruitless attempts, the chimpanzee gives up and begins to play with a stick lying in the cage. In his playing the chimpanzee puts the stick into the tube and knocks out the banana. This is a lucky chance; we will not speak of insight in this case.

The following day, the chimpanzee again has the tube and the banana in his cage in the same position. There is again a stick in the cage, but it is a different one and it lies in a different place. The chimpanzee immediately grasps the stick and with it pushes the banana out of the tube. Now we are willing to speak of insight, for the action was not bound to a special stick lying at a special place.

3.   The following problem is given to children in a geometry lesson: Within a square *ABCD* an isosceles triangle *CDE* is placed such that side *CD* of the square is the base of the triangle. The base angles are 15°. Prove that triangle *ABE* is equilateral (see Figure 22.1).

One of the pupils finds the following solution: If within square *ABCD*, equilateral triangle *ABP* is placed, then the triangles *ADP* and *BCP* are both isosceles with vertex angles of 30°. With the help of this it is easy to calculate that triangle *CPD* is isosceles with base angles of each 15°. Because only one isosceles triangle with the base *CD* and base angles of 15° can be drawn within square *ABCD*, *P* must be the same point as *E*. With this the proposition was proved.

The proof is perfectly exact and shows quite a lot of insight into what "proof" means, but the pupils of the class do not like it. Still no other, more satisfying proof is found. It remains an open question whether there exists a better proof.

After some weeks the following proposition is given: The area of a regular dodecagon is equal to three times the area of the square described on the radius of the circle circumscribed about the dodecagon. The proof is given as follows (see Figure 22.2): Pentagon *MABCD* is one-fourth of a regular dodecagon. We have to prove that the area of square *MAKD* is one-third of the area of the regular dodecagon and therefore we have to prove that this area equals the area of four triangles each of which are equal to triangle *MAB*. So it has to be proved that pentagon *DCBAK* has the same area as triangle *MAB*. Inside triangle *MAB* a point *L* exists with the property that triangle *ABL* is equilateral. It is easy to prove that triangles *MAL*, *MBL*, *DKC*, and *AKB* are all isosceles triangles with base

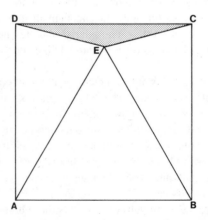

Figure 22.1

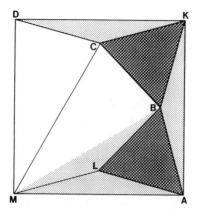

Figure 22.2

angles of 15°. They are all equal. Triangle *BCK* is equilateral and therefore equal
to triangle *ABL*. From this it is obvious that triangle *MAB* has the same area as
pentagon *DCBAK*. With this the proposition is proved.

One pupil says: "Now I am able to prove the former proposition concerning
the square and the isosceles triangle with angles of 15° (see Figure 22.3). In the
interior of triangle *BEC* a point *F* exists with the property that triangle *CEF* is
equilateral. Then triangles *DCE* and *BCF* are equal (side-angle-side). But from
this we know that angles *BFC* and *BFE* are 150° and therefore that triangles *BCF*
and *BEF* are equal (SAS). Hence *BC* = *BE* and angle *ABE* = 60°, so triangle
ABE is equilateral.

It is clear that we here have a form of insight: The proof is very original. We

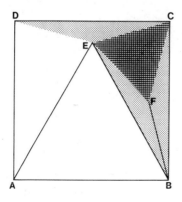

Figure 22.3

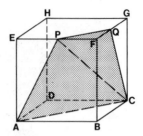

Figure 22.4

can also understand how this insight has been brought about: In the picture of the dodecagon the pupil recognized the part he needed for the proof of the square with the isosceles triangle. The class liked this proof very much. Now they could *see* that it was true.

4.   A class is given the task of constructing different cross sections of a plane with a cube (see Figure 22.4). The teacher is not content to call *ACP* a section. "No", he says, "*ACP* doesn't make the cube fall into two pieces: The real section is *ACQP*." A pupil remarks that splitting up of a cube into two parts more resembles physics than mathematics. Moreover, the planes bounding the cube do not really end in the edges of the cube. She suggests that we draw the intersecting lines of *ACP* with all bounding planes of the cube and that we not stop at the edges. If we do that we get the picture in Figure 22.5. Indeed may we speak here of a demonstration of insight into the structure of stereometry. The teacher can profit from this: Using this concept, one can make constructions better.

From this range of cases we can determine the following:

1.   Insight can be observed when there has been an adequate action in a new situation.
2.   Insight can be ascertained when there has been action on the strength of an established structure from which the answers to new questions can be read.
3.   The best examples of insight happen unexpectedly; they are not brought about by planning.

PROBLEMS AIMED AT INSIGHT

In the preceding we have seen that insight can be observed (1) by an adequate action and (2) in a new situation. The second point, especially, may produce difficulties for testing insight. For presence of insight can only be tested if it is

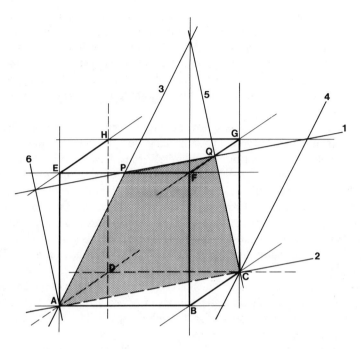

Figure 22.5

sure that the situation in which the pupil is put is sufficiently new. If the pupil and teacher are on sufficiently good terms, this condition can be fulfilled: The pupil can inform the teacher. It is not unreasonable to suppose such a relationship: Each teaching–learning situation ought to be founded on such cooperation. In practice, however, it can be quite different. In many cases the pupil will try to hide lack of insight and knowledge as much as possible by learning by heart the answers to questions that might be asked. In this way, the pupil escapes from the difficulty of having to act in a new situation. On the other hand, the teacher must try to ask questions that the pupil does not expect and that are characteristic of the insight to be determined. Such questions we may call questions aimed at insight.

Let us suppose the following familiar theorem: In every triangle the bisectors of the angles pass through one point. To test insight we can then ask the following questions:

1. Do the bisectors of the angles of every quadrangle pass through one point? Justify your answer.

This question investigates whether the pupil has insight to an auxiliary theorem: If the bisectors of the angles of a triangle pass through one point, a point exists that is at equal distances to all sides of the triangle. This theorem has implicitly been used with the proof of the theorem to be learned without mentioning that its validity surpasses triangles. To answer question 1, one must only know that there exist quadrangles with no point at equal distances from the sides, and this is the case with every rectangle that is not a square. We may therefore consider the question characteristic of the insight to be ascertained, though it is rather difficult.

The difficulty consists in the following. A pupil who gives the answer "No, the bisectors of the angles do not pass through one point in every quadrangle, for quadrangles do not have an inscribed circle," must have seen in the first place that he can draw a quadrangle with a circle touching three of the sides but not the fourth; but in the second place he must have understood the law of contraposition leading to the theorem: If in a polygon no point exists at equal distances from all the sides, then the bisectors of the angles do not pass through one point. So the question raised really is a question aimed at insight, but it is a rather difficult one; there is a great possibility that the pupils will fail in their answer and still have some insight.

2.   If it is known of a quadrangle that the bisectors of three of the angles pass through one point, this quadrangle has an inscribed circle. Develop a proof.

With this task insight is tested for the following auxiliary theorem: In every triangle a point exists at equal distances from the sides.

3.   If a quadrangle has an inscribed circle, the bisectors of all angles made by any two sides of the quadrangle go through the center of the circle. Develop a proof.

With this task insight is tested of the implicitly applied theorem that if in a polygon a point exists at equal distances from all the sides, the bisectors of all the angles pass through one point.

From the above examples we may conclude the following:

1.   There is a possibility of investigating whether a pupil has insight into a definite theorem. But the insight is complicated, we have to distinguish between insights into various parts of the *proof* and insight into the theorem as a whole. If the obtaining of insight is used as a norm for the progress of the pupil, it is possible to express this by a grade.

2.   For the above-mentioned investigation the cooperation of the pupil is desirable, if not necessary. It is difficult to constantly invent questions that pupils have not been able to prepare for by memorization.

3.   Pupils with a good attitude like to have their insight tested. Questions of this kind have a great charm for them. Still, the pleasure of the testing will be spoiled if the tests are too difficult and grades are given for the results.

4.   It is easy to have inappropriate questions when testing insight. After analyzing the test, it very often appears that the question has a complex nature and therefore evokes more difficulties than were expected.

ABSENCE OF INSIGHT

It is well known to insiders that pupils think that questions like those discussed above are very difficult. This means, then, that some of the pupils have not been able to obtain the insight that is tested by the questions. So it is reasonable to ask the following questions:

1. Should we avoid dealing with a subject matter if insight into it fails to appear in most pupils?
2. Are pupils to whom insight fails to appear unfit for this type of school?
3. Was the subject matter given at the wrong time?
4. Is it possible that insight fails to appear because of an overburdening of curricula?
5. Have the pupils had an inadequate explanation of the subject matter?

People who have to answer these questions must be very honest. For if the teacher has done his best, and usually this is the case, he will not like to give affirmative answers to these questions. He might rather throw the failure onto the pupils, their lack of intelligence. This is a simplification that will not do.

There are many questions that can be asked to demonstrate that a pupil has insufficient insight into a specific part of a subject matter. One of the steps of a proof can be chosen, or the bald contents of a theorem, with little change of wording. If the pupil does not know what to do with it, there is a good chance that he has not understood the theorem or the proof. Here are some examples:

The pupils have studied second-degree functions and have found by the equation $-\frac{1}{2}x^2 + 3x - 13 = -\frac{1}{2}(x - 3)^2 - 8\frac{1}{2}$ that the function $f(x) = -\frac{1}{2}x^2 + 3x - 13$ has a maximum value at $-8\frac{1}{2}$. Then, to determine insight, the following questions might be asked: (1) Has the function $f(x) = -\frac{1}{2}x^2 + 3x - 13$ any positive values? (2) What is the range of the function? Explain your answer. If, for the solution of question 1, a pupil makes use of any other means than the fact that $-8\frac{1}{2}$ is the maximum value, then from that it can be concluded that this other means has a stronger attraction to the pupil than the theorem he has just studied. From this it is not certain if insight, in the sense of "maximum value," is missing. If the pupil, on the contrary, does not know the answer to either question, we can be sure that insight is missing.

One may suppose that in elementary education children have obtained some insight into the idea of 'area'. In order to test this, the following problem may be given: A square is divided by its diagonals into four equal parts. It is possible to join two of those parts in such a way that a new square comes into being. Make a drawing of such a square. What is the ratio of the area of the original square to the new one?

If the pupils are not successful in doing this problem, lack of insight must be taken very seriously. Difficulties in understanding geometry later on may be the result.

Sometimes nearly all pupils show a lack of insight. I give an example: In a lesson, it is proved that the medians of a triangle intersect one another in the ratio 2 : 1. How can one use this information to prove that the three medians of a triangle pass through one point? The question appeals to mathematical insight and the absence of a reasonable answer proves the absence of mathematical insight. It is possible to see this by analyzing the problem. What is given consists of six parts:

m_a divides m_b in the ratio 2 : 1;
m_b divides m_a in the ratio 2 : 1;
m_b divides m_c in the ratio 2 : 1;
m_c divides m_b in the ratio 2 : 1;
m_c divides m_a in the ratio 2 : 1;
m_a divides m_c in the ratio 2 : 1.

In the above the, median drawn from point A is denoted by m_a, and so on. Now the question is which of these six given data are necessary and sufficient to prove that the three medians pass through one point? It appears that most students lack insight into the problem as a whole.

It is much easier to find questions establishing a lack of insight than to find those establishing positive insight. A correct response to questions of the former type gives no guarantee to the existence of insight, although the probability of such insight is very high, especially when many such questions have been asked and the percentage of the right answers is high. However, if the questions are no longer new, they test something other than insight.

DIFFICULTIES WITH TESTING INSIGHT

The second condition mentioned earlier for the existence of insight—that action ought to be appropriate—may also lead to difficulties.

The first difficulty is the possibility that the teacher has an inadequate solution in view. In this case the insight of the pupil will often not be evident. More often it occurs that teacher and pupil both have an adequate solution in view, but the former does not recognize that of the latter. In examinations, the examiner sometimes gives instructions not fitting the outline the examinee has in view, and usually the results are unfavorable. It also occurs that the examiner permits the solution of the examinee but afterward concludes evidence of a lack of insight has been given because the examiner likes his own solution more. We may hope, for the examinee, that someone else is present who is able to demonstrate that one solution is as good as the other.

THE INTENTION OF THE PUPIL

The examination situation enables us to add another important notion to insight. Acting adequately in a new situation obviously does not characterize insight sufficiently. To explain this I first cite how Prins approaches insight:

> The solution of relatively difficult problems usually begins with the ordering of the data, the consideration of the consequences; in short, there is wrestling with the problem, characterized by Thorndike as "trial-and-error behavior." . . . She approaches the solution more closely by correcting the obtained result and at the end she is able to give a summary, an abstract, a real coordination, and after she has shown the capacity to embody the investigation in a clear answer we may say she gives evidence of insight. (Prins, 1951, p. 30)

Many examiners will justifiably not consider the *result* as a proof that insight exists. They will only admit that insight exists if the examinee intended just this conclusion and did not merely run into it accidentally. Nor does recognition of a solution after having it demonstrated indicate intuition. This may be very valuable, but it does not prove insight into the totality of the problem. In order to investigate whether the examinee has come to total insight, a new problem of the same structure is given to him, but with another form. From the manner this new problem is tackled, it can be concluded if insight exists or not. What we miss in the description of Prins and what we now recognize as essential for the existence of insight is the intention of the examinee to choose just this solution. So now we can give the final description of insight: *Insight is always recognized as such, if a person acts adequately with intention in a new situation.*

A MORE PRECISE ANALYSIS OF INSIGHT

With the addition of "with intention," the character of the means to recognize insight has been importantly changed. Whereas "adequately" and "in new situations" are closely related with behavior and therefore can be used in behavioristic theory, "intention" belongs to quite another vocabulary. Intention is related to our own mind; we only know of someone's intention after that person has informed us of it. It is true that in animal psychology intentional movements are spoken of; by these are meant preliminary movements, for example, taking up a certain position that precedes a completely developed pattern of conduct. But though this may be a useful concept in animal psychology, it is unrelated to human intention.

Our only means to know ourselves and other people is the exchange of internal experiences. In behaviorism, objections are made to narratives of private experiences, because it is supposed that these are not objective. We have seen, however, that at examinations objectivity about intention can be obtained. It can be observed, objectively, that an examinee has difficulties connecting parts of his reasoning. Then he often will have to be helped, and he can be if he has the right intention—by giving him a problem of the same structure but of another form.

The great difference between human and the above-mentioned animal intention is that the intention necessary for insight is not always followed by action. We know that sometimes we have excellent ideas, which, should we execute them, would manifest an important insight, but unfortunately we fail to execute them. This also undermines the position that chimpanzees have insight, for there is little reason to suppose that chimpanzees can think, and without thinking intention is impossible. So in this stage of my semantic analysis of insight I must leave my former point of view that the chimpanzee, by solving the problem of the tube with the banana, has shown insight.

If we compare the above characteristics of insight with the notion at the beginning of this chapter—an action on the basis of an established structure from which the answers to new questions can be read—we now see more points of resemblance. Acting on the basis of a structure presumes an intention; the "having been established" of the structure can only be stated by a new situation. "Adequately," however gives us some problems. This need not alarm us, for whether something is adequate or not depends on conformity to an existing culture or custom pattern of a group. It is difficult to express this in general terms.

There are two reasons why the word "structure" so preeminently fits. In the first place, many structures are visual; we can see them in many places, just as someone may have insights in various domains. Moreover, a field may have different total structures, just as someone may have different insights in one total domain. In the second place, there is a phenomenon that has struck many mathematicians; namely, that many visual structures correspond with thought structures; to every structure of the observation some insight is added. There are, however, many examples of insight that cannot be read from a structure in a visual field. By the application of schematic representations we may attempt to make such nonvisual structures visible. In any case, we can now understand why geometric problems are so often used to study insight.

THE MOMENT AT WHICH INSIGHT
DEMONSTRATES ITSELF

We have seen that testing insight entails certain difficulties that can be overcome if a sufficient bond of confidence between teacher and pupil exists. Another kind of difficulty results from the special character of examinations. There are always examinees who cannot activate the right insight at the right time: The examinee cannot decide what insight must be used in the given case. Often the day after the examination we hear: "The night after the examination I found the solution in half an hour." That is why some people think examinations are unsuitable for testing insight. And indeed, in many cases the best way to prepare for an examination is to carefully study the possibilities of testing offered by the subject matter in order not to be put in a new situation that requires insight. In the more favorable case, in which the pupils have not been coached for the examinations but have found the solutions themselves beforehand, we get a reproduction of the results of former insight at the examination. In the unfavorable case, in which they have been coached, we get a reproduction of other people's insight.

Must we conclude that it is a mistake to prepare pupils for examinations by having them study the test papers of previous years? For without such a preparation, the examination papers preserve the character of tests of insight. But the teacher giving an examination without such training would seriously deceive himself and his pupils. First, the test can be difficult precisely because the examinees are acquainted with the papers of former years; every examinee can prepare himself with the aid of former papers, and every examinee must perform well relative to the others. Second, is it not at all bad that pupils prepare themselves for a certain number of examination papers. Ultimately the point of examinations is to test insight, and by preparing for those tests, an existing structure with some hazy patches can made clearer. A teacher, who for years has done his utmost to impart insight to his pupils, who has not scrupulously limited himself to the subject matter of the examination, will satisfy the curriculum well if during the last three months he seriously prepares for the coming examination.

COOPERATION BETWEEN TEACHER AND PUPIL

Insight is, as it were, the foundation for later thought; success for a great part depends on it. It should be one of the aims of instruction to develop insight, and the conditions should be established that render it testable. A relationship between teacher and pupil, in which the former does not act as judge but as confidant, should be strived for. After the establishment of such confidence, a test of insight will give information just as desirable to the teacher as to the pupil. At the end of a study of one subject, series of short tests should be given to guide the insight that has been attained. The purpose of the such tests is to guide, not to hinder. There are working methods (Dalton, Mastery Learning) in which the subject matter is divided in sections. There is a control test at the end of each section, and a pupil who fails such a test is not allowed to begin the next section. This is not a good method. Failure in the test of a certain section does not imply lack of understanding in the next section. It is even possible to understand an earlier section by seeing how the subject matter is continued. It is better to have the pupils go on with their work and to repeat difficult subject matter after some time—and then for all the pupils. Most pupils like it to have their subject matter repeated. This approach is called *telescoped reteaching*.

CONCLUSION

1. A condition for insight is the ability to act adequately in a new situation.
2. Testing insight requires cooperation of teacher and pupil.
3. It is just as important for the pupil to know if he has obtained insight as it is for the teacher.
4. In examinations, usually the only insight demonstrated is that which the examinee has previously obtained. One can only guess if it is a reproduction of the results of the examinee's thinking or of the thinking of other people.
5. Acting adequately in a new situation only implies insight if the adequate action results from the intention of the pupil.

23

A Phenomenal Introduction to Geometry

se p. 4

AIM AND SIGNIFICANCE OF MATHEMATICS INSTRUCTION

Why do we teach mathematics in secondary education? At the end of the 1940s Beth (1955, p. 45) studied this question extensively. His conclusion was as follows: "It seems to me that the role of mathematics education in secondary school nearly exclusively consists in making the pupils familiar with the deductive method."

It seems to me that this thesis must not be gratuitously accepted. The thing we have to look at is not as much the significance of the deductive method as the claim that the educative value of mathematics exclusively or even principally is found in the deductive method. The manner in which Beth defended his thesis may itself be used as an argument against his thesis. Beth begins with a number of postulates, of which the first pair are pronouncements qualified by the expression "among other things." I cite here the important theses and the important part of the conclusion (Beth, 1955, p. 35):

1. "Every institution of secondary education is among other things intended to prepare future [university] students."
2. "Mathematics forms a part of the normal program of the institutions of secondary education."

3.   "From our postulates [there were four of them] it results that one may expect a rather intensive interaction between mathematics programs of secondary and university education."

The fact that the premises are not part of abstract logical propositions forces Beth to express himself very carefully in his conclusion. The suggestion, embodied in the expectation, is not logically justified even though Beth chooses the form of a syllogism for his reasoning. Just here lies the danger of the thesis put forward by Beth. For with familiarity with the deductive method one may clothe reasoning in syllogistic *form,* of wrongly giving an impression of the truth of the conclusions.

Still, we need not doubt the fact that pupils' acquaintance with the deductive method has a certain value. This acquaintance can be useful to them in two respects: first, to be able to use this method in suitable cases, and second, to be able to recognize when others use of this method incorrectly. But it may be seriously doubted that the value of mathematics nearly exclusively consists of a familiarity with the deductive method. Beth came to this conclusion because he saw the mathematics education as a problem principally defined by mathematics itself and by psychology. He therefore did not take into account that in determining the aims of education, pedagogy is also engaged with other factors of special character. Psychology, too, was soon put aside by Beth, because it appeared to fail in supplying a satisfactory axiomatic foundation for mathematics (this argument seems me to be of little import). The above reasoning brought Beth to the conclusion that the mathematician is the only person with the right to decide the aims of mathematics education, and therefore it is clear, or at least understandable, that acquaintance with the deductive method is seen by him as the principal aim of education.

In learning the deductive method, the pupil will also have to learn under what conditions a method is applicable. This can be done by a phenomenal approach, to which the beginning of geometry lends itself very well.

At the moment that instruction in geometry begins for the pupils, they are not completely unaware of the objectives of the instruction. For geometry is engaged in the study of space, and the pupils have dealt with space since childhood. It is true that space will now be studied in a very special connection, namely, in the geometrical context, but this does not alter the fact that pupils, during their study, will continually be obliged to fall back on earlier experiences. It seems that there have been attempts made to oppose such "falling back" because associations with a world of experiences have been thought to be unfavorable for abstract thinking. Those who want to change to such an "abstract" form of education ought to have very conclusive evidence that they can do so without seriously damaging the child's development. For there is a great danger that the child will get totally flustered in trying to deal with an artificially built up domain, in which there are ideal objects having the same names as and the same relations to the world of experience, without being allowed to connect one with the other.

Because I do not know if such education in mathematics, detached from every experience, ever has succeeded, and inasmuch as the above objection against such an education has never been refuted, I now take the starting point that in mathematics education we have to take into consideration the earlier experiences of the pupil. So we will have to construct a curriculum in which the beginning, though not mathematical, is nevertheless of great educational value.

Because a child has for many years observed objects in space and has also learned to move in space, he has acquainted himself with many spacial relations. These relations, however, such as 'in front of–behind', 'above–below', 'fitting', 'far–near', 'high–low', are of quite another nature than the logical assertions in geometry—although they often form part of corresponding structures. In a deductive system the most important concept is 'implication', in which "A implies B" is equivalent to the statement excluding the simultaneous occurrence of A and not-B. The child's spatial concepts have a much less imperative character: They indicate no more than that the phenomenon A is often accompanied by the phenomenon B.

It is of great importance that we carefully observe the difference between the two types of connections, especially because the second connection is sometimes termed "implication." If this difference is not observed, misunderstandings in mathematics can occur, because "mathematical implication" will not be carefully dealt with. In an examination the question is asked: "If in a triangle, cos C = −cos $4B$, does this imply that $A = 3B$?" The answer is given: "Yes, the implication is true; but also $A = 3B - 360°$, $A = 360° - 5B$, $A = 720° - 5B$." This conclusion is not in accordance with the *logical* meaning of "implication." The answer should have been: "The conclusion is not true. It is true that one of the following four relations has to be true: $A = 3B$, or $A = 3B - 360°$, or $A = 360° - 5B$, or $A = 720° - 5B$." Modern mathematics has an easy notation for such implications.

Just this strict demand that has to be made for "implying" makes the learning of geometry so difficult. The essential nature of much of the reasoning in mathematics is not understood by the pupils because they only know of "implying" in a global context. The significance of a definition, the difference between a theorem and its converse, an indirect proof, are all only partially understood by a child who does not possess the correct concept of logical implication.

At the beginning of mathematics teaching, the teacher has to face the following dual problem: (1) Starting from the knowledge the child possesses of spatial ordering, he must give the child experience in mathematical spatial ordering. (2) He must lead the child to experience how far mathematical concepts differ from those the child has experienced before. These problems can be solved in a neat way by an introductory curriculum. Before moving to a description of it, I first summarize the ordering structures of space the child may be more or less globally acquainted with. These structures are of special importance because their extension and analyses are useful for most pupils. The structures generally determine the geometrical concepts that should have to come up for discussion in mathematical learning over the years:

1. recognition and naming geometric figures
2. partitions of plane and space
3. the use of congruent figures
4. similar figures
5. piling of figures
6. mapping of figures
7. symmetry with regard to a plane
8. symmetry with regard to a line
9. symmetry with regard to a point
10. area and volume
11. movements in space: translation, rotation, screw movement
12. trajectones
13. lack of congruence of spatial figures that are reflections of one another
14. mappings from space onto a plane
15. intersections of figures
16. determination a point by means of coordinates

This chapter would become much too extensive if for every item I should have to indicate in which way the structure is already present to most pupils and why its analysis contributes to their learning. Therefore I restrict myself to some illustrative points:

Item 2 is connected with tiled and parquet floors, with the partition of space with cubes, with regular hexagonal prisms (honeycomb). With 5 you may think of a complete filling of space, as with the stones of a wall; you may also think of stacks in which there is some space left, like the stacking of congruent or noncongruent spheres. Solids may be obtained by the stacking of other solids. A house, for instance, can be thought of as the result of the stacking of a rectangular parallelepiped and a truncated triangular prism. The building up of a solid with the help of its network may also be considered as a very particular form of stacking. Items 2 and 5 have a certain resemblance—still, they must be seen as different. In structure 2 a totality is split into congruent or noncongruent parts; in structure 5 a totality is built out of parts—the totality need not be known beforehand. In elementary school, structure 2 forms the foundation for the concept 'fraction' and structure 5 forms the foundation for addition and multiplication.

Item 6 is connected with seeing: A square can, from visual observation, be seen as a trapezoid, a rectangle, a rhomb, a quadrangle, and so on. It is also connected with mechanical transformations: compressing, bending out of shape, and so on. Items 7, 8, and 9 are of importance when figures from nature or mechanics are studied. They also contain an aesthetic element: A symmetric formation often gives the impression of stiffness; a figure having an axis of symmetry but no plane of symmetry gives the impression of being dynamic. A structure as meant in 15 may be developed by the observation of the effect of a meat-cutting machine or the like. This structure can be used effectively when the principle of Cavalieri is applied. It seems absurd to suppose that these originally global structures should not play an important part in geometry instruction. Of course the teacher can totally ignore the existence of such structures in his instruction. Some of his pupils, however, will discover global isomorphisms between the mathematical structures and the above-mentioned structures and they will use them successfully. Many others will develop a badly functioning global system of calculating that, because it misses every link with observation, cannot or can only with difficulty be applied.

The beginning of geometry instruction should call the attention of the pupils to one or more (but by all means not too many) of these subjects and discuss them in a geometric context. With this a double goal is aimed at: (1) with the discussion of the subject, the meanings of the concepts and their interrelations are determined. Perhaps it is better to say that just by the interrelations the meanings of the concepts are fixed. There is still no possibility of fixing concepts by means of definitions, because, as Kohnstamm (1952, p. 84) has strikingly remarked, "A definition of a concept is such a description that the place, owing to this concept within an as-given accepted system of concepts, in this way uniquely is defined." So we must take care to create a sufficiently marked out system of concepts, with which we provisionally must renounce definitions, but with which we have to choose such clear examples that everyone can easily recognize the concepts that are meant. (2) by the choice of interrelations, we make clear what is typical for a geometric context. So our method totally differs from the blind classification of characteristics derived from observation. This latter would be nothing new to the child: Ordering and classifying according to observed characteristics is essential for human thinking and a child has done this (partially unconsciously) from his early youth. The second aim is closely connected with the first: The field of concepts is just as sharply marked out by the context the connections act in as by the connections themselves.

Here we have to apply a phenomenal analysis of space in a very special (viz., the geometric) context. Pupils of about 12 years of age are well able to understand this context, because for them the originally very complex spatial structures have long since been differentiated in different directions. So, for instance, we need not fear that pupils will question very important emotional experiences of space. I mention this possibility because phenomenological analysis especially is applied to get objectivity about emotional experiences. This is surely not our intention here. But, as I remarked, for children this confusion practically is excluded.

When, after some time, the concepts are sufficiently clear, pupils can begin to describe them. With this, the properties possessed by the geometric figures that have been dealt with are successively mentioned and so become explicit. The figure becomes the representative of all those properties: It gets what we call the "symbol character." In this stage, the "comprehension" of the figure means the knowledge of all these properties as a unity. So, for instance, an isosceles triangle has the properties of having two equal sides, an axis of symmetry, and two equal angles. The knowledge included in the symbol character enables the pupils to do some simple logical operations. Here we have a total equivalence: Not only does an isosceles triangle possess these properties, but also the children may always call a figure having all those properties an isosceles triangle.

The symbol gives thought the points of support that are necessary: When once it is decided that a given figure is an isosceles triangle, then the pupil also knows that a certain number of properties are applicable without being obliged to memorize them. In the beginning the properties can be read from the representation; the symbol has the character of an "image" (see *Meyerson, 1932,* p. 502). In the end, the properties will be called up more directly by the word alone.

Because in this stage the concepts are only defined by the sum total of their properties, it is only possible to operate mathematically with them in a very simple manner. For instance, one can decide that half a rhomb is an isosceles triangle, because in the half rhomb all the properties of an isosceles triangle are found. Usually it will only be possible to judge that a figure can be indicated with a certain symbol after deriving empirically the existence of the essential properties. So in this stage the relation between geometry and perception is strengthened; in the mathematical domain, however, only little progress is made.

When the symbol character of many geometric figures have become sufficiently clear to the pupils, the possibility is born that they also get a *signal character.* This implies that the symbols can be anticipated. Then, on the basis that a figure possesses some of the properties of a rhombus, the pupil may begin to suppose that he has a rhombus. But we can only rightly say that the figures act as signals after the pupil has been able to *orient* himself with the help of the properties of figures in geometry. When this orientation has been sufficiently developed, when the figures sufficiently act as signals, then, for the first time, geometry can be practiced as a logical topic. For the orientation implies that the pupil begins to see, on the basis of a *combination* of properties, what can be concluded about the existence of a certain geometric figure. So the pupil is able to recognize a rhombus, because he knows that he has a quadrangle all sides of which are equal, or because he knows that it is a quadrangle in which the diagonals bisect each other perpendicularly.

In this stage, however, the possibilities of logical thinking must not be overestimated. Still the figures are the objects of thinking, not the relations between those figures and still less the character of these relations. Now the pupil is able to conclude about a certain figure that two angles are equal because they can be regarded as opposite angles of a rhombus (because of the symbol character of the rhombus), after he has concluded that the figure is a rhombus on basis of the figure being a quadrangle in which the diagonals bisect each other perpendicularly (signal character of the rhombus). But it is improbable that at this level the pupil surveys the whole of the reasoning, because the relations between the figures have not yet obtained a symbol and a signal character. That figures possess a symbol and a signal character has been well known for some time. A figure in which the symbol and the signal character have been recently studied is the parallelogram.

After the pupils have attained the second level of geometry, that is, when they become oriented with the help of the properties of figures (rhombuses, rectangles, isosceles triangles, regular polygons, etc.) those figures have for them a symbol and a signal character; only then does it become possible that the relations get a symbol and later on a signal character for them. When they do, pupils can study the properties of congruence, reflection, similarity, parallelism, and others. And in this stage only the *extrinsic* properties of these relations are studied—the properties of congruent triangles, similar rhombuses, parallel lines, triangles being each others reflection with regard to a line, and so on. The study of the *intrinsic* properties of relations leads to the third level of thinking.

The symbol and signal character of relations is studied in many places in mathematics. For instance, it belongs to the symbol character of the relation 'line perpendicular to a plane' that the line is perpendicular to all lines of that plane; it belongs to the signal character of that relation that we only need to know that the line is perpendicular to only two intersecting lines of the plane to be able to conclude about the perpendicularity of line and plane. In general, it does not appear from the textbooks that there is sufficient recognition of the fact that a pupil does not readily understand the signal character of relations and therefore can not readily operate with them.

As soon as the signal character begins to become significant for the pupils, implication also begins to get its proper sense. For now the equality of the pairs of opposite sides of a quadrangle implies that it is a parallelogram and this again implies that in this quadrangle the diagonals bisect each other, the opposite angles are equal, and the opposite sides are parallel. The first implication has the meaning we ordinarily attach to the term and is not evidently reversible; the second implication has a more psychological content: It contains the identification of the name of a figure with the whole of its properties. From a logical point of view, the intermediate proposition "this quadrangle is a parallelogram" might be omitted; still, educational practice has taught us that children very much need

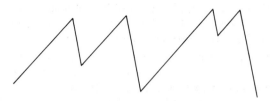

Figure 23.1

it. The real significance of such an intermediate proposition becomes clear if we also insert some of such propositions into discussion of parallelism. Figure 23.1, which we can call a "saw," has following properties of symbol character: (1) There are two sets of parallel lines in it. (2) All angles of the saw are equal. The signal character of the saw is given by the statement that each of the properties (1) and (2) is sufficient to establish the saw. By the introduction of the intermediate proposition, the pupils can be prevented from mixing up the proposition and its converse.

Though we have now given a means to avoid the difficulty of incorrectly using propositions and their converses, we still must realize that the pupils have not yet understood this difference and in general cannot understand. The signal character of geometric figures forms an introduction to the learning of this difference. After the pupils have examined the signal character of various figures, they will discover that some combinations of properties produce the desired figures and that other combinations do not. The parallelism of one pair of sides of a quadrangle and the equality of the other pair of sides together are not sufficient to ensure that the figure is a parallelogram.

The signal character enables pupils to operate with geometric figures. With these operations, relations are also objects, namely, the relations between the properties that a geometric figure has and the properties that define the figure. The operations will flow more easily, the more the pupils see as a totality the properties leading to a geometric figure (so belonging to the signal character) and the properties the geometric figure has (so belonging to the symbol character). This "totality character" gradually results in the completion of a direct link between the properties leading to the figure and those issuing from it. The figure itself can more easily be pushed to the background, and at last only the name remains as a symbol for a set of syllogisms. With a figure like "saw" the name is usually no longer made explicit, and a direct link is laid between the equality of alternate interior angles and the parallelism of lines.

From the preceding it should be clear how, by condensation the concepts, the symbol and signal character of "saw" can be abstracted to the symbol and signal character of the relation 'parallelism'. Other relations, like congruence and similarity, can only become symbol characters after the figures these relations refer to themselves have sufficient symbol and signal characters. Such relations need not come up for discussion before it is certain that nearly all the pupils have attained the second level of thinking.

Only after pupils have progressed far enough to see the symbol and the signal character of a figure as a totality are they able to conceive of 'implication' in its intrinsic meaning. Then they know that a quadrangle in which the diagonals bisect each other is a parallelogram, and that from this, among other things, it may be concluded that one pair of sides are parallel and the other pair equal. However, they also know by experience that not every combination of properties leads to a parallelogram, and therefore they will know that in a quadrangle in which one pair of sides is parallel and the other pair equal, it is not necessary that the diagonals bisect each other. In other words, after they have learned how it is possible to give relations an implicatory character, they experience that this character sometimes only exists in one direction. The understanding of the intrinsic properties of implication will be dealt with later. For this understanding it is also necessary that the relations themselves have symbol and signal characters. After the intrinsic ordering principles of concepts like 'implication' have been studied, new global structures can come into existence from which, gradually, symbols and signals are developed. This ends in a new level of thinking. At this point there is indeed not much difference between geometry and formal logic. But one must admit that only few pupils will be able to cover the long path of thinking that culminates in this level.

A careful examination of the above outlined development will make clear that there is little sense in introducing implication in the beginning of geometry instruction. For this concept cannot have the meaning needed for the pupils to be able to operate with it. And still clearer, we can understand the impossibility of developing a deductive system in the beginning of geometry instruction. For to understand such a development, it is necessary that groupings and sequences of syllogisms are seen as totalities—that these totalities have symbol and signal characters.

It seems to me that the global character of the concepts forming the foundation of a theory is essential. When in a later stage of development the global concepts derived from empirical investigation are analyzed, there will be a possibility of understanding an axiom system. Then the originally global conceptions will have a logical foundation. This means that though they may have kept the same place in the network of relations, they now have a new function—they finally have logical significance. But still, the axiom system forming the foundation contains global elements.

When in the beginning of geometry instruction the pupils are carefully familiarized with a logical deductive system (without, however, having analyzed the relations derived from observation), the global structures only have the appearance of mathematical structures. These structures are global because they are not connected with other structures with the aid of analyses. If the teacher has begun with axioms, then in the beginning only verbal structures are formed, because in this situation the pupils do not know how to orient themselves. Afterward, the actions of the teacher will have global structure for the pupils. It is also possible that the teacher passes over the first axiomatic part and consciously aims at the development of global pseudomathematical structures. In both cases, however, he plays a risky game. From the global structures, new structures of action are developed by means of symbols and signals forming more and more automatically. The original global structures lose their meaning and may be lost. This course of events should be well known to many teachers of mathematics. A good example is fractions, which for many elementary-school pupils were never linked with the world of experiences. In the first class of secondary school, these pupils know no more about fractions than a few algorithms.

When geometry is based on originally global observation structures, the risk that this base will be lost is much smaller. For these structures retain their sense, even when abstract thinking structures and automatic action structures are developed from them. It will also be possible in due time to analyze those observation structures and their relation to axioms. Starting with observation structures therefore gives a better introduction to the deductive method than starting with only apparently deductive structures.

The assertion that geometry developed from observation structures should be based on experiments does not appear to me true. Even the investigation made by the pupils when they try to pave a floor with congruent nonisosceles triangles does not have the character of an experiment. They do not carefully determine whether everything fits, and they do not investigate whether every triangle will fit into the available space on the floor. After having put together a number of triangles, they see the structure of the totality that has been formed. They see, for instance, a set of parallelograms or lines, or even still more primitive structures. And in the later restructurings, the question of whether the original structures exactly filled the plane hardly comes up for discussion.

Beginning geometry instruction with observation structures has the advantage that pupils can experience how a domain of knowledge of which one has global structures can be made accessible to objective contemplations by analysis. For the way indicated here for geometry can also be used for other domains of knowledge. The nature of the field determines whether the final knowledge of the field can be made mathematical. This can happen only if the relations are not distorted by transformation. It will be much easier for those who have once participated actively with such a working method to recognize the limits than for those who have had to accept the logical deductive system as a cut-and-dried subject.

With this we see a value to be obtained from the instruction of beginning geometry, one of great importance for the aims of education. The greater part of students do not advance to the deductive system, and a still greater part will not later go to the university. It is a significant question whether it is right to direct the introductory instruction of geometry to something appropriate to university education—especially since the aim is of use only to those who will study one of the exact sciences. So it is a happy circumstance that the method of teaching that best prepares pupils for the logical deductive system also gives important training to the large group of those whose familiarity with the deductive system is of dubious value.

So the development of logical thinking must be considered as the result of a learning process. Experiences of teachers acquainted with teaching processes affirm this. This is important to remember when interpreting the results of tests concerning the development of logical thinking in children. These results are not to be considered results of a spontaneous (biological) development; they are obtained by incidental learning, appearing from the intercourse of the pupil with more experienced people. Moreover, our analysis shows that the pupil acts on grounds of global, not logical, structures. With this I especially think of investigations about the ability of children to construct syllogisms or to give correct definitions.

Beth (1955) has also claimed that the subject matter to be instructed should be sufficiently interesting to teachers; otherwise they are not able to give their lessons with conviction. To some extent, I can agree. I can understand that some teachers will have trouble when they are asked to "do kindergarten work," to cut, to glue, or to fold with their pupils. But it seems to me very improbable that teachers, as a result of their training, have lost links with the material world to such an extent that they are no longer able to develop interest for this material world or to help children transform it in logical structures.

The development of the symbol and signal character of geometric figures, of the symbol and signal character of relations, and finally of the insight into the deductive system I have called in other chapters of this volume the development of the levels of thinking of geometry. A further analysis of these levels makes clear that in every next level of thinking a higher degree of formal logical thinking is necessary. So we can say that in the end we have some agreement with Beth's statement. It is really true that knowledge of formal logic can lead to a better understanding of common difficulties in geometry instruction and consequently can lead to better teaching methods. Still, Beth did not draw the right conclusions–because he chose a wrong starting point: He should have started from learning situations.

In the above, I described the teaching of geometry with "logical thinking" as the final purpose. It is not necessary to agree with this purpose. Many pupils will be happy if they are only taught geometry aimed at the attainment of the descriptive level. With such geometry many things can be done and even some branches of university mathematics can be studied with it. The visual and the descriptive levels are by no means inferior to the theoretical one.

24

The Significance of Intention in the Learning Process

MATURATION, LEARNING, AND DEVELOPMENT

Introduction In many cases it appears to be necessary to differentiate between maturation and learning. This happens, for instance, when it is necessary to decide if children are capable of keeping up with the education in elementary school. One may ask oneself in such a case if they are already mature enough for school. By "maturation," I think, we imply that a certain autonomous process has taken place—a process very difficult to guide, or perhaps a process one is not accustomed to guiding. It may be important to clearly distinguish these two possibilities, for if, as with biological maturation, influence from the outside is not possible, one must wait until the child has sufficiently mentally "grown." If, on the other hand, incidental learning processes are involved, that is to say, learning processes introduced by more or less incidental circumstances, then it is always possible that a school can overcome the shortage with the help of guided learning processes.

Still, it is difficult to distinguish between cases of maturation and a series of incidental learning processes. Roth (1957) makes a serious attempt in this direction, but he is not able to give better examples of obvious maturation than skills such as the climbing of stairs. Finally he is obliged to acknowledge that in many cases a distinction is not possible.

Perhaps the distinction can be clarified by the introduction of a new definition:

Learning is the acquisition of new skills under the influence of an intention to learn. I do not pretend that such a definition is totally in accordance with ordinary language (though it is not clearly contrary to it), I even admit that in other chapters I have written about incidental learning processes in which absolutely no intention to learn was present. This definition of learning was a suggestion of M. J. Langeveld, a prominent pedagogical psychologist: I here try to determine whether it holds. So in this chapter we distinguish learning processes and development processes. A learning process is characterized by an intention to learn a specific subject matter. With a development process an increase of knowledge or an acquisition of new skills also takes place, but in this case it happens independently of an intention to learn that knowledge or those skills.

Concept of Number in a Guided Learning Process   At the elementary school, a child must learn, by means of the arithmetic lessons,

1. to consider addition, substraction, multiplication, and division as actions that can be considered apart from the objects with which those actions were experienced;
2. to have some results of those actions as ready knowledge;
3. to understand that the ordering of a quantity in groups of equal numbers has something to do with multiplication and division;
4. to understand that these actions can be simplified by grouping the numbers in a special manner. Only after 4 has been accomplished are the children able to understand upon what the operations multiplication and division are based.

It is easy to see the resemblance between the learning process concerning these operations and the former development of the concept of number. Again only the results of 2 can directly be learned; for the activities mentioned in 1, 3, and 4, a "proper insight" is necessary. Here too one is tempted to speak of a development, though we are considering a subject matter that is taught in school. In other words, it is obviously possible to guide those development processes in such a way that they still get the character of learning processes.

Phases in a Learning Process   In earlier chapters I have discussed the levels of thinking in geometry. Apparently at the end of the development of the concept of number, the second level of thinking in arithmetic has been attained, and at the end of the learning process of operations, the third level of thinking in arithmetic has been attained. If we call the learning process leading from one level to the next a "period," then we find in one period the following phases:

1. information
2. bound orientation
3. explicitation
4. free orientation
5. integration

In the first phase, *information*, the child is acquainted with the context of the field of study involved. In arithmetic in the second period, this happens by the grouping of quantities denoted by numbers. In the second phase, *bound orientation*, the child comes in contact with the principal connections of the network of relations to be formed. For instance, two rows of three may be read as "three and again three," as "two times three," or, if seen from another side, as "three times two." In the third phase, *explicitation*, the relations that have been found are discussed; the child recognizes that three times two is the same as two times three. In this way he learns to speak a technical language. In the fourth phase, *free orientation*, the child learns to find his way in the network of relations with the help of the connections he has at his disposal. Thus, for instance, he learns what he can do with multiplication and division and in what cases these have to be used. In the fifth phase, *integration*, the child will procure a survey of the various thinking paths. In this fifth phase, for instance, the necessary tables of multiplication are memorized.

Of course the above must only be understood as a scheme: It may very well happen that one operation has progressed to a much later phase than another; it may also happen that for a certain operation a pupil has already progressed to a certain phase and then must complete his knowledge with some material out of a former phase. Still, the classification of phases may serve us well, because we know that learning as well as teaching go on differently in the different phases. For those who have accustomed themselves to the above ideas it is easy to see which phase a given learning process is in.

A teacher can guide a learning process by the following:

1. in the first phase, by placing at the children's disposal (putting into discussion) material clarifying the context;
2. in the second phase, by supplying the material by which the pupils learn the principal connections in the field of thinking;
3. in the third phase, by leading class discussions that will end in a correct use of language;
4. in the fourth phase, by supplying materials with various possibilities of use and giving instructions to permit various performances;
5. in the fifth phase, by inviting the pupils to reflect on their actions, by having rules composed and memorized, and so on.

So memorizing only appears at the end of the fifth phase. Only then do we see "ordinary learning." Explanation by the teacher is only possible after an ordered field of thinking has been formed in which obscurities can be cleared up by means of many already existing connections. So we see that in a guided learning process the aid of the teacher is principally indirect: He creates a situation effecting an accelerated development.

In the above analysis, I have not mentioned a specific form of instruction. The ideas that have been used here have a place in every method of teaching. It may be observed that in one method this phase and in another method that phase plays an important role. So may it happen that in classroom teaching the fifth phase is stressed, in Montessori teaching the second phase, in Socratic teaching the third phase. But all these forms of teaching are good, as well as many others that are not mentioned here, if they use all phases to full advantage—and they fail if they place too much stress on one single phase.

Phases in the Development Process   We now return to the development process in order to see if there too the five phases are discernable. For this we again choose the development of the concept of number.

1.   A child gets information about number by seeing adults or older children counting, stacking, ordering.
2.   A child experiences bound orientation by exploring. During the bound orientation, the world abandons its mysteries, networks of relations are formed.
3.   The child on his own accord seeks out an explicitation: He confronts his own language and his discoveries with the world of the adults.
4.   With the aid of the relations that have been found, the child tries to move within the world; by this he better learns to find his way within the network of relations.
5.   The fifth phase, integration, we cannot easily find in such a development process. So we may see that the actions effecting integration are usually stimulated by the teacher in the elementary school. This makes it seem as if the teacher alone has taught the children the principles of the concept of number.

As long as a child experiences the inviting character of the world, as long as he wants to join in the environment, development having a great resemblance to guided learning will take place. When the development process ends in a differentiated action, an integration takes place. This happens, for example, with many manual skills and with speaking. In cases in which the integration only can be brought about by means of conscious thinking about the action, integration will not usually occur in the free development process. This explains why children of preschool age seldom pass the second level with their skills and it also explains how it is possible that the teacher in many cases can begin the teaching process with something resembling an integration. Only the control of the mother tongue continues a good distance in the direction of the third level, but in this development process, thinking about the acting is stimulated by many activities.

THE DIRECTION OF THE INTENTION DURING THE LEARNING PROCESS

In the above we could recognize in broad outline similar structures in a learning process and a development process. The differences are determined by the intention present in the learning process. We now investigate the objects of this intention in the different phases of the learning process.

Information   To understand at what intention is directed during the information phase, we first must ascertain how, in many cases, the information is gained. As late as the 1950s, it was common to give the information directly. A textbook of geometry could begin in the following style:

> *"Definition*: The *definition* of subject indicated by a certain term is a short and accurate description of that subject by which it may be distinguished from all other subjects.
>
> *Proposition*: A *proposition* is a property that will have to be proved. Every proposition is composed of two parts: (1) the *premise*, in which it is indicated what is given as true in connection with the matters that are discussed in the theorem; (2) the *conclusion*, in which the truth of that which has to be demonstrated is summarized.

From this example it is immediately clear why we begin in another way. For by such talk the pupil is informed of nothing. If a pupil has never before heard of a definition, he will not be able to make one up himself, and if he is given an example, this information will hardly help him understand it. Even clearer is the insufficiency of the explanation of a proposition. The identification of "proposition" and "property" will only cloud understanding, and it is only possible to understand "proof" after it has been made clear what a proposition is. This is why nowadays one usually begins with exercises; after the pupils have been busy for a time and have developed a certain action structure, one can say, "Look, what we have been doing here is typical geometry and the statement you just now uttered is a proposition. The reasoning you gave with it was a proof." So the information comes last, in an afterthought about the actions that have already been done. But this also implies that the information was implicitly given by the material in response to the actions to be executed; the explicitation made the information explicit!

So we may venture to say that intention usually is not directed at information itself. The old-fashioned geometry textbook was written with an eye to a so-directed intention, and therefore missed its aim. It is not quite clear why textbooks were arranged in this way. Was it perhaps that the author felt himself obliged to give this information, even though he knew that it could not have the desired effect? Or was it that the concepts that are used in the information were him so familiar that he could only consider them as self-evident? Or was it that an adult always asks for such information, even when he missed the necessary base of it? Probably this is a common habit with an origin in a mixture of the three causes. It is much worse that many teachers do not realize that their information cannot be understood by the pupils.

Bound Orientation   We find an example of *bound orientation* in language lessons when the pupils are asked to transpose into the past tense a paper that has been written in the present tense. Here the intention of the pupils is directed at accomplishing the task: putting the paper into the past tense correctly. The teaching aim differs; it consists in confronting the pupils with the differences of the verb forms. Here the intention cannot be directed, for the task is only aimed at calling attention to the verb forms. Before the task has been done, these verb forms do not appear to the pupils in this sense. Just as in this case, it is practically always the situation in bound orientation that the aim is to render visible the principal relations between the concepts, but the students' intentions are not aimed at this target, because at the beginning of this phase the target is invisible.

Explicitation We find a good example of explicitation in physics when at the beginning of the chapter "Heat" the pupils are asked to give their opinions about the ways in which transfer of heat can take place. Here we are dealing with an explicitation of knowledge the pupils have acquired by means of a development, for they have acquired this knowledge before the guided learning process has begun. By imagining how heat is distributed in living rooms, the pupils can easily find the three types of distribution: radiation, convection, and conduction. Various simple relations can be deduced from remembered experiences. The intention of the pupils is to give opinions about the relations they have seen; the object of teaching is still the recording of such relations in the proper language.

Free Orientation We have a good example of free orientation when pupils are asked to write an essay about some aspect of a subject they have studied. Here they have to bring well-known relations into an often somewhat new connection. The intention of the pupils is to express the materials of the essay in the correct sequence; the object of teaching is to constitute a coherent network of relations.

In many cases free orientation will have a less distinct character and will coincide with the bound orientation of a new subject. So it is possible to teach pupils operate with letters by having them occupy with long division. For the learning of the long division the exactly defined task has the character of a bound orientation; the freedom the pupils have to choose the way in which they subtract and multiply gives this special facet of the task the character of free orientation. It is, however, easy to convince oneself of the equality of the relation between intention and object of teaching in the latter case and that which we have analyzed before.

Integration In integration the intention is for a summary of the things that have been learned. The way in which the past tense of a verb may be formed is fixed; the multiplication tables are memorized; a rule giving the values of x for which a given quadratic function of x is positive is memorized. This is the phase in which intention coincides with the object of teaching. So it is no wonder that pupils like to begin their learning process with this last phase. And it is clear why many teachers switch too quickly to this last phase: They satisfy the wishes of their pupils and they take a shortcut to the goal. However, such a shortened learning process never can lead to real understanding of a concept; the pupils will get the use of a verbal network of relations not based on an experience of action. Such a network of relations not rooted in the personality of the pupil is in danger of quick dissolution. Moreover, because of the absence of connections with other activities, it can not have any educational value.

INTENTION IN VARIOUS LEARNING PROCESSES

Intention in Learning a Skill Our analysis has shown that generally the learning intention is not aimed at the object of teaching. This means that generally the pupil learns something other than what he expected. The cause of this phenomenon is simple: It is not possible to intend something you do not already know about. However, for didactics this simple phenomenon is of great importance: It explains why help from other people is necessary for so many learning processes. How annoying the real objects of learning can be are seen when young children want to learn certain skills. They, for instance, want to learn to ride a bicycle. But for this they need balance, the correct use of the pedals, and the ability to steer. The ability to ride a bicycle is based on the acquisition of a coordination of the three mentioned skills, but this coordination cannot be the child's intention. For a child who wants to ride a bicycle immediately, the learning process is an awkward business: He is continually confronted with a total impotence in attaining his aims. The child who takes the matter slowly, who doesn't mind a push from behind, and who trusts the strong arm of his father riding next to him is much better off. Gradually he will get a feeling for balance, and after some time he will feel free enough to pedal for himself.

Intention in Other Learning Processes We see that with learning processes with a skill as their outcome, too strong an intent toward the final goal can have an adverse result. With learning processes of a more intellectual character, a similar intent can have much more serious consequences. A child who learns to multiply will have attained a certain level of thinking when he is able to accomplish smoothly all sort of multiplications. The action is supported by the ready knowledge of multiplication tables. If the attention of the child is turned directly to the knowledge of these tables before he has been made familiar with their sense and structure, then after the child knows the tables well, the way to an understanding of the structure will be blocked. Van Parreren once conjectured— and an analysis of different learning processes bears this out—that the final result of a learning process consists of the constituting of a valence (association) structure, that is, that most learning processes have a tendency to form valence systems that substitute for the concept structures that are first built up. If one would have a child constantly repeat the multiplication tables without showing him the way to a higher level of thinking, then gradually the child would loose every basic concept of those tables. And much more quickly would this happen to a child who has learned the tables without ever really having had at his disposal such basic concepts.

The choice of the right moment for integration by memorizing and the conscientious dosage of this task is of the greatest importance for quality in teaching methods. Only if the teaching process is aimed at a practice well supported by a strong motivation, for instance, in order to master a language, can intention have a favorable effect and prolonged exercise at the same level improve instruction and learning.

When a teacher does not sufficiently realize how results are achieved, his own intention too strongly aimed at the object of teaching may lead to adverse effects on the learning process. In the first place, the teacher may consider the results of an action structure accompanying the learning process to be the proper teaching object. The teacher, for instance, may have established that pupils who have done many arithmetic problems with fractions eventually know many results like $5/8 = 0.625$, by heart. If he insists on having such facts as ready knowledge—whereas they are no more than by-products of the learning process—then he promotes formation of a valence structure that perhaps afterward will block the way to a higher level of thinking. In the second place, the intention of the teacher may be aimed at a too-early attainment of a higher level of thinking. In that case he promotes algorithmic thinking, a verbalism. We must as teachers strive for a situation in which we know and aim for the proper teaching object, but in which, moreover, we have such insight into the learning process that we are aware of the detours the children must take before they can attain the teaching object.

Often the Intention Should not Be Toward the Final Goal   I here give another example from the development of the concept of number. It is highly undesirable that pupils just beginning with fractions should have their objective directed toward the performance of problems like $2/3 + 1/6 = ?$. Rather their attention should be directed toward the meaning of $2/3$ and $1/6$. This meaning they will have to recall in many different forms. There will come a time—but not too soon—at which they will join two fragments representing the values $2/3$ and $1/6$, and then they will read the value of the result from the figure. But even then attention will have to fall on the sense of such an addition and *not*, at least for the present, on the attainment of the result.

There are many learning processes presenting themselves to the teacher as a totality. For the pupil, however, they do not appear as such—which is probably best. For if the final goal was visible to the pupil, then the path to this goal would often seem much too long, with the result of a premature abandonment of the trials leading to attainment the goal. In a normal case the intention of the pupil is about neither provisional nor intermediate purposes. He creates himself, perhaps influenced by a wise teacher, purposes within his reach, which we can call "apparent purposes." So these purposes are not characterized by the fact that having attained them means achieving a phase in the learning process, they merely have the function of aiming the intention. As we have mentioned before, it will often happen that such an apparent purpose in one learning process is an intermediate or even provisional purpose in another learning process.

THE DEVELOPMENT OF AN ADULT

The Attainment of New Properties of Behavior   The attainment of new properties of behavior in man does not stop with adulthood. Here too we can see a difference between intentional and unintentional changes. In the first case we can speak of ''learning,'' but in the second it would seem very artificial to speak of ''maturing''; the expression ''developing'' would certainly be better for the latter. But this does not alter the fact that sometimes we say that adults have insights and ideas that have matured.

Let us for a further investigation first imagine the case in which a person attains a certain manual skill. When this skill has developed optimally, the person will generally act according to an action structure principally determined by valences. However, in cases in which the circumstances strongly vary, that person will have to think about the action, and a more differentiated structure may develop, enabling automatical actions in a greater number of cases. Generally these cases have to do with a real learning process in which, from the beginning, the intention is to learn the action. When the learning process nears completion, the intention decreases, so that by the end it is only to start and finish the action. There is even a possibility that in the long run this intention will be absent.

Learning Intention with Self-Instruction   Of quite another quality is development man passes through when he passes to a higher level of thinking. In this case he develops with the action structure a system of language symbols interlinked by a network of relations. Now his action happens on the basis of the existing connections between the symbols. Such a development may be brought about by means of self-instruction. In this case we are also dealing with a learning process, for the self-instruction points to the existence of an intention. Again, I here trace the objects of intention during the five phases of the learning process.

The first two phases, information and bound orientation, may be given by textbooks when a study of an already developed field of knowledge is concerned. The explicitation usually happens by going over the given material for oneself and by confronting the given technical language with the proper language. In the fourth phase one may try to use the given material in self-chosen examples. Difficulties appear especially in integration. If the study material is tuned to the higher, still-to-be-attained level, there is a great chance that by studying one only gains a verbal understanding of the network of relations. This will happen particularly when the explanation of the subject matter is so complete that there is little material left for free orientation. However, if the study material itself is not tuned to the higher level, the student himself is expected to do creative work with the material.

From the above it may be concluded that self-instruction, if it is to lead to something other than an empty result, must form a certain habitude with the student. For in the third phase he will have to feel the need to bring the given study material into a connection with his life, he will have to feel the necessity to make the material meaningful for himself. When the material is given to him at a higher level, he has to try, practically by his own force, by again and again analyzing and transforming intuitively appropriate matter, to take his thinking so far that at the end he is able to get to the bottom of the given material. If the material has been given at a lower level, he will have to try to find out, by continually analyzing and transforming the given material, what he really has been studying, and he has to try to emerge so far above the material that he will be able to see it as a totality.

It is well known that typical education does not generally promote the cultivation of this habitude. When a pupil has some difficulty understanding, when he lacks insight into a subject, then explanation is usually thought of as the suitable means of teaching. However, the possibility of explaining is based on the existence of a practically complete network of relations; the explanation consists, for example, in pointing out where the passage that has not been understood is placed in the network of relations. As long as this network has not yet been formed, explanation is not possible. If, nevertheless, explanation still is tried—in practice this happens repeatedly—then this has to be considered as a level reduction; a verbal relation has been put in the place of what should have been insight. The absence of the proper habitude causes a tendency to use the given study material verbally rather than structurally. It causes impatient requests for explanation, even if the necessary foundation of understanding is totally absent. There was once a very popular slogan in education: "If you are not able to explain something, then you have not understood it." Pupils were sometimes told this when they had not quite finished the third phase and had faltered in their explicitation. So in this case little value was attached to implicit knowledge of the material. The slogan was sometimes also directed at the teacher, who in this way was reproached for insufficient knowledge of the subject matter. Such reproach merely demonstrates a failure to appreciate the true function of explanation.

It is important to investigate how one passes through the phases of the learning process in a new field of study in which there are no textbooks. Here we can speak of a learning process, for we may suppose that there is an intention to decompose the field of study involved. Though the instruction giving rise to the study may be defined very accurately (for instance the framing of a method for some topic at a specific type of school), still the information is rather incomplete. For the instruction gives little or no indication of the structuring determinants of the field of study (how in general a method is framed, what the purposes of the topic involved in the type of school in question are, etc.). Just as with guided learning processes, here too the information has to come for the most part from the explicitation after the event. If the problem is studied by a group of persons, they will soon try to pass to the phase of bound orientation (other methods are studied, how far they can and must be transformed for the intended purpose is investigated); in short, one tries to replace the hazy instruction by other instructions that can be carried out immediately, even though they may be less directly aimed at the goal.

When the bound orientation has brought in enough material, the group may change over to explicitation. In this free learning process, there is much more question of an exchange of very different opinions than in a guided learning process. Now no teacher is present, so the sorting of useful and useless material is brought about with much more trouble and the technical language is only adopted on grounds of its usefulness in practice. Moreover, every member of such a study group is aware of the pioneer character of their task and does not want to come too quickly to results with the help of a differently orientated thinking field from an adjacent field of study. After the group has formed the beginning of a network of relations, free orientation happens of itself. Everyone interested in the subject will try to put the available structures into practice in selected situations. This also implies that, if anywhere, it is just in this learning situation that the phases appear mixed. So this means that free orientation appears at a time when rather much bound orientation and explicitation must still take place.

If the learning process is successful, integration will come at the end; the possibility of varying the solution of the posed problem in accordance with circumstances will have been created, the total problem can be looked over. If, however, one wants to have people from outside the group profit by this result, then the result must definitely not be given in the last integrated form. Whoever wants to master a certain thinking structure will have to pass through a learning process. But now this learning process can proceed toward the goal, because, unlike that process of the pioneers, guidance has become possible.

CONCLUSION

As mentioned early in this chapter, we are faced with the question of whether it is sensible to distinguish, as I have done, between maturing processes and learning processes. In any case, the analysis of the directions of intention during the development process (by which I now mean learning and maturing processes) has deepened our insight into learning and the function of the guidance of learning. The analysis, however, has also made it clear that an intention aimed at the teaching object is not always conducive to favorable progress. This implies that we need not consider it a disadvantage that so much development is left to what I have earlier called "incidental learning processes" and what in this chapter was temporarily termed "maturation." On the contrary, many things will have to be learned in periods in which the intention is directed toward other purposes. But one important point remains: Such a maturation may not in the least be understood as biological maturation, as maturation the educator only can see and await. Though we cannot speak of "conscious" learning of the child, guidance is possible and even desirable if the maturation developes too slowly.

At the same time, resemblances and differences between the development processes in the period before and the period during the elementary school have become clear. In both periods the development is often brought about by an intention to explore, an interest that demands nothing in particular. But whereas the child who yet does not go to school is stimulated to exertion by his desire to become great, that is, to be able to join adults, the adults on the contrary have much difficulty realizing that there are things that cannot be directly explained to them, that in order to participate in a discussion of such things they at first must become familiar with a new world of thought. Rather than assenting to such a situation, they believe that they lack a required bump on the skull or that they are unable to generate the required interest in the subject. In some favorable cases, an adult discovers for himself a part of the to him unknown area by free exploration, and after that an exchange of thoughts with other persons is possible. In any case, it becomes clear that in a lifetime many things are "learned" in periods in which the intention is not aimed at a specific goal and even not at learning itself. Such a period begins especially when strenuous learning is replaced by exploration. It might be considered a task of didactics to find out in what way man might be induced to alternate more consciously these activities. In such a case, exploration and intention to learn would not necessarily exclude each other.

If we would designate a development of mind with which no intention to learn is present as "maturation," this would have the advantage that enrichment of mind would be clearly distinguished from intentional learning. On the other hand, the goals of the teacher would then be equally aimed at development of his pupils by means of "maturing" as of "intentional learning." Common parlance resists so strongly against such a conception that such a use of the word "maturation" is not be recommended.

25

The Problem of Motivation in Education

INTRODUCTION

There have been many discussions about motivation, but enough confusion about this subject exists to warrant even more discussion. Our chapter title here "The Problem of Motivation in Education," evokes a series of difficult issues: Is there really a problem of motivation in education? Does the concept of motivation belong to education? Can one fruitfully operate with the concept of motivation? What exactly is motivation?

Let me begin by answering the last question. In the Netherlands, De Groot, in a 1954 lecture, once put this problem before us. At that time he gave the following description:

> Motivation is a concept used for the strength as well as for the structure of the intellectual drive. By "structure" I mean the way this drive can be derived from definite tendencies and wants of the personal pattern. The concept of motivation not only refers to conscious motives, but also to unconscious ones, as far as it is necessary to accept such unconscious motives . . . . Why, on the ground of what motives, conscious or unconscious, is a pupil in general willing to exert himself? Which of their needs can he (or she) satisfy by their work? (1955, p. 26)

The wording of this explanation is for the most part in a psychological context, for De Groot is a psychologist. But is it important to know if, by broaching the problem of motivation, one must necessarily enter the domain of psychology.

For we can begin by noticing that the problem also has a pedagogical aspect; in concerning oneself with motivation, one must first decide which motives for child development are desirable and which are not. From this point of view, motivation is directly connected with the aims of instruction.

Still, another approach is possible: we can widen the domain of investigation and study instruction in general. Then also adults, pupils who have already passed the period of education, can be brought into discussion. Motivation is also important when an adult learns. There is much to be said for such an approach, because the structure of such instruction has many traits in common with a pedagogical situation. To this we may add that motives inspiring intellectual effort can be—and in many cases have to be—found in the structure of the subject to be studied. Still, by bringing this into play we have left the domain of pedagogy and have entered one of special didactics of a topic.

REWARD AND PUNISHMENT

Unfortunately, some pupils today are motivated by aims that are neither pedagogical nor didactic. Such motivations are connected with somewhat obsolete psychological theories. The motivations in question are based on reward or punishment not connected with the goal of instruction itself. The foundation of such applications of motivation can be found in animal psychology. If we want an animal to do something, we reward it after a correct performance. But if we want a child to do something, the reward must be found in the performing itself. Learning things at school must be meaningful to the child; if not, we cannot expect the skill to last long. Motivations consisting of good grades, praise by the teacher, or rewards for good reports may have temporary success, but they will not work in the long run. The same can be said about discouraging with bad grades, scolding by the teacher, and so on (see Heikkinen, 1957, for such a psychological approach).

The idea that an association might develop between a more-or-less accidental action and a reward (one of the variants of the stimulus–response theory) is now even mistrusted in psychology. Some psychologists have observed that an association between stimulus and response may be obtained by a reward, but also by a punishment. It is possible that a pupil, having been punished because of a mistake, will continue to make the mistake in the future more obstinately. From then on his attention will be especially drawn to it. He will know that something is afoot in the subject, but he will have lost the possibility of finishing it automatically.

Instruction supported by motivation ruled by reward or punishment is common. Many things have to be learned by heart: series of words, dates, towns, rivers and countries, propositions in mathematics (with or without proofs), and others. In these cases we usually think of reward and punishment. Certainly the learning of words results directly from an intention of the pupil; he has asked to learn it because he thinks he may become better by it. But it is reasonable to suppose that in most cases memorizing is not chosen by pupils with motives concerning the subject matter itself. To demonstrate this it suffices to examine the textbooks or to ask the pupils themselves. Many exercises have the same foundation. To give a foundation for piano lessons, the following agreement is often made with the parents of the pupil: "You must make sure that the children perform the finger exercises, study the scales, and so on. Every day for half an hour at the keys, you must see to it."

Two questions are of great importance. First, must we accept that for much subject matter, such motivation is necessary because we have none better? Second, is it possible that such an approach has advantages? We begin by answering the second question. By learning things through force—performing exercises—pupils accustom themselves to discipline. Often afterward, disagreeable things will have to be done. In the long run, one learns many subjects; it is even possible that when schooling is done, there will still be a desire for new instruction. In short, every subject matter may be associated with certain subjective goals directed at character building. On the other hand, this kind of discipline is not one of the best kinds. The best discipline is one that can be accepted as a necessity founded on the welfare of the community. Such discipline, founded on the apprehension of the situation, does not consist in servile obedience to given instructions; it allows for adaptation to changing circumstances. People who have been educated by forced discipline without insight will later have difficulties learning discipline with which insight is needed.

The question of whether we can do without motivation by reward and punishment is not easily answered. In any case, we may look for better motivations. There is a great chance that such a search will succeed, for it has not often been undertaken.

RECOMMENDING THE SUBJECT MATTER

A second form of motivation may be found in the recommendations of the subject matter. Here the utility of the subject matter is shown to the children. The arguments are well known: Mathematics is learned because later you can build bridges with it; French is learned because later you can speak it in Paris; geography is learned because later on you will know that oranges and lemons can be bought on a large scale in Spain or Italy but not in Iceland. Perhaps you will say that I am presenting this point too ridiculously; but it cannot be denied that such motives are never very realistic, because it is difficult to demonstrate how in practice or in professional work the subject-matter is really applied. To know these things you first have to investigate how the subject matter is practiced and you also have to know something about the professions. This type of motivation cannot be of great importance, at least not in high school. It very rarely occurs that a pupil sets for himself an aim in life so that the attainment of this aim gives him continual support for the performance of less agreeable work. Perhaps there are exceptions in technical instruction. If in such instruction a deficiency of knowledge of mathematics or physics stands in the way of complete understanding, a discussion in a mathematics or physics lesson can fill a need and therefore be of sufficient importance. The subjective value of this motivation can be described rather accurately with the word *self-discipline*. In many biographies you can read how far some people have advanced with self-discipline.

Even if the two above-mentioned motivations give sufficient driving power, they each have the deficit of not aiming attention at the subject itself, but rather at something lying outside it. The pupils hardly feel themselves personally engaged with the subject matter. The most positive form of the above-mentioned motivation appears when pupils throw themselves upon a subject matter because it is necessary for the understanding of another, better-motivated subject matter; for example, when pupils begin memorizing words because they have noticed that the contents of a book about which they are very curious cannot be read without a better knowledge of those words.

PROBLEM SOLVING

The third form of motivation is totally different. The teacher opens the discussion with a problem interesting to the pupils, and the solution can only be found by studying a certain subject matter. Now the intention of the pupils is related to the subject matter itself: learning in order to get acquainted with this subject matter is the aim of exertion. The so-called Socratic method may be based on this principle (a well-known example is the story of Socrates and the slave of Menon).

The Socratic method is not without risk. In the first place, the teacher must be sure of the interest of the pupils; necessarily, the problem must have their attention from the very beginning. Often a given problem is only interesting to a special group because of their history. In such a case it is only possible to make it a real problem to all the pupils if it is possible to have them all go through that history. In the second place, the effectiveness of the Socratic method is only guaranteed if the pupils meet the solution by working on the problem. If the solution is given to them prematurely by an impatient teacher, the problem might just as well never have been posed. In the third place, it is important that quicker pupils do not cut the ground from under the others. During this work pupils should not help each other too much, and class conversations should be carefully guided in order to leave the slowly working pupils enough to do. Moreover, the problem must not be so difficult that pupils forget the heart of the problem before its solution comes up for discussion. This situation can be anticipated by putting a simpler problem before the students. The Socratic method may have very good results, but to succeed with it you must prepare your lessons well, and even then there may be no positive results. The subjective value of this motivation consists in the possibility that pupils will *realize the strength of proper reflection.*

DESIRE FOR EXPLORATION

A fourth form of motivation is of a still higher degree: Here, too, the lesson itself fills a desire—in this case the desire for exploration. Of course it is well known that every child, from very early childhood, wants to explore the world. If the subject matter is arranged in such a way that pupils can discover all sort of things in it, if those discoveries give them the sense that the subject matter reveals its secrets, a driving force has come into existence without outside help. The subjective value of this motivation lies in the *exercise of the inventive power.*

This method also contains dangers. One must pay attention to the fact that the exploration must be aimed at the subject matter itself. The materials must belong to the subject matter to be taught. The problems given must not be attempts to guild the pill. You may, for instance, teach the names of the U.S. states by making a jigsaw puzzle of the map of the United States. With this you try to give the pupils a motivation very closely related to a desire for exploration. Still the pupils will learn very little of topography by this method, for their attention is directed at something else. This mistake occurs more frequently than one might imagine. Many mathematical problems contain a puzzle element that has very little relation to the subject matter to be exercised. Often the puzzle element is carried too far; for example, when in an astronomy lesson about the sun, the earth, and the year, one asks, "Has there ever been, in the Christian era, a year with a number of days other than 365 or 366?" The answer involves the year in which the Julian calendar ended and the Gregorian calendar began. In England and its colonies that year was 1752 and had 354 days. This is a curious fact, and the pupil who gives this answer understands the subject matter very well, but I do not see that every pupil who has studied well should be able to give such an answer.

ZEST FOR WORK

Before beginning the fifth form of motivation, I discuss "zest for work," in which pupils are said to love all sorts of learning, cheerfully setting themselves to carry out any instruction. They surely do not always do this in the hope of reward or the fear of punishment. They are usually unconscious of the future profit of their knowledge. They work because they like working—or to express it less strongly—because they are not in the least against working. I have no confidence in such undifferentiated enthusiasm. It seems to me that in such cases, working has become acceptable not because of the love of work for its own sake but because one has got used to it. Such work is the result of habit. But that which is done by habit is usually soon forgotten. Therefore I cannot share the pride of teachers whose pupils learn by such habits.

THINKING AND STRIVING OF OTHER PEOPLE

The fifth form of motivation consists in bringing pupils into contact with the thinking and striving of others by means of the subject matter. It is possible, for instance, that someone who admires a very old vase will wonder what went on in the mind of its maker. In mathematics, one can ask oneself about the world of thinking of the Greeks, which led them to such important results in geometry and such poor results in algebra. The subjective value of this motivation may be described as development of *appreciation of fellow man*.

Such a motivation is found when pupils are ambitiously working in groups. These must be fair working groups; pupils must trust each other and they must be aware of each other's share in the work. Therefore, the teacher arranging such group work is not finished when he randomly assigns the groups. He must be fully aware of the aim of the work groups. If he assigns work groups only because the type or the modernity of the school happens to use this approach, effects without any intrinsic value will follow.

In the work groups the fifth motivation is found in a simplified form. The pupil is confronted with the thinking and striving of his fellow pupils. Often this will be less than the thinking and striving of adults who have already assimilated the subject matter. Still, working in groups may be a way to attain an understanding of the subject. Of course, there are many other ways to enter the world of thought of other people, such as a play in which life of other people is depicted.

CONCLUSION

The classification in this chapter must be considered as an attempt to bring some order to 'motivation'. I am not at all sure that with these five types the topic is exhausted, nor do I pretend that this classification is the most appropriate. But it is important to distinguish the different values of various types of motivation. I would, moreover, profit teachers to recognize the kind of motivation they want to appeal to in their instruction. A teacher setting tasks without a sufficient reason appeals to a motivation outside of the topic and has little reason to hope for lasting success. Much of teaching of grammar in first-year Latin, for instance, might be considered to be a weak part of the method in that topic. Series of words, formulas, towns, exceptions, dictations with increasing obstacles— this all is subject matter of doubtful value.

When subject matter or tasks are given that actually surpass the comprehension of the pupils, it must be seen that a true motivation is missing. In such cases, teachers might quiet their consciences by pretending that although, at the moment, true comprehension is missing, the pupils will later remember with gratitude the subject matter the teacher is now forcing on them. This fault is found in practically all topics: in algebra, in calculation with letters when pupils do not yet have any notion of their meaning; in physics, with applications of definitions and laws when the children cannot understand them; in biology, with all sorts of physical and chemical laws when the children know practically nothing of physics and chemistry. And it is just the same in geography: Papers have to be written on subjects about which the children can only guess. In history, profound considerations of constitutions are demanded when the pupils do not even know how government in their own country is arranged. School, in the first place, should develop a desire to know. Children often bring such a desire with them, but with unsuitable instruction in school, such a desire soon will be extinguished.

It is my opinion that in instruction too little has been done to find a correct motivation. For those who want to renovate instruction, this is a great domain in which to do important work.

26

System Separation and Transfer

TERMINOLOGY

System separation is a term from psychology that can be illustrated by a short story: Mr. Johnson travels by car to a conference where he is expected to deliver an address. While driving, he thinks about his lecture, taking it through point by point. Meanwhile he reacts to the traffic, traffic lights, and signs. Both activities require thinking, but the two streams of thought do not disturb each other. They take place in separate systems. Pupils might think in the same way in mathematics and physics: In the mathematics lesson they learn about vectors, which also occur in physics instruction, though they are not aware that the two are the same.

SIGNALS

The example of the driver shows that thinking in separate systems may be useful, but in teaching vectors it is not. Usually it is not that bad in education, or rather if it is that bad, something is wrong with the instruction itself. Because vectors pervade all mathematics, the word "vector" works as a signal. This signal calls up a long series of subsidiary concepts, such as 'number pair', 'direction', 'norm', 'parallel', 'nonparallel', 'normal vector', and 'inner product'. In the course of training the concept vector gets more content. When my colleague in physics complained about pupils' not knowing what vectors were, he meant that they could not give a definition. I replied that many people can work with numbers, though they do not know what numbers are. This gave him food for thought, and for a quarter of an hour I got the opportunity to satisfy his curiosity about numbers.

It is no wonder that signals often do not call up the definition of a concept, since most definitions are side issues. Knowing a definition of a thing is not a precondition of knowing the thing itself. For a long time in the method I co-authored, vectors were ordered pairs of points, or line segments with heads and tails distinguished. Now they are numbers, or number pairs, or number triplets, according to whether they are one, two, or three dimensional.

If a mathematical concept is to be called up in a physics lesson, it matters that the physics teacher has given the right signal and that the mathematics teacher has established such a signal. When my colleague had difficulty with proportions, I advised him to put the numbers into a proportion matrix, and after the next lesson he told me enthusiastically that ''proportion matrix'' worked as a magic word.

Though I had the habit of teaching integration as the inverse of differentiation, I did not use the integral sign, lest it complicate things. This, however, was a mistake. The integral sign works as a signal; as soon as they see it, pupils react. The associations with summation are particularly useful.

AVOIDING SYSTEM SEPARATION

As we have seen, system separation may be worth while in many cases. It is annoying if a teacher starts teaching in an eighth grade class as though it is the ninth grade because some signal misled him—perhaps seeing a girl that looks like her older sister—and system separation is a good means of preventing such blunders. But if system separation is to be avoided in teaching mathematics and physics, some measures must be taken. In teaching introductory physics, it does not pay to spurn mathematical tools. Of course, the fact that the mathematical apparatus is still in a developing state must be taken into account, but even so it can be useful. Proportions occur in physics from the beginning. In former days, even before the proportion matrix had been taught, proportion could be shown on the slide rule. In every position the C- and D-scale of the slide rule form a proportion matrix; the physics teacher could use this as a table to be consulted when needed. Now calculators are used instead of slide rules. There are two sorts of calculators: ordinary calculators and calculators that can be programmed. With the latter, proportion matrices can be demonstrated. But to explain the use of programmed calculators with the view to the teaching of mathematics would carry me too far afield. For the physics teacher, it would mean a new difficulty; he would have to learn the new signals belonging to this new skill.

Almost all textbooks introduce kinematics with rectilinear or even uniform rectilinear motion. This is the best way to cut off 'velocity' from the vector concept. In no respect is a vector in one dimension distinguishable from a scalar, and a constant vector is as dead as a doornail. A marvelous start in kinematics is with uniform circular motion. Here the concept of mean velocity is a source of surprise. It would not be wise, however, to continue this subject with differentials. This is better learned with a two-dimensional place vector, both components of which depend quadratically on time. The parabolic motion $\mathbf{r}(t) = \mathbf{r}(0) + \mathbf{v}(0)\,t + \frac{1}{2}\mathbf{a}t^2$ is a better start than uniformly accelerated rectilinear motion.

ARTIFICIAL SUBJECT SEPARATION

Teachers often favor separating mathematics and physics. This starts with the phrase "applying mathematics in physics." A mathematics teacher does not speak about applying vectors in trigonometry, or in solid geometry—or does he? Rather, he there develops a new piece of vector algebra, and this is what should be done, more or less, in physics.

A physicist may choose to use the formula $b^{-1} + v^{-1} = f^{-1}$ for mirrors and lenses. This bears all the characteristics of a formula concocted by physicists. A mathematician would write $(b - f)(v - f) = f^2$, which shows immediately the graphic representation of a hyperbola and the solution $b = v = 0$. In instruction for opticians, the first formula would not be too bad. Their terminology includes not only the dioptrics of a lens, but also the convergence and divergence of the entering and leaving bundle. In any case, whenever reciprocal values must be manipulated the calculator is the most useful tool. Do not get angry if pupils lack skill in manipulating fractions. Mathematics cannot guarantee the needed transfer, because there fractions are avoided.

The integral is introduced earlier in physics than in mathematics. I recommend interpreting work as an integration from the start, and writing it in the same way. To do this, it is not necessary that pupils can integrate mathematically. The basic work for the concept of integration can be laid here as solidly as in mathematics. One can determine difference of place by an integral of velocity as a function of time, and the pupils will experience the connection between finding differentials and integrating—concepts with as much physical as mathematical meaning. With the notions of electrical and magnetic flux it is obvious how little it matters if the integration can be carried out mathematically. In textbooks these notions are defined by integrals of inner products, although they are not actually computed.

POSSIBILITIES AND SUGGESTIONS

Some textbook series in mathematics go quite far in vector algebra. The inner product is a universal topic, but some methods include vector products and tensor products. The Lorentz force can be defined as a vector product. With a bit of cooperation between mathematics and physics instruction, potential fields and gradients can be prepared by the mathematician and elaborated by the physicist. In the higher grades of secondary school, the pupils get acquainted with differential equations belonging to the system of lines of a magnetic field. They also learn how orthogonal trajectories are obtained, and this applies to equipotential surfaces. This arrangement creates the opportunity for dealing with this subject matter at the most appropriate moment in the course of physics instruction, with fields of central forces rather than the gravitational field, where it is of no use.

THE POSSIBILITY OF COORDINATED APPROACH

I do not believe that coordination between mathematics and physics instruction can be effective as long as it reaches no farther than agreement about the timing of certain subjects and the use of mathematical notations. One should realize, rather, that by being used in physics a certain part of mathematics becomes part of physics itself. Rather than applying old things one creates something new. Mathematicians and physicists must cooperate in this creation; together they must examine the problems and look for the solutions that are didactically most recommendable. This requires work and time, but it is the only way to build properly; anything else is patchwork.

27

The Relation between Theory
and Problems in Arithmetic
and Algebra

---

see p. 4

HOW CAN THEORY AND PROBLEMS
BE DISTINGUISHED?

As in any other part of the didactics of mathematics, to discuss or even describe the distinction between theory and problem is a difficult task because a certain indifference has prevented us from developing a language in which things can be formulated adequately. Even such terms as "theory" and "problem" are not without ambiguity, leaving room for a variety of interpretations.

There must be some sense in distinguishing theory and problem. This appears from the fact that in textbooks one can readily assign that part of the "theory" to which the "problems" of a set are related. However, this linguistic distinction is not clear cut. If the teacher attaches special importance to some type of problem, he is inclined to say that this problem is so important that its solution can be considered as part of the theory. The line between theory and problem is quite distinct in some textbooks and rather vague in others. It is distinct when in each chapter the theory is first developed and afterward the problems are set. It is vague when the theory is implemented by means of problems. In the first case, "theory" means a group of propositions that are proved by the teacher (or under his guidance), whereas "problems" might comprise other propositions that have

199

to be proved by using the "theoretical" group of propositions. This means that the propositions are classified according to their value as tools in deriving new propositions. Propositions that are likely to be met by the student in his further learning process belong to "theory." The student, however, will not grasp the contents of the theory until the chapter of arithmetic or algebra to which it refers is integrated. Then he will see the theory as a system of laws, methods, and rules that tell him how to act according to the theory. If someone "knows the theory," the integration has taken place, he conceives of the subject matter as a whole, or, in a more sophisticated terminology, he has reached the second level of thinking.

We can illustrate this exposition by the example of substitution of binominals in algebraic expressions. Any teacher who has taught this subject knows that this technique is acquired by a learning process. The exercises are not matched by an adequate program in which they are put into words. Verbal explanations are not of significant help. Nevertheless, if the learning process is finished, the students have achieved an important theoretical insight. They have acquired a certain skill based on insight and not on automatic action. A student who has acquired this insight will be able to carry out quite different substitutions. Even if he is confronted with similar tasks after many years, he will appear not to have lost the ability of carrying them out. If, however, the student has acquired no more than automatic behavior, he will have to learn every kind of substitution anew, and finally he will forget all he has learned. This is an example of a theory that is wholly implied by the integration of the teaching matter and is not presented explicitly.

PROBLEMS

Problems are clearly a tool of the teaching method. As far as they are a part of the integrated teaching matter, they belong to theory. A problem is sometimes not significant in the integrated teaching matter in which it originally occurs; it may nevertheless play a significant part later on. Completing the square for $ax^2 + bx$ is quite insignificant for the subject "squares of polynomials," but this skill gathers momentum when quadratic functions are studied. It is better to deal with such a problem at the point at which it becomes functionally significant. Otherwise it will be forgotten.

THE FUNCTION OF PROBLEMS

Problems are tools of instruction. The theory, as integrated teaching matter, is the aim of instruction—or rather an aim preliminary to knowledge of arithmetic or algebra.

In the different phases of the learning process problems have different functions:

1. In the phase of *information,* problems help discovery of the field of knowledge. For instance, in arithmetic, distributing a bar of chocolate may be an introduction to fractions. In algebra, combining congruent triangles to get larger triangles may lead to the discovery of certain number sequences.
2. In the phase of *bound orientation,* problems serve to uncover the bonds that form the system of relations. As an example in arithmetic, take half a bar of chocolate, add a quarter of a bar, and tell how much you get; this helps with addition of fractions with different denominators. In algebra, problems with even numbers, odd numbers, and prime numbers introduce different number sequences.
3. In the phase of *free orientation,* problems help one find one's way in the system of relations. An example in arithmetic is the variety of problems of adding fractions with equal or different denominators; in algebra, problems on the intersection of two number sequences, such as the sequence of the squares and the sequence of even numbers.
4. Finally, problems can serve to test whether *integration* has taken place (short problems that have to be answered readily).

In these cases the problem was a tool in the learning process. But problems are also used to test

5. how far the student has progressed in the learning process;
6. whether the student is able to continue his study.

THE PURPOSE OF PROBLEMS

Problems have to be chosen and answers have to be evaluated with a view to the purpose they are meant to serve.

1. A problem that aims at information must be simple, but it must also incite curiosity. It must not admit of accidental solutions. Most of these problems cannot be given as homework, because they require the guidance of the teacher.
2. Problems used for bound orientation must generally admit of just one solution. They may be somewhat more involved, but then indications are needed to steer the student into the right direction.
3. Problems for free orientation must generally have more than one solution because they are designed to make the student find a way in the system of

relations. But the student who moves in the right direction should not meet with unexpected obstructions.

4. Problems set to check integration must be simple. They are not to test the intellectual ability of the students, but their vision of the topic.

5. Problems set to check how far the students have progressed in the learning process should not be complicated. They must be designed to show clearly the gaps in the knowledge. Generally these problems depend largely on the details in the instruction given to the student.

6. Problems that test the ability of the student to continue his study should appeal to the insight of the student, not to automatic operations.

THE USE OF PROBLEMS

It is a general requirement that the teacher know how to make use of problems. It does not make much sense to discuss the usefulness of problems in textbooks in an abstract way without regard for the teacher.

1. Information problems cannot function properly unless the teacher gives a good introduction, invites a class discussion, and steers the activities in the right direction.

2. The same is true of bound orientation problems, although, in these, class discussion is not always indispensable.

3. The greater part of the problems set for free orientation can be worked by the students independent of direct help from the teacher. They can be given as homework. With bound orientation problems, this is only possible after an extensive discussion. Classroom discussion of the different solutions shows the different ways through the system of relations.

4. Problems of the integration phase are suitably given orally in class.

5. While the student works on problems given to check the progress of the learning process, the teacher should ask him informative questions.

6. Interference from the teacher makes little sense and may even be undesirable if the student works on problems to test ability for continuing study.

METHODS AND TEXTBOOKS

Algebra can be taught in many ways. The students' classroom activity can be mainly confined to listening to the teacher. Problems are in this case generally given as homework. But the teacher rarely addresses the class as a whole. So independent work on problems is also a part of classroom activity. Different kind of textbooks are required to meet the needs of these different approaches. Textbooks are used by teachers in various ways. Among Dutch textbooks on algebra there are examples of all kinds, from those reflecting problems of only one phase to those offering various combinations.

There are many points of view regarding textbooks. One is to arrange the teaching matter in a logical order from the beginning, for instance, natural numbers, independence of the counting result from the counting process, zero, negative numbers, and so on. Another view considers these subjects too difficult for initial instruction. Then the stress is laid not on the mathematical context of negative numbers or fractions, but on their everyday use; it is expected that the mathematical context will become clearer once the everyday use is better understood. Often teachers use the first kind of textbook though they are not convinced that students can understand the material. As mathematicians, they feel obliged to stick to the deductive arrangement, and sometimes they argue that students will remember and understand later. There is no evidence to justify this optimism.

READY KNOWLEDGE

A certain amount of ready knowledge is indispensable in the progress of the learning process. We consider knowledge of a more permanent importance, not restricted to one specific learning process. To be meaningful, ready knowledge has to satisfy certain conditions:

1. It results from integrated teaching and it does not consist of rules that are only mechanical.
2. It has a clear function in the learning process.
3. It proves continually useful, and in any case immediately after memorizing.
4. It cannot be derived so easily as to make memorizing superfluous.
5. It can be formulated in entirely understandable terms.
6. Memorizing this knowledge must be so easy as to exclude mistakes.

Subjects of ready knowledge are

1. technical terms needed for expressing and understanding linguistic structures;
2. properties like commutativity, associativity, distributivity;
3. relations between various operations;
4. properties of powers;
5. properties of fractions;
6. the rules of signs in products and quotients;
7. some properties of equations and systems of equations;
8. some properties of proportional number sequences;

9. the square of a polynomial, and the product of sum and difference of two numbers;
10. some properties used in simplifying roots;
11. the formula for the roots of a quadratic equation.

TESTING

Testing the learning process is continually required. There are various aims of testing:

1. investigation into the ability of the student to continue study;
2. investigation into the progress of the learning process;
3. investigation into integration;
4. investigation into insight as a result of the learning process.
5. investigation into the functioning of the teaching method;
6. investigation into the functioning of the textbook;
7. investigation into whether the teaching method (the kind of school) is suited to the student.

Problems, however, are not the only means for such investigations. Others include observation of the reactions of students in classroom discussion, or outside of class, psychotechnic tests, and analysis of papers written by the student. With a view to the different aims, one has to distinguish between problems set after due preparation, problems set in the classroom not based on preparation, problems to be worked by the student at the blackboard, and home-work problems.

ADEQUACY OF THE MEANS OF TESTING

The adequacy of the means of testing can only be judged if the kind of instruction the student has been given is known. When investigating whether the student is able to continue study, one must know whether and to what degree the student is already familiar with the test problems or with that special kind of test problem. Investigation into the learning process requires a testing method strongly depending on the method of instruction. Investigation on integration can give adequate results only if it is known which rules have consciously been memorized. The investigation into insight is only possible with test problems that are sufficiently new to the student. The functioning of teacher and textbook can be investigated only if the aims of instruction and the preconditioning of the student are known.

28

Proportion and Fraction

MULTIPLICATION INSTEAD OF DIVISION

It is customary to read a proportion as the equality of two quotients: $\frac{2}{5} = \frac{6}{15}$. Often this is written in the form $2 : 5 = 6 : 15$. This manner of presentation makes the theory of proportions more difficult than is necessary. Fractions have two disadvantages: (1) the denominator cannot equal zero, and (2) calculation with fractions is more complicated than calculating with products. Such calculation is easy to do differently. Many didacticians concerned with calculating in primary school have already broken with tradition by operating with "proportion blocks" (see Drenckhahn, 1962; Turkstra & Timmer, 1953). Two sequences of numbers are placed one under the other.

$$\begin{pmatrix} 2 & 4 & 7 & 12 & -2 & -5 \\ 6 & 12 & 21 & 36 & -6 & -15 \end{pmatrix}$$

The second sequence is obtained from the first by multiplication of each number of the first sequence by the same number. The importance of this method is that there is no operation mark: The numbers are placed in a rectangular block; they form a proportion matrix.

PROPERTIES OF A PROPORTION MATRIX

To obtain general validity of the properties of a proportion matrix, we must first exclude the number 0. This is sometimes a disadvantage. Therefore, we

later see how to reintroduce 0. The definition of proportion matrix is as follows:
(1) We have a system of n rows of m numbers, which are ranged in a rectangular
block. (2) The second and following rows can be obtained from the first row by
multiplication by a certain number. So the matrix looks as follows:

$$\begin{pmatrix} a & b & c & d & e & f & \cdots \\ ka & kb & kc & kd & ke & kf & \cdot\cdot \\ ma & mb & mc & md & me & mf & \cdots \end{pmatrix}$$

$a, b, c, d, e, f, \ldots, k, m, \ldots$ are elements of $\mathbb{R}/\{0\}$. Every proportion matrix
may be continued infinitely to all sides.

The first property of a proportion matrix is that any proportion matrix is
transformed into another proportion matrix if rows and columns are interchanged. The preceding matrix, transformed, is also a proportion matrix.

$$\begin{pmatrix} a & ka & ma & \cdots \\ b & kb & mb & \cdots \\ c & kc & mc & \cdot\cdot \\ d & kd & md & \cdots \\ e & ke & me & \cdot\cdot \\ f & kf & mf & \cdots \end{pmatrix}$$

The second row is obtained from the first by multiplication by b/a; the third row
is obtained from the first by multiplication by c/a.

The second property of a proportion matrix is that every row can be obtained
from every other row by multiplication by a certain number and every column
can be obtained from every other column by multiplication by a certain number. I
will leave out the proof; every beginning pupil can find it.

The third property of a proportion matrix is that for every four elements on the
vertices of a rectangle in a proportion matrix, the product of the elements belonging to one diagonal of the rectangle is equal to the product of the elements
belonging to the other diagonal of the rectangle.

$$\begin{pmatrix} a & b & c & d & e & f \\ ka & kb & kc & kd & ke & kf \\ ma & mb & mc & md & me & mf \\ na & nb & nc & nd & ne & nf \end{pmatrix}$$

It is clear in this matrix that $kb \times ne = ke \times nb$

The fourth property of a proportion matrix is that every proportion matrix may
be extended with a new row by adding p times one row with q times another row
(under condition that no zeros appear). A similar property holds for the columns.

Indeed, $(pk + qm)a$ $(pk + qm)b$ $(pk + qm)c$ . . . may be added as a new row under condition that $pk + qm \neq 0$.

THE CALCULUS OF PROPORTIONS

Example 1   Two numbers are in the ratio of 3 to 8, and their sum is 34. What is each number?

If we denote the numbers by x and y, we have the following proportion matrix:

$$\begin{pmatrix} 3 & 8 \\ x & y \end{pmatrix}$$

After extension according to the fourth property

$$\begin{pmatrix} 3 & 8 & 11 \\ x & y & 34 \end{pmatrix}$$

With the help of the third property, we compute

$$x = \frac{3 \times 34}{11}, \, y = \frac{8 \times 34}{11}.$$

Example 2   For the numbers x, y, z, and t it is given that $x : y = 4 : 7$, and $5z = 3t$ and $x = 3z$. What is the proportion of those numbers?

The proportion matrix gives the following:

$$\begin{pmatrix} x & y & z & t \\ 4 & 7 & - & - \\ - & - & 3 & 5 \\ 3 & - & 1 & - \end{pmatrix}$$

We have to fill some open places. The fastest way is to work with the last row; the second place becomes $3 \times 7/4$, the fourth place $1 \times 5/3$. After filling and completing we get the following:

$$\begin{pmatrix} x & y & z & t \\ 4 & 7 & - & - \\ - & - & 3 & 5 \\ 3 & \frac{21}{4} & 1 & \frac{5}{3} \\ 36 & 63 & 12 & 20 \end{pmatrix}$$

Example 3   Two numbers are in the ratio 2 : 5, and their product is 20. What are these numbers?

The proportion matrix can be set up and completed as follows:

$$\begin{pmatrix} x & 2 & xy & 20 \\ y & 5 & y^2 & y^2 \end{pmatrix}$$

We have gained some space by writing y under x. The rule of the diagonal products gives $2y^2 = 100$; thus $y^2 = 50$. So $x = \sqrt{8}$ and $y = \sqrt{50}$ or $x = -\sqrt{8}$ and $y = -\sqrt{50}$. Of course this can be done with $x = 2k$ and $y = 5k$, but then it is a teacher solution. Pupils themselves found the solution above.

Example 4   In a right triangle, there are equations relating to the segments that some people think very important. How can one deduce these equations?

The triangles ABC, ACD and, CBD (see Figure 28.1) are similar, so the following proportion matrix holds:

$$\begin{pmatrix} c & a & b \\ b & h & q \\ a & p & h \end{pmatrix}$$

The rule of the diagonal products gives $a^2 = pc$, $b^2 = qc$, $h^2 = pq$, $ab = hc$. After addition $a^2 + b^2 = pc + qc = (p + q)c = c^2$. And so the Pythagorean theorem, $a^2 + b^2 = c^2$, can be proved.

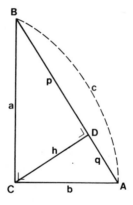

Figure 28.1

THE SLIDE RULE

After the development of the calculator and the computer, the slide rule has lost importance. Therefore I will be very brief about this subject. The most important property of the slide rule is that in every position of the slide the numbers of the C-scale and those of the D-scale form a proportion matrix. So if x = ab/c must be computed, we set up the following proportion matrix:

$$\left(\begin{array}{cc} a & c \\ x & b \end{array} \right)$$

The number c of the C-scale is placed above the number b of the D-scale. The answer x can be read on the D-scale under the number a on the C-scale. With this, multiplication and division can be done:

$$x = ab = \frac{ab}{1}, \quad \text{and } x = \frac{a}{b} = \frac{a \times 1}{b}$$

In this manner $x = abc$ can also be computed. We write $x = ab/c^{-1}$. So we know the following is a proportion matrix:

$$\left(\begin{array}{cc} a & c^{-1} \\ x & b \end{array} \right)$$

The number c is placed on the CI-scale ($=$ inverse C) above the number b of the D-scale, and x is read on the D-scale under the number a from the C-scale.

FROM PROPORTION MATRIX TO MATRIX OF RANK 1

In geometry we often work with two- and three-dimensional vectors. If a line in a plane has direction vector (a, b), then it also has direction vectors (ka, kb) and (ma, mb). We can place those numbers in a matrix:

$$\left(\begin{array}{cc} a & b \\ ka & kb \\ ma & mb \end{array} \right)$$

This may be a proportion matrix, if there are no zeros in the matrix; but if there are zeros, then it is not. We must allow zeros in the matrix, because in a direction vector only one of the coordinates must be other than zero. To solve this difficulty we pass from the proportion matrix to the matrix of the rank 1. First we write a matrix of four elements:

$$\left| \begin{array}{cc} a & b \\ c & d \end{array} \right|$$

The two straight-line fences instead of parentheses indicate a *determinant;* such a determinant has a value $ad - bc$. If the matrix is a proportion matrix, the value of the determinant is 0 according to the rule of the diagonal products. The following matrix also has a value of 0, but it is not a proportion matrix:

$$\begin{vmatrix} 5 & 0 \\ 2 & 0 \end{vmatrix}$$

In a matrix of m rows and n columns in which m or n is greater than 2, we have many matrices of 2 rows and 2 columns built up by the vertices of rectangles. All these matrices are also considered determinants. If the original matrix is a proportional matrix, then all those determinants have a value of 0. From this follows a definition: A matrix has the rank 1 if in such a matrix all determinants of 2 rows and 2 columns equal 0. Every proportion matrix has the rank 1. But matrices that are not proportional, such as the following, also have the rank 1.

$$\begin{vmatrix} 2 & 3 & 0 \\ 4 & 6 & 0 \\ 6 & 9 & 0 \end{vmatrix}$$

IS COMPUTING WITH FRACTIONS NECESSARY?

In the above I have shown that proportions can be dealt with without using fractions. This evokes the question: Can fractions always be avoided? Everyone knows that computing with fractions does not go very smoothly in elementary school. Addition of fractions with unlike denominators gives pupils a lot of trouble. Multiplication and division are taught as tricks, and we see how fast those tricks are forgotten. In secondary school, fractions return, sometimes as a repetition, sometimes with letters in the numerator and denominator. Computation with fractions often is postponed till the second grade because in the first grade success is negligible.

We need not wonder why elementary school children so soon forget computation with fractions. For what is their practical application? Decimal fractions, in practice, are not presented as fractions and also are not calculated as fractions. One who has to add $27.12 and $0.48 does as if it were dollar and cents; one who has to compute 5 times 12.36 meters, does it with centimeters. If a method of decimal fractions is set up in the right way, a transition to another scale is used. In such a case, 12.3 + 9.24 = 1230 hundredths and 924 hundredths = 2154 hundredths = 21.54. Those hundredths have a concrete meaning when one thinks of centimeters or dollar and cents. A milkman who works with eighths of liters, quarters of liters, and so on also works with a graduated scale: If he has to add, he uses all eighths of liters. Of course in this manner $2/7$ and $3/5$ can also be added; the weak spot in this extension, however, is the fact that a corresponding concrete situation does not present itself and probably never will. The problems constructed in textbooks have no real significance; the above examples borrowed from practice demand calculations so simple that for this no special method needs to be developed.

To be honest, we should admit that being able to calculate with fractions has no practical utility. That is why so many people long out of school have for the most part forgotten the techniques of calculating with fractions. If we replace $\frac{2}{7}$ + $\frac{3}{5}$ by $\frac{31}{35}$, what have we achieved? We know then, to be sure, that we have something less than 1, but what percentage of 1? To know this is often important. With a calculator we can immediately determine that it is 29% + 60% = 89%. So it is much better to learn to determine such things very early at school.

In secondary teaching, fractions with letters are introduced. Here it is taught that $a/b + c/d = (ad + bc)/bd$. Here, too, fractions are a source of misery for children. The above reduction is read as follows: instead of adding the quotients of a and b and of c and d, we can first add the products of a and d and of b and c and afterward divide the result by the product of b and d. If you reflect on this result you might come to the following conclusion: "Indeed is it possible to get the same result in two different ways, but why should I be happy knowing this?"

In mathematics many identities, such as that above, are found. We have always supposed that such identities are useful, but now we begin to doubt it. Does the form $(ad + bc)/bd$ simplify further calculation? It would be worth tracing what is done with fractions in algebra; I presume that the reduction of $a/b + c/d$ makes us lose as much time as we gain in many cases. If the result has to be used in a programmed calculator, it is bad to apply such a reduction. We then lose a part of the memory of the calculator, which is not recommended.

This is not the first time in secondary teaching that we have begun to doubt of the profit of identities. In trigonometry there was a time when all sorts of identities concerning line segments in a triangle—expressed in the radius of the circumscribed circle and goniometric functions of the angles—were taught. In the Netherlands it was said that these identities were very suitable for solving problems on final examinations. (Whether those problems were meaningful, I will not discuss.) One day I wanted to convince a class of the use of those identities, and I began a class discussion. Looking at an examination problem, I asked the pupils what a person first coming across such a problem likely would do. The pupils came to the conclusion that such a person would at first think of the sine rule. I entered into this thought, as one ought to do in a class discussion, though I hoped afterward to be able to demonstrate that with the help of identities we could save much time. However, my expectations were not met: With the help of the sine rule, the problem was solved in four lines. A second and a third problem were tackled, and each time we finished quickly. From that moment on, I was no longer willing to explain identities with the radius of the circumscribed circle of a triangle.

There was a time when we spent many hours with the simplification of expressions with radicals. The pupils were taught how to deal with forms like $\sqrt{(6 + 2\sqrt{5})}$ and $\sqrt{6}/(\sqrt{3} + \sqrt{2})$. Now many people like it to write $2\sqrt{5}$ instead of $\sqrt{20}$, $\frac{1}{2}\sqrt{2}$ instead of $1/\sqrt{2}$. I agree that it is necessary to realize that those forms are equal; nevertheless, it is not necessary that the pupils themselves be able to execute the reduction. If you have to calculate with expressions with radicals, the reduction is of little or no value, and if you have to find approximations, the calculator does not require such reductions.

So, before we begin to express our regret about the fact that pupils are so poor at calculating with fractions, we first have to see whether calculating with fractions is really necessary. Could we perhaps find a way by which calculating with fractions might be kept to a minimum?

THE CONSTRUCTION OF A LOGICAL SYSTEM IN ALGEBRA

The construction of a logical system in geometry has always been a rather dreary matter for pupils of secondary school. It was an inheritance of Greek mathematics and so had all the qualities of old-fashioned science. Because it was science it was not given in the order that is necessary for a curriculum; because it was old-fashioned it did not satisfy the conditions we ask from a logical system. Therefore, geometry begun with such a system generally came to nothing. Reasonings that were no more than simulations had to be applied so often that pupils were made unfit for logical thinking more often than they profited by it. In my discussion of the levels of thinking I demonstrated that such a beginning for geometry, from a didactic point of view, has to be disapproved. An intuitive introduction for geometry has also been used, but this too has failed: Either too many axioms were introduced, or only a very small chain of theorems was developed. The crux of the matter is that the system of theorems in geometry is much too complicated to be attractive to pupils of secondary education. I add to this that even for most university students the matter is too complex and of too little importance.

In algebra it is quite different. Here it is possible to obtain, with the help of five axioms, a complete system for the addition of real numbers $\mathbb{R}$:

Axiom o1:   For every two real numbers a and b there exists a real number $a + b$ that is their sum.

Axiom o2:   Addition is commutative: For every two real numbers a and b, $a + b = b + a$.

Axiom o3:   There exists an identity element $0 \in \mathbb{R}$, such that for each element $a \in \mathbb{R}$, $a + 0 = a$.

Axiom o4:   To each element $a \in \mathbb{R}$ there exists an additive inverse element $-a \in \mathbb{R}$ with the property $a + (-a) = 0$.

Axiom o5:   Addition is associative: For every three elements a, b, $c \in \mathbb{R}$, $(a + b) + c = a + (b + c)$.

With the help of these five axioms it is easy to prove that there is exactly one element x with the property that $a + x = b$. Of course, to introduce such an axiom system we have to wait for the right moment as determined by the levels of thinking: It is only possible for pupils to understand such a system after they have reached the third level of thinking. The first acquaintance with algebra should not involve such an axiom system.

For multiplication we have a corresponding set of axioms. I can also use the terminology of structure: The axiom system of addition and that of multiplication are (mathematically) isomorphic.

Axiom v1: For every two real numbers a and b there exists a real number $a \times b$ that is their product.

Axiom v2: Multiplication is commutative: for every two real numbers a and b, $a \times b = b \times a$.

Axiom v3: There exists an identity element $1 \in \mathbb{R}$, such that for each element $a \in \mathbb{R}$, $a \times 1 = a$.

Axiom v4: To each element $a \in \mathbb{R} \setminus [0]$ there exists a multiplicative inverse element a^{-1} with the property $a \times a^{-1} = 1$.

Axiom v5: Multiplication is associative: For every three elements $a, b, c \in \mathbb{R}$, $(a \times b) \times c = a \times (b \times c)$.

The set $\mathbb{R} \setminus \{0\}$ mentioned in v4 is the set of real numbers with exception of the element 0. So if we want the axiom system of multiplication to be completely isomorphic with the axiom system of addition, we must make an exception for the element 0 with the former system.

With the help of the multiplication system we can easily prove that there is exactly one element x with the property that if a and b are elements of $\mathbb{R} \setminus \{0\}$, $a \times x = b$. I will prove with the help of the axiom system that $x = a^{-1} \times b$

According to axiom v4, the element a^{-1} exists.
According to axiom v1, the element $a^{-1} \times b$ exists.
According to axiom v5, $a \times (a^{-1} \times b) = (a \times a^{-1}) \times b$.
According to axiom v4, $(a \times a^{-1}) \times b = 1 \times b$.
According to axiom v2, $1 \times b = b \times 1$.
According to axiom v3, $b \times 1 = b$.

There is only one element x for which $a \times x = b$, for if there were another element y such that $a \times y = b$, then $a \times x = a \times y$; but also $a^{-1} \times (a \times x) = a^{-1} \times (a \times y)$, from which $x = y$ can be derived.

All algebraic theorems of addition, substraction, multiplication, and division can be derived with the help of the former 10 axioms if we add an eleventh axiom:

Axiom d: For every three elements a, b, $c \in \mathbb{R}$, $(a + b) \times c = a \times c + b \times c$. This axiom is called the distributive law.

With such a construction the pupils learn better and more naturally what a logical system really is. Later we can give a corresponding axiom system for vectors, from which a foundation for geometry can be found. Such a construction has many points of similarity with the construction of a system in algebra. The systems of addition and multiplication can be seen as two varieties of Abelian groups. We can see the Abelian group as a more-inclusive structure than the first two structures.

COMPUTING WITH FRACTIONS AS PRODUCTS

If we use the construction above, we can replace a/b by $a \times b^{-1}$. This way of thinking can be easily introduced in elementary school, especially if the pupils are allowed to use a calculator. If they have to compute $4 \div 7$, they can either directly find 0.5714285714 or take 4×7^{-1}, finding $4 \times 0.1428571429 = 0.5714285714$. If fractions are introduced in this way it is necessary that pupils become acquainted with the properties of inverses of numbers immediately after they have been introduced. They will have to know that if $a > b > 0$, the following inequality is true: $b^{-1} > a^{-1} > 0$. The fractions a/b and c/d are multiplied as if they were products: $(a \times b^{-1}) \times (c \times d^{-1}) = (a \times c) \times (b^{-1} \times d^{-1})$, and if one needs it, this also equals $(a \times c) \times (b \times d)^{-1}$. The quotient of two fractions can be found as follows: $(a \times b^{-1}) \div (c \times d^{-1}) = (a \times b^{-1}) \times (c \times d^{-1})^{-1} = (a \times b^{-1}) \times (c^{-1} \times d) = (a \times d) \times (b \times c)^{-1}$. The sum of two fractions is rather complicated: $(a \times b^{-1}) + (c \times d^{-1}) = (b \times d)^{-1}(a \times d + b \times c)$. But is there any important reason to factor out $(b \times d)^{-1}$?

On a final examination in the Netherlands the following problem was given:

For a convergent geometric sequence t_1, t_2, t_3, . . . , t_n, it is given that $t_k = (1 + \log_2 x)^{-k}$.
  a. What are the possible values of x?
  b. The sum s of the sequence is a function of x. What are the possible values of s?

a. To answer question (a) we have to think the following:

1. x belongs to the domain of the function $\log_2$, so $x > 0$.
2.   For $(1 + \log_2 x)$ the inverse is taken, so $1 + \log_2 x \neq 0$; hence $x \neq 2^{-1}$
3.   The sequence is convergent, so the common ratio $(1 + \log_2 x)^{-1}$ suffices $-1 < (1 + \log_2 x)^{-1} < 1$, so according to the properties of inverse numbers: $1 + \log_2 x < -1 \vee 1 + \log_2 x > 1$; hence $x < 2^{-2} \vee x > 1$. From (1), (2), (3) we deduce $0 < x < 2^{-2} \vee x > 1$.

b. The sum of a convergent metrical sequence with common ratio r and first term t_1 is $t_1 \times (1 - r)^{-1}$. For question (b) this gives $(1 + \log_2 x)^{-1} \times [1 - (1 + \log_2 x)^{-1}]^{-1}$. For this we may write $[(1 + \log_2 x) \times (1 - (1 + \log_2 x)^{-1})]^{-1} = (1 + \log_2 x - 1)^{-1} = (\log_2 x)^{-1}$. The range of $(\log_2 x)^{-1}$ for the domain $0 < x < 2^{-2} \vee x > 1$ is $-2^{-1} < x < 0 \vee x > 0$.

As can be concluded from this conversion, it is especially necessary to know the following properties:

1. $a^{-1} \times b^{-1} = (ab)^{-1}$.
2. $a \times a^{-1} = 1$.
3. The function $x \to x^{-1}$ is, in both of the coherent parts of its domain, a continuous monotonous decreasing function.

CONSEQUENCES OF GIVING UP FRACTIONS

The abolition of fractions in secondary education would of course have the consequence that they also would have to be given up in primary education. The habit of writing 4^{-1} instead of ¼ would perhaps cause some difficulty. But one might begin by writing 4* or something of the sort. Because, as we have already seen, fractions are seldom used, we could restrict ourselves to fractions like 3×4^{-1} and 2×5^{-1}. The question of how fractions have to be ordered could be restricted to very simple cases, like parts of regular polygons or rectangles. To a question like "which is greater, 4×5^{-1} or 7×8^{-1}," we can give this advice: "Multiply both numbers by 5×8, you will get 4×8 and 5×7. Thus 7×8^{-1} is greater." I would prefer to have my pupils do this with a calculator. The calculator gives $4 \times 5^{-1} = 0.8$ and $7 \times 8^{-1} = 0.875$, and so we see directly that 7×8^{-1} is greater.

At some time pupils will have to be able to write a number like 17×83^{-1} as a decimal number. Most pupils leaving primary school cannot do such a thing, though this conversion is more important than any other conversion of fractions. It must be decided where this conversion should be learned—in primary school or in secondary school. I prefer primary school, but then in a very easy way: by using the calculator.

In secondary education, calculation with negative numbers and fractions may be an introduction to work with groups: $(+6) + (-13) = (+6) + (-6) + (-7) = 0 + (-7) = (-7); 12 \times 4^{-1} = 3 \times 4 \times 4^{-1} = 3 \times 1 = 3$.

There are advantages and disadvantages to giving up of fractions. Advantages are:

1. A piece of mathematics will be given up that contains only an isolated technique.
2. Theorems will be presented more frequently in the form of a product than in the form of a quotient, which will benefit exactness.

3. The concept of group will have a more central position.
4. In differential and integral calculus it will no longer be necessary to first convert fractions with the help of negative exponents.

Disadvantages are:

1. One will have to break oneself of a habit.
2. There will be some resistance to replacing ¾ by 3×4^{-1} or by 0.75, and $4\frac{1}{2}$ by 9×2^{-1} or 4.5.
3. It will be necessary to struggle against all those who do not like change.
4. We have not yet tried this in practice, so the consequences for the entire field of mathematics are not quite known.

It is only an idea, so we are not obliged to switch over at once to the new manner of writing. Still, it seems to me that it is worth considering the abolition of operations with fractions (cf. Freudenthal, 1983, pp. 133–177, on the subject of fractions).

29

Objectivity

OBJECTIVE AND SUBJECTIVE

In order to know what "objective" is, we could begin by contrasting it to "subjective." We then run the risk of not being able to avoid the emotional element that is sometimes associated with the concepts of 'objectivity' and 'subjectivity'. Often a judgment is called "subjective" by one who intends to reject it. On the other hand is the "objective," proper judgment that one wants to put in its place. In order to avoid this emotional element, we go to a domain of supposedly objective judgments: mathematics.

More and more sciences begin to make use of mathematics. One only has to think of physics, chemistry, biology, economics, and sometimes even linguistics. There is an expectation that when a problem has been put into mathematical form, objectivity has been attained. As was mentioned, the objective judgment is contrasted to the subjective judgment. If someone thinks that a certain painting is fine, this judgment is subjective. He thinks it so and this judgment is not open to discussion. We get a greater objectivity in the judgment of a painting if a great number of people appoint a committee of experts to set up norms according to which the painting will be judged. Nevertheless, the judgment still retains a measure of subjectivity: Are we sure that the correctness of the norms have been discussed long enough? What is the weight of each norm? How is it possible to gauge the norms? Has an expert whose judgment is significant been missed? From such issues, criteria for a judgment that might be called objective can be deduced:

1. the judgment is discussable;
2. the judgment is testable;
3. a sufficient number of people agree with the judgment.

These three criteria indicate that objectivity never can be absolute. For during the discussion—which may always be continued—it is always possible to change one's mind because new arguments are introduced. There also may be cases in which the results of a test turn out in another way. When the group giving judgment is increased or changed, a judgment may change as well.

LIMITS OF OBJECTIVITY

Experience teaches that a judgment of great objectivity is not necessarily true. Some judgments are discussable and testable within a large, private group. Within the group, these judgments have great objectivity. Still, there is the possibility that other people outside the group are not willing to accept the presumptions of the group and therefore do not agree with the judgment. Norms that have been valid for centuries now appear not to suffice in newer applications. Statements that were unassailable a century ago are now considered out of date and incorrect.

Sometimes to avoid long discussions, operational norms are established. As long as the group working with such norms handles them as axioms, the conclusions based on them are objective (assuming, of course, that the reasoning based on these norms is valid). Still, it may be that at the end one arrives at statements that are unacceptable. In that case one will have to adjust the norms, and with this some originally objective judgments will fail. It may also be that another group starting from other operational norms appears to have a greater influence. In that case one will also be often obliged to change the norms. So we may say that operational norms within a certain group result in rather great objectivity, which, however, is strongly tied to the group and is usually not very lasting.

OBJECTIVITY OF MATHEMATICS

On grounds of the above considerations it can be concluded that mathematical judgments are highly objective. They are discussable, testable, and accessible to a great number of people. Moreover, the content of mathematical symbols is so much reduced that there is little chance of a misunderstanding. An important issue is how it is possible to get certainty about the content of the symbols.

The first possibility is that within the context of a group, a similar action structure with those symbols is developed. Remainders of such a conception are found in sayings like "With two terms of an equation *it is allowed that* . . .''

There is a certain relation between this objectivity and that which is based on operational norms.

The second possibility is that the symbols have been developed in a larger field of knowledge in which the relations between the symbols are sufficiently known. The "defining of the symbols" is based on this second possibility. For a definition is only possible in a well-ordered field of knowledge. But this field can not be the field of mathematics, because we want to use the definitions in order to embody mathematics. If mathematics does not lean on an action structure that has been developed within a group, then it is founded on a sufficiently ordered field of nonmathematical, or perhaps not yet mathematical, knowledge.

An action structure, having been developed within a group, may have within the group a great measure of objectivity: the judgment is discussable. ("We *always* do it in this way!") The judgment can be tested. (Within the context in which the symbols are used, a contradiction has never occurred: the use of the symbols has been arranged in such a way that all contradictions have disappeared.) A sufficient number of people have agreed with the judgment. (Everyone wanting to apply the symbols gets a text in which he is shown how to act.) But a mathematician is not happy with a foundation based on an action structure: A mathematical judgment ought to have a better foundation than one based on custom and imitation. Still there is no harm in realizing how the practice of teaching mathematics is sometimes based.

The "better" mathematics has its foundation in not yet mathematical knowledge. However it is definitely not emphasized that the definitions of the symbols are not yet mathematical. This of course is related to the reputation mathematics possesses with respect to objectivity. This reputation can only be maintained if the fact that the roots of mathematical knowledge are outside of mathematics is concealed.

But, as we have indicated earlier, this reputation with non-mathematicians is in general founded on the ability to conclude uniformly on grounds of an action structure. With the truth of $2 \times 2 = 4$ other truths are tested. For we say, "It is as true as two times two equals four." Still, the statement "$2 \times 2 = 4$" is for practically everyone a lesson learned by heart, and not a judgment deduced from mathematics.

OBJECTIVITY IN GENERAL

To obtain objectivity in a non-mathematical field there is the following possibility: One begins an exchange of views about the subjects of the field. A characteristic object of the context involved is chosen and is described as exactly as possible. With this description, relations with other objects characteristic of the context come into discussion. All aspects will have to be avoided that are not characteristic of the context. (For "set in a mathematical context," the activity of "setting up a collection" is not characteristic.) Moreover, in order to avoid circular reasoning, all higher abstractions must be avoided. So in the first discussion about the not yet mathematical foundation of mathematics, mention of "definitions," "theorems," and "axioms," is not desirable. These concepts ought to be *developed* in a primitive mathematical context and so are not appropriate to a discussion serving to constitute language symbols of a primitive mathematical context. All words that eventually will be used in definitions (and the first mathematical reasonings) must first work in primitive contexts connected with the definitions to be treated.

After an understanding of the fundamental ideas is possible, one is able to (1) build up a language in which the fundamental relations are connected, and (2) lay an objective basis for the constituting relations of the topic involved. Here we have been busy with language development; the development of the language of the first level of the topic involved. The activity of the development of this language is accessible to every one; the advanced as well as the beginner ought to participate in the discussion. The assertions in the language are completely objective because they satisfy the three criteria mentioned above. The beginner is a necessary participant in the discussion. The beginner of today is advanced afterward. His judgment of today influences his judgment afterward. To avoid a condition in which science changes its character each time a practitioner begins to think about truths formerly gratuitously accepted, it is necessary to admit such practitioners during their study as active participants in the scientific discussions.

After the development of the language, one can seek the explanations of the connections; a higher level of abstraction can be attained. When differences of opinion present themselves, one has to determine if they issue from (1) an indistinctness not before perceived in the description of the first level, (2) an indistinctness in abstraction of a definition, or (3) unsufficient orientation in the first level, so that abstraction was not yet possible. It is in the interest of objectivity that no argument be delivered that the participants are not able to follow. Many people break this very simple rule. More often than not lecturers in mathematics change to a higher level of abstraction after a low-level introduction. Only those who are generally aquainted with the content of the lecture are able to participate in the discussion. The others are obliged to remain silent in order to conceal their lack of comprehension, or they have to restrict themselves to unimportant questions that merely testify to their interest. Afterward they must try to determine from their notes what the lecture was actually about.

We know that if a good teaching method is used every mathematical subject can be made comprehensible to almost everyone: The simplicity of such a subject shows itself in secondary education when good instruction and a suitable transformation have taken place. The role of didacticians of secondary education is not inconsiderable, and more interest in didactics in higher education is desirable. Something like this holds for every other science as well: Objectivity is not developed by expressions in hardly understandable jargon or by discussions within a select group of supporters. Objectivity of science benefits from open discussion with the usually large group of those concerned.

OBJECTIVITY IN PHYSICS

In physics, mathematics plays an important role usually. If a physical law is to be determined, one will try to abstract it into a mathematical form. The results can then be obtained in a mathematically objective manner from the law. Of course these results are only correct if the law is correct. They must be tested by practice. A physical law gives a mathematical model in order to describe phenomena. Afterward a hypothesis can be set up to explain the law. With more exact testing, the mathematical model may deviate from that which is observed; it will then be necessary to look for a new mathematical model. The first mathematical model may then be considered as a first approximation of the second. The hypothesis will also be correspondingly extended.

Two questions are therefore significant to objectivity of natural sciences: (1) How is it possible that a natural law has an objective content? and (2) What sort of test can be considered objective? A natural law originates in a concept that has to be affirmed by experiment. This experiment must be accessible to everyone; that means it must be repeatable. It must be set up in such a way that neither supporters nor opponents are able to falsify it. The authority of the experimenter should have no influence on the credibility of the result. When an experiment leads to a certain result, this result must be interpreted. About this interpretation discussion must be possible. Often the interpretation of the result is the feeblest link in the reasoning. It is important here to account for all seeming exceptions to the law, including these suggested by opponents.

These conditions for objectivity are typical of the second level of thinking in the natural sciences. At the first level, the not yet scientific knowledge, the approach is the same as that of not yet mathematical knowledge.

It is clear why mathematics cannot replace experiment. Mathematics is engaged with the structure and mutual connections of mathematical concepts. These are pure constructions of thought. They are tested by investigations for internal contradictions. Such tests do not have the character of experiments, because no "question is asked of nature." If one tries to fill a tiled pavement with pieces of cardboard having the shapes of congruent irregular quadrangles, and they fit, then this is not an experiment; for as soon as the structure of the tiled pavement appears, one can say, "Of course it can be done; it is possible to prove that it can." It is a mathematical structure that presents itself: physical imperfection is not important.

OBJECTIVITY IN THE SCIENCES OF MIND

It is hard to imagine that a first approach to the first level of thinking of sciences of mind would take place in a manner other than that of mathematics and natural sciences. Here also it is possible to obtain objectivity by exchange of views about subjects characteristic of the ground level of the topic involved. However, with the transition to the higher level, obvious differences appear. Because human behavior is an essential factor in the sciences of mind, not only objective judgment, but also other human actions and ways of thinking, play a part in the transition. If, for instance, to translate a play by Shakespeare into French, one must be familiar with (1) the use of language at the time of Shakespeare, (2) Shakespeare's use of the language, (3) the life-style at the time of Shakespeare, (4) the material out of which Shakespeare drew his data, and (5) the French language and its use in the subjects involved. All these points contain a great deal of "fellow-man-like" thinking, and they come under discussion at a higher level of thinking in translation. In a first approach to translation from one language in another, these concepts are not yet present. (It is hard to believe that a translating machine could take the above points into account.)

Objectivity in history presents a different problem. At first one might strive after objective historical writing. Soon it will be discovered that this is not possible: The political inclinations, nationalities, and philosophical attitudes of writers of history all determine their concepts of a historical event. To eliminate these factors, historical writers must restrict themselves to a reproduction of the facts without comment. Such has been tried by some writers. But it does not give a satisfying solution. In the first place, the facts as such have little significance; much more important is how people concerned directly or indirectly with these facts experienced them. And with a description of such experiences, the personality of the writer of history plays an important part. Moreover, those who want to describe the simple facts have to choose what is worth mentioning, and this cannot be done without subjectivity.

So even if we are intent on being objective, we have to accept the subjectivity of the writer of history. But we can agree about why, when biographies or descriptions of the same event are compared, writers give such different reports. Of course the results of such a comparative study will vary from one period to another, but such a change of objectivity does not differ much from that which we have met already with other sciences. So a historian may gain objectivity, not in giving a description of an event, but in analyzing descriptions of other people. A historical work containing many articles of authors of various vision may with an honest selection have a certain objectivity.

PHENOMENAL APPROACH

The first approach to every science, which in principle is always the same in the sense described above, we may call a *phenomenal approach*. First there is always the fixing of the context of the topic, the development of the technical terms by speaking (or writing) as clearly as is possible. If somebody begins to present a theorem, he must suppose that a phenomenal approach already has taken place. If he is not sure that it has, then the time for a theorem has not yet come.

Phenomenal analysis is used in phenomenology. It is no wonder that Husserl, the founder of phenomenology, was a mathematician who tried to give mathematics a foundation. Remarkably, this means of gaining objectivity is more appreciated in sciences of mind than in mathematics. Of course a phenomenal introduction takes time. It is more direct to begin physics with "Every substance consists of molecules . . ." or economics with "Everyone agrees with the pronouncement that human striving is directed at enlarging social prosperity . . ." These, however, leave no room for an objective discussion.

A phenomenal approach need not always be used as a means of establishing relations at a higher level of thinking. If such a high level of thinking has already been attained, it is possible to use the symbols and concepts that already have significance. If, however, it is the first time that such a high level has been attained, the phenomenal discussion cannot be spared. The fixing of concepts of the higher level of thinking must be done with the help of language symbols that have just gained their correct significance. This new significance can only be ascertained by discussion. Those who have not yet attained the level of thinking cannot participate in the discussion: They cannot speak about the phenomena because they have not yet seen them.

A phenomenal approach also may render good service when cooperation between students of different sciences is desired. Such a circumstance can occur when philosophy is studied. For it is improbable that the language symbols developed in different sciences have exactly the same significance. With the help of a discussion, such differences can be overcome.

WHAT IS SCIENTIFIC THINKING?

From the above it appears that the development of a science is something quite different from the search for the truth. The constructive character of a science becomes especially clear in the development of language that attends it. Some language symbols are so suggestive that they alone are able to evoke complete constructions of thought. The absence of language symbols sometimes makes discussion very difficult. In a language (like French) where the words "insight" and "thinking pattern" are lacking, it is difficult to explain how a higher level of thinking is brought about. The words "insight" and "thinking pattern" evoke a coherence of concepts that very much enlightens the discussion.

Molecules and atoms are not discovered; they are constructions of the mind enabling us to better understand the world. If a further refinement of the description is necessary, this construction is no longer sufficient. The ancient Greeks' lack of a distinction between molecules and atoms was not based on an error of thought: Their knowledge of nature was not refined enough to urge them on to construct a model in which this distinction was made. At that time, the concept '*atomos*' had enough objectivity.

It sometimes seems that Piaget was investigating how far his subjects had advanced toward an absolute truth. He investigated whether they had already discovered that the volume of a liquid is constant, that five beads put together is just as much as five beads spread apart, that with a very fine division of a segment, points are obtained. With the latter case, they had discovered something that for Piaget, but not for mathematicians, was an objective truth.

A phenomenal approach does not try to find answers to these questions: How *are* things? How *is* nature? What *is* the truth? For this way of thinking, these questions are not meaningful. What it does ask is this: How is it possible to understand phenomena? How can we understand each other by a description of phenomena? About what answer to a question are we able to agree? A question about the *cause* of an observed phenomenon is often not meaningful, because in many contexts 'cause' cannot be described phenomenally. Then we have to restrict ourselves to questions about the regular co-occurence of phenomena.

TECHNICAL CONTROL

As we saw at the beginning of this chapter, it is possible to obtain uniform results if one has learned within a group to command perfectly a structure of actions. In this manner algebra has sometimes been taught. For example, one may think of schemes in order to calculate with the help of logarithms. Such uniformity has little to do with objectivity; it has not been developed by objective judgments. On the contrary, just because an action structure has been developed, the judgments have withdrawn from objectivity. Only an analysis and a description of the actions might be able to procure objectivity for the structure.

Parallel to this is intuitive acting and judging. It is possible to arrive at a practically unfailing judgment by intuition. This is based on an insight that has not (yet) become objective. Important parts of theories have been developed in this way. Forced by necessity, an action structure has been developed—has been learned in order to make decisions intuitively. By analyzing actions, reflecting about the motives, and making this all explicit, one gives other people access to one's "gift"; the "power" passes from a subjectivity in an objectivity.

CONCLUSION

Objectivity is only possible through language development. A mathematical language with little variation in interpretation leads to great objectivity. This, however, is limited to the exactness of the symbols; if the symbols are related to nonmathematical concepts, objectivity demands long discussions about their relation. It is possible to put many kinds of research into a mathematical format, and usually the mathematical analysis will be correct (objective). But often the relation between the object to be investigated and the mathematics is a weak link.

If mathematics has been partly transferred by action structures, paradoxes may occur that require a renewed mathematical approach for their solution. The earlier obtained objectivity is then replaced by a new one.

In sciences other than mathematics, a language may have been developed within a certain group. This leads to an objectivity within the group. For instance, is it possible to use a definition of 'maturation' within a certain group, such that a child may become more mature if given adequate teaching. The reasoning set up with the help of this 'maturation' loses much objectivity if other researchers using the concept of 'maturation' only think of preordained biological maturation. At this point it is no longer possible to speak of objectivity in a greater field of research.

Working in select groups, which for practical reasons is very common, carries the danger of limiting objective results to the group. Because of a shortage of exchange of thought with other groups of independent researchers, a general objectivity fails to appear. Sometimes such a condition has the result that after the dissolution of a group, the greater part of their work falls into oblivion because the language in which their reports have been stated is not known by others. Working scientifically means developing a language with which discussion about the investigated subjects becomes possible. The language must be developed within a sufficiently large group. It fails to develop if it is not spoken—if it is not used to exchange views. Those who begin to learn to speak the language have an important part in the construction of the language. Therefore it is of the greatest importance that students actively participate in the teaching–learning process, and that their opinions be heard.

In the preceding I have never mentioned a priori judgments. I do not think we need them. Even the truth of $2 + 2 = 4$ is found in a certain context, and to come to this result a discussion was necessary. The result could be read from a structure of the second level, but this structure first had to be built up with the help of discussions—many of them. We see the connection more clearly when a judgment of logic is concerned, like "It is impossible that A and not-A are true at the same time. Here we have a judgment concerning structures of at least the fourth level of thinking. The judgment is only true in a very special, fabricated structure; in daily life, it often is not true. Of course, there are action structures that might be considered a priori—part of our human inheritence is instinctual. But it goes much too far to suppose that inherited structures surpass the first level.

30

A Step in the Direction of Philosophy

INTRODUCTION

I have always avoided occupying myself with philosophy. One of the reasons is that if you are to talk with philosophers you must first learn an extensive jargon and you must read many books very closely. And, just as in psychology, there are many branches of philosophy, and the followers of one branch have difficulty reading the works of another branch and have even more difficulty listening to the others. Another reason is that philosophy is generally not aimed at practical utility, whereas my work is aimed at the improvement of our conduct in many ways. Sometimes, however, it is impossible to ignore philosophy. Sometimes sciences are influenced by philosophy, and where this influence is contrary to my views, I must react.

In order to be easily understandable, I use in this chapter, as much as is possible, the terminology of Popper (Popper, & Eccles, 1981). In the first place, Popper has written very clearly and gives a plain survey of the various philosophies he deals with. In the second place, Popper uses a World 1, World 2, and World 3, which correspond to three of my media of structure: the world in which we live, the mind, and common human knowledge, respectively.

MATERIALISM

Popper describes various types of materialism. He says that all of them assert that the physical world, what Popper is calling World 1, is self-contained or 'closed'. By this it is meant that physical processes can be explained and understood, and must be explained and understood, entirely in terms of physical theories. Popper suggests that we are faced with prima facie dualism or pluralism with interaction between World 1 and World 2; moreover, he suggests that by way of the mediation of World 2, World 3 can act on World 1. By contrast, the physicalist (materialist) principle of the closedness of World 1 either asserts that there is *only* a World 1 or implies that if there is anything like a World 2 or a World 3 it cannot act on World 1.

From this I can conclude that, though there are many points of consonance between the worlds of Popper and my worlds (media of structure), there also is an important difference. To make this clear I use a semantic analysis. If someone wanted me to introduce World 1, I would show him something—for instance, a tree. I would ask, "Do you see this tree?" The fact that we have called the thing a tree, makes "tree" a part of World 3, but even if we had not known the name for it, we would still have been able to see it. The thing we see, and what we are able to see before we can speak, is of World 1. We see many things without giving names to them: We could call this seeing an act of World 2. But it is possible to attract the attention of other people to the things we see. If we want to speak of them, we speak of parts of World 1.

If a physicist is developing a theory, he is working in World 3. Sometimes he carries out experiments and then asks questions about World 1. The answers to the questions are given by the results of the experiment. But after this I can no longer understand the supposed closedness of World 1. For what the physicist wants closed is not World 1 but World 3! And general physical laws are constructed in such a way that the so constructed world is closed. About this we need not be astonished.

The structures of World 1 are all of the first level. These structures exist, for different people are able to observe them. We know that they have observed them, because we are able to discuss those structures and thereby transfer them to World 3. For such a transference, in each person, World 2 must have been brought in. You see, I cannot prove the existence of the three worlds, I can only hope for some comprehension of my reasoning if I use these terms. Without the intermediary of a World 1, I cannot understand that a correspondence of the minds of two people is possible. But what they construct and what man constructs during his whole life is (a part of) World 3.

The world of the physicists, therefore, is World 3, and there can be no doubt that this world has been influenced and always will be influenced by World 2.

But can World 1, the world we see, the world we live in, also be influenced by World 2? To answer this question I continue my semantic analysis.

THE SIGNIFICANCE OF EXPERIMENTS

Physicists have a very practical attitude, contrary to philosophers. Archimedes carried out his experiments about upward forces in liquids in order to find out if a substance was really gold or some alloy of metals. Optical systems are constructed to do things that otherwise could not be done. Experimenting means intervening in nature, so the physicist is always working with his World 2 upon World 1. And doing so he creates a new part of World 3. So it is clear that even the physicist, though he may be a true materialist, is busy influencing World 1 by World 2.

Here all materialists will say that they are not to be understood in this manner. I should have painted the picture more simply: The physicist, being part of World 1, has carried out the experiments; World 2 had nothing to do with it. What we have is the influence of World 1 on World 1. However, this reasoning is contrary to what is said in the lectures: They themselves had an idea (World 2), they devised an experiment (World 2) to prove their theory (World 2). So, by carrying out the experiment they proved that there is an influence of World 2 on World 1. If afterward they say that we have to understand this in quite another way, they are applying a theory that they themselves are not able to conceive the consequences of.

WHAT IS THE MEANING OF WORLD 1?

In the preceding, I have very much diminished World 1. After so many things have been placed in World 2 and World 3, it is reasonable to ask if there is something left of World 1. But as we have already seen with the physicist, nature (World 1), not theory, determines the outcome of experiments. Many experiments have results that are not expected; in such cases we have an influence of World 1 on World 3. Before the experiment, the result is not yet part of World 3. When I see a poplar, there is a part of World 3 in it, for I know it is a poplar. But I cannot analyze (in World 3) why it is a poplar, I read it from the gestalt, which is also something of World 1.

We may sometimes think that World 1 plays a small part in our life, but this is partly the fault of teaching. As I have emphasized many times before, all learning should begin with the things we see: in mathematics, physics, chemistry, geography. Sometimes this is difficult, for instance in history, pedagogy, or economics. Still, even in such topics we should begin with visual things; if we do not, we will never be sure of what we are talking about. So every topic has to begin somewhere in World 1, every science should have its roots in World 1. It is very often done otherwise, and this is the cause of many misunderstandings.

How our thinking is influenced by World 3 we can see when the pictures in this book are looked at. Many people ask, "What does it represent? What would you like me to see in it?" There is a psychological rule that if a paper with something on it is shown you, be it an inkblot or a picture of a piece of marble, you will always be able to see something in it. If not, the psychologist will be very worried about you. The pictures I have presented generally have clear structures, but when I made them, I often had no name for them. If I see a painting at some distance, I often know that I like it very much before I have seen that it also represents something. Sometimes such a picture has a name, for instance, "The War of the Two Kingdoms." I may not understand why it has such a name, I do not see the kingdoms and I do not see the war, but I am not troubled about that: I like the picture and that is enough. So you may say that, in such cases, my mind (World 2) is very closely related with World 1; World 3 is for the most part left out.

It is not always easy to draw a clear distinction between World 1 and World 3. Language never does. If we speak of the continent of South America, it is part of World 3. But what if we see a map of this continent? The making of the map belonged for the greater part to World 3, but if I see the map, it is part of World 1. What I see is World 1; its significance is World 3. But an astronaut, if there are only few clouds, may see the whole continent; then it is World 1. Only the knowledge that what is seen is called South America belongs to World 3. It is no wonder that we attribute many things to World 1 that really belong to World 3.

THE ROLE OF LANGUAGE IN THE RELATIONS AMONG WORLDS 1, 2, AND 3

If we want to communicate with others, we generally use language. So we need not be astonished that language plays an important role in the mingling of the three worlds. If we see a tree, this action is part of World 1 because the tree (without its name) belongs to it; the action is part of World 2 because our mind takes part in the action; the action is part of World 3 because we know that it is a tree we see. For those three actions language has only one expression. When I was a child, I was once asked by my schoolteacher, "Do you see that this liquid is troubled?" I did not, and he was very angry, because the liquid was troubled and he had every reason to suppose that I was not blind. Still, I did not see it, for I did not know what "troubled" meant. The Worlds 1 and 2 worked well, but I was not well enough acquainted with World 3. Geologists accompanying me in

Iceland saw many things that I did not see—naturally, for I had not yet learned to see them.

The important question is whether the troubling of the liquid, the properties of a tree, the things geologists see beneath Iceland belong to World 1. My answer is that they do not. What we see as parts of World 3 are interpretations of World 1; they are creations of our mind. With the laws of Einstein you can give a very fine description of World 1; still it is a mental description and thus part of World 3. With such descriptions you can make predictions; with the help of the theories of World 3 you can make atomic bombs with which you will be able to destroy a great part of World 1. World 3 gives you the opportunity to do many things you have already foreseen; still, your actions are governed by World 3 and not by World 1. So if you fail in your attempt to destroy the world (and I hope you do), this is not the fault of World 1 but of World 3.

If you see the matter in this way, you will have no trouble understanding why we, with our mind, are able to do things in World 1. All theories about cause and consequence belong to World 3; they are constructions, and if they give us no possibility of acting with our will, it is a deficit of the theory. The theories of Newton, Huygens, Bohr, Einstein, and many others are comprehensive, but they are all developed in closed systems and do not extend to everything. So, though we may be impressed by their extent, we can limit our awe: the laws need not stretch to the laws of our mind. The former should have some modesty: they must always account for their own production by our minds.

The people who developed the theories of physics, chemistry, and so on did not tell us to which world their theories belong. In their language, a distinction between the worlds was not made. But in the nineteenth-century view, the investigating of nature was an investigation into absolute truth.

Of course it is a reasonable desire to be able to predict the effect of all our actions. Most of our actions are aimed at a certain effect, and if we are disappointed we change the action a little. If we are in a completely new field, we first try to orient ourselves by performing arbitrary actions; we hope that by doing so we will eventually see some structure in their effects. After some time we may say that we are able to act adequately in the situation, that we have gained some insight. We must be careful when claiming to have insight. It is difficult to predict the weather of a certain day in the Netherlands three years from now. We know that in a specific month there will be some rain and also some sunshine, but we do not know how much or when. And now a materialist may say, "If we knew exactly the situation on earth, the coming and going of sun spots, and the status of all other things that influence the weather, we would be able to predict the weather at all places for years and years. But the materialist knows that the acquisition of such knowledge is impossible, so he is talking of a hypothetical situation; he is talking of a World 3 giving an impossible description of World 1.

All our theories are constructed for limited domains, and if you are a determinist you have to extend them to the universe. But this is an illicit generalization. Happily, human mind has helped itself in such difficult situations. If we have a vessel filled with air, we do not know the positions and the velocities of the molecules in it; but with the help of statistics we are able to predict tolerably accurately how the air will react if we change the circumstances. We do not know what the weather will be on a certain day three years from now in the Netherlands, but we know pretty well between what limits the amount of precipitation in the month of that day will be. In the same way, we know many things about stars and galaxies with the help of statistics. But in all these cases we have exchanged domains for which there is exact knowledge for other domains in which other, more global, laws are in effect.

We may conclude that it would be very pretentious to say that a World 3 has been developed that more and more will be able to give a perfect description of World 1. We are able to give more and more partial solutions in World 3, and with those partial solutions we will be able to make better and better predictions, but the solutions are doomed to remain partial. So the problem of how it can be possible that World 2 influences World 1, this latter world being closed, does not exist. If there were a world that was closed, it would be World 3, and we have seen that it is not closed at all.

EXAGGERATION OF THE EXTENSION
OF THEORIES

It is a common mistake for someone with a new theory to exaggerate the extension of this theory. It is easy to understand this mistake, for if you have found something new, you are so happy that you are inclined to believe that you can reconstruct the world. The physical laws that were found in the nineteenth century are so beautiful, so fertile for prediction, that you might have the illusion of being able to predict everything with their help. You also see this mistake in other sciences. At one time people believed that with "association" psychology it was possible to explain human conduct and even human thinking. Followers of psychologists of thought were of the opinion that with such theories all thinking could be explained, and they even tried to build a theory of learning with them. Psychologists of learning, studying the learning of meaningless things, thought that they could advise teachers about the teaching of meaningful things. Sociologists often try to extend their theories to domains in which they are not valid. It would be good if such scientists were a little more modest.

If you want to study a certain phenomenon, you must first determine in what context this phenomenon exists; after that you can investigate whether this context belongs to some already developed science. But there is a great chance that the context belongs to no existing science, and then you will have to develop a science yourself. After you have finished, you can see if it is possible to place your theory in some existing science.

My theory of the levels of thinking refers to the learning of pupils trying to understand theories. "Pupils" must be understood in a broad sense; anyone trying to understand new theories is a pupil. I think you will not find such ideas in the publications of psychologists of thought, psychologists of learning, or developmental psychologists. It is not their fault; they wanted to study thought in general, learning in general, or development in general. If you want to study the psychology of the learning and teaching of mathematics (or physics, chemistry, or economics), you must do so with the development of the language in those topics—and this is a specialization. Such a specialization cannot be found as a part of other theories; it represents an absolutely new problem. As you have seen, I was obliged to borrow ideas from the above-mentioned psychologies, but still I had to add my own ideas.

Every theory has its limitations. We should never try to apply one to too large a domain. If we have developed a theory and someone else has found astonishing things in an adjacent area, we should not immediately think that he has attacked our ideas. Perhaps the situation he has described does not belong to our territory.

ATTEMPTS TO FIND A SUPERSTRUCTURE

Often people do not trust their own tools. Practioners of a science sometimes try to find protection in another science. Mathematicians have done so. They failed to find the foundations of their topic in mathematics itself, and so they tried to find them in logic or in psychology. With logic they made a very bad choice, for logic can be understood as a higher level of mathematics: Mathematics does not proceed from logic, logic does proceed from mathematics. But it is just as impossible for mathematics to proceed from psychology, for the elements of mathematics cannot be found in psychology. Teachers engaged in the practice of their profession have tried to find the solution of their problems in psychology or pedagogy. It is useful for teachers to know much of these topics, but most of their problems will not be solved by them. Didactics, the theory of learning and testing, is a topic in itself.

There are two reasons for an attempt to find a master science. The first of them results from the level structure of the topic. In the old view, every topic should be built from truths that are sure. In mathematics, such truths are called axioms. In other topics they are called principles, and they are strengthened by definitions. With the principles and the definitions the whole pattern of the topic is given. Of course this is an authoritative construction; the pupil has nothing to say about it. Still, the teacher, by acting in this way, must have a more powerful authority to lean on, and therefore he uses another topic from which the principles are borrowed. If you consider the level structure, the course of things will be quite different. First there are discussions with the pupils about the subject. After many such discussions the pupils develop a structure at the second level. Then this new structure can be discussed and studied. The constituting principles of this structure form a new structure, and after studying these principles it is possible to find the principles on which the whole topic is built. Such an approach requires quite a new attitude for the teacher. By acting in this way he has to show that the principles are reasonable; they are not merely accepted.

The second reason for a search for a master science is a shortage of knowledge. Sometimes we want a theory when there is none. It is often so with didactics. The teacher has bad results. He is willing to acknowledge that this is his own fault; his teaching was bad but he does not know how to correct it. And there is not much literature that can help him. Of course there are magazines in which teachers tell of their own experiences; such magazines are of great importance, for they tell us something about the practice of teaching. But most of these experiences are very individual; generally the distressed teacher cannot repeat them, and if he could he would have to change them according to his own case. There is also an extensive literature of psychology and pedagogy. So it is no wonder that the teacher tries to find help in these sciences. A much better remedy is talking with colleagues. If they are sincere, they will admit that they also have difficulties. Exchanging ideas about the subject will help them all. When I was teacher, we held a weekly meeting at which we exchanged our bad experiences. We called it "weeping ourselves out." After some time with such meetings it will not be difficult to acknowledge your problems and mistakes, and if you and your colleagues are sincere there is a great possibility that you will be able to correct them.

Trying to find a superstructure starts with the supposition that somewhere there must be a great truth governing the whole domain of your topic. In reality there are many problems, each having its own solution. Many times these solutions are connected, but often it takes a long time to find this connection. If most of our problems have solutions that are clearly connected, we can say that we understand the structure of our topic—in this case we have attained the third (theoretical) level. Then indeed we have found a superstructure governing the problems of our topic. But this superstructure has been built up by our own working and puzzling and by discussion with other people also struggling with the material. So, if we have problems, we should not seek a closed theory to solve them: closed theories usually suit only a very limited domain.

A PRIORI KNOWLEDGE

Many philosophies work with a priori knowledge. Here and there I have found examples—"two and two is four," "every event has a cause," "the propositions A and not-A cannot both be true." All these statements belong to a higher level than the first, so it is obvious that I cannot agree to their self-evidence.

Let me begin with "two and two is four." In an old Arab tale there were once two men intending to make a long voyage together. Each of them said that he would like to take a friend with him. "So," one of them said, "we will go with four, because two and two is four." "No," the other said, "I think we will go with three." It is evident that the other supposed that they both thought of taking the same person as a companion. In mathematics there is a solution for such a situation: a theorem that tells us that with the union of two sets the addition of cardinal numbers is only allowed if the two sets have no elements in common. But again, we are on a higher level of thinking. "Two and two is four" tells us something about cardinal numbers. Those numbers then have been removed from visual structures. The properties of such numbers are not a priori; they have been developed in the discussion about such numbers.

In a general way, I have already touched on the proposition "Every event has a cause" in this chapter: in the discussion of our intense desire to be able to predict everything. Elsewhere (1981, p. 117) I have shown in a semantic analysis that we do not know what we are speaking of when we talk of cause.

"The propositions A and not-A cannot both be true": This is a statement of logic. It presupposes of every proposition that it can be said to be either true or false. In logic this is very easy: We exclude from the beginning the propositions about which we are not sure. But in daily life it is otherwise. "Yesterday the weather was fine." Some people will say this is true; others will deny it. Sometimes even in logic we have doubt, and then the rules are changed in such a way that the doubt is removed.

If my levels of thinking are accepted, we will have no need for a priori knowledge. Just as materialists suppose that in nature laws are waiting to be discovered, so mathematicians and logicians suppose that in their topics laws are waiting to be discovered. The medium, however, has to be different. The medium for mathematicians and logicians has to be mind. So in their supposition, laws are waiting for us to be discovered in our mind; this therefore must be a priori knowledge. So when they teach they begin with the a priori knowledge that is expressed in axioms. Starting from these axioms, the whole topic can be developed. For the teacher, this is a fine starting point. Discussion is basically useless; everything is fixed beforehand by the axioms.

On the basis of the levels of thinking, this order is reversed. We begin with the first (visual) level and the theses can be seen. Afterward the theses can be applied, and in this way the second (descriptive) level is attained. This descriptive level has its own structure, after discussion it is possible to make its laws explicit. These laws also have a structure, and by examining and discussing this structure we are able to find the axioms. But then we are at the third (theoretical) level of thinking at least. In this way we understand that the axioms do not issue from a priori knowledge, that they can be discussed and even rejected.

An important reason for the adoption of a priori knowledge was the fact that there exist truths that cannot be deduced from visual structures. If it was not possible to deduce them from visual observations and we still needed them, what else could be done besides accept them as a priori knowledge. Now, with our levels, we do not see such a difficulty. Every law of the second or higher levels has its origin in something other than the visual field. But this knowledge need not be considered a priori; it is knowledge we can read from the structures at the higher levels. Such a reading is not visual, for the structures at the higher level are too abstract to be visual. For the constitution of such structures, discussions were necessary. The theory of levels of thinking thus explains how knowledge can be attained that is neither derived from visual fields nor accepted a priori.

THE ROLE OF LANGUAGE

We have seen that for the constitution of higher levels, discussion is an indispensable phase. By discussion, the higher structures are formed; laws governing the lower structure are discovered after discussion. So would it not be possible to discover the laws of the higher structures by carefully examining the language that is used, or perhaps to deduce the language of the higher level from the language of the lower level?

Ir mathematics such an effort has been made. Attempts have been made to builu a system of geometry by just using a language, with the words of this language seen only in their mutual relations. If a line, a point, or a circle is spoken of, there is never a thought of a visual figure. A true mathematician plays this game when he builds geometry axiomatically for himself. If he says, "There is exactly one line that has two given different points as elements," he does not think of a visual line and visual points. If you draw two intersecting lines and say those lines are given the name "points" and the point they have in common is given the name "line," he will say, "This is a possible conception of what I have said, but I have intended nothing in particular about the visual world." But the game cannot be maintained. In the first place, we have to make various agreements about the order of the words, for we know that a sentence may have a quite different meaning if we change the order of its words. But second, we could never find new things. For new things require new words, and these are not in the game. The only things we can find are contradictions, on the basis of which we can state that a theory we thought to be correct is in fact not. To be clear of many of the difficulties of language, mathematicians use signs, with which they make formulas. They have learned that ordinary language is generally too dangerous.

I have given the above exposition because it shows us the feebleness of the foundations of each science. For these foundations are the last things we find, just at the highest level of thinking, after discussing and considering at each transition from level to level. The differences of opinion in many sciences demonstrate that such discussions often remain undecided. And even if a community of opinion has been established it may be only that an important person has pressed his own idea to acceptance.

PROBABILITY AS A CONSTITUTING FACTOR

Since the theories of Boltzmann in the middle of the nineteenth century, we have learned to live with probability. Not that Boltzmann was the founder of theories of probability; this science was already founded by Pascal and Fermat in the seventeenth century. But Boltzmann has shown us that though we know neither the positions nor the velocities of the molecules of a gas, we still know with great certainty what the pressure is if mass, temperature, and volume are given. What I have said here is a quite conversion of the facts: The relation between pressure, volume, temperature, and mass was known long before Boltzmann introduced his theories, but he made clear, using statistics, how it is possible that a very great number of molecules with very different velocities together exercise a constant pressure. If you have a great number of individuals each linked with some quantity, it may be that the average of this quantity is very predictable. We know this from elections: After the results in some districts have been counted, the whole result can be rather accurately known.

This knowledge can help us to live with uncertainties. We may die at any moment, but it is still useful to act as if we have many years to live. Any automobile driver we pass may be mad and do terrible things, but it is useful not to expect this. Probability tells us that the chance of such things occurring is too small to justify attention to them. In this way our whole life is pervaded with probability. Our senses tell us something about a "reality" that is only an interpretation. We believe them because until now everything fits the structure we have constructed. On the higher levels we have ourselves built new structures; we believe in them because we have been able to remove all contradictions. Perhaps at some time our belief will be nullified by some new contradiction. But until that time we act as if we were certain of the structure, probability gives us the right to do so.

Though we have to live with probability, we must not exaggerate. In the preceding examples we always had a rigid structure to rely on. Probability supported us in our expectation. But this certainty falls away without such rigid structures. There are many reasons to suppose that smoking is a cause of lung cancer. Statistics may support this supposition. If the results of statistics pointed in another direction, we would not be obliged to give up the suspicion of a relation between smoking and lung cancer, but there would be reason for doubt.

But if statistics indicate some correlation between matters that do not yet appear together in one strong structure, we are not obliged to suppose that there exists a relation between them. Of course it is sensible to investigate whether there is some overlooked structure constituting a relation between those facts, but if we cannot find one, we provisionally conclude that the correlation is merely accidental.

In mathematics and physics the probability that the laws we work with are right is very great. Though in mathematics, just as in any other science, the higher levels have been formed by interpretion, discussion, and integration, we seldom have to change our minds in this topic thanks to the possibility of reducing the level by using signs that make the higher level again visible. As there should be, there remains an insecurity when we apply this reduction: We are not always sure that the visible structure we have attained by reduction completely covers the situation of the higher level. We know that this danger always threatens, for beginning pupils often use the reduced visible structures in the wrong way. But in practically all cases doubt can be removed by discussion.

In physics the higher levels are tested by new experiments. They succeed in so many cases that at the higher level very strong structures have been formed. Whereas molecules were in the nineteenth century abstract products of the mind, we now work with them in so many ways that they have become very concrete. In many and various experiments we "see" them. Giving up 'molecules' and exchanging them for some other concept would be tremendously more difficult than introducing the metric system to a nonmetric society.

But in the mental sciences like psychology, economics, and pedagogy the laws of the higher levels are much more debatable. In the first place, the discussions used to attain the higher level have often been poor; the authority of the teacher has generally decided. But also the testing of results in practice is often contestable. So there is no reason to be astonished if a theory in these topics is soon followed by another quite contrary to the first.

THE UNCERTAINTY OF HUMAN KNOWLEDGE

In this discussion I have belittled many certainties. Facts of a higher level, like "2 and 2 is 4," often considered to be a priori knowledge, appear to be things worthy of discussion about which we have come to some agreement. The World 3 we have built up with those agreements is merely a human construction; it gives a fine interpretation of World 1. What World 1 really is, is not a very sensible issue; what we have to deal with is always World 3, which must be changed and rechanged every time World 1 does not give the expected answer.

We are not sure about the language we use; language must always be interpreted. There may be a misunderstanding any time we change the order of the words of a sentence. The words we use can seldom be defined, for if a definition is possible it always implies that we already know what we are speaking about. There is no sense in trying to make language more rigid, for it is just the flexibility of language that enables us to extend structures, to apply a global isomorphy, and to find superstructures. So we will have to live with the vagueness of language, it is one of its necessary properties.

We must be suspicious about the extent of the sciences: Most of them try to extend their territory beyond their limits. There are many physical, chemical, and biological laws that we may use when we study brains, but we have to be aware that with these we are not studying mind. When we apply one science to the domain of another science, we must be aware of being in a new situation. Even a book of differential equations of physics does not directly give the solutions to physical problems: After the use of the differential equations, the result must still be interpreted.

We also have to be suspicious of the use of statistics. Statistics may be very useful in a rigid system. If I have a lottery ticket, there is not much chance that I will win the first prize. But I know with certainty what my chances are, and I also know with certainty that someone will win the first prize. And we are similarly certain of the laws of behavior of a gas in physics, which also obey the laws of statistics. In these cases we know the distribution of chance very well. But when we try to put these laws into practice in economics or pedagogy, we must be very careful. Generally the distribution of chance is not at all certain; often, on the contrary, statistics is used to determine this distribution. But if such a distribution is very variable and we do not know the constituting factors of the problem we want to solve, the results of our research will be contestable.

My summary of this analysis is that no science can glory in the certainty of its results. Our highest certainty is in the results of mathematics, physics, chemistry, and biology. In those sciences the structures are so rigid that there is a great probability that they are right. But it is otherwise with the results of the mental sciences. There the higher levels of thinking have been often attained by the authority of important people, and generally this supplies an insufficient argument.

References

Beth, E. W.
   1955   Réflexions sur l'organisation et la méthode de l'enseignement mathématique. In *L'Enseignement des Mathématiques*. Neuchâtel, Switzerland: Delachaux et Niestlé. Pp. 35–46.

Bos, W. J. & Lepoeter, P. E.
   1955   *Wegwijzer in de Meetkunde*. Amsterdam: J. M. Meulenhoff.

Bos, W. J. & Lepoeter, P. E.
   1946   *Het denken van de schaker*. Amsterdam: dissertation. Noord-Hollandse Uitgevers Mij.
   1955   De psychologie van het denken en het meetkunde-onderwijs. In *Het aanvankelijk meetkunde-onderwijs*. Purmerend: J. Muusses.

De Jong, L.
   1974   *Het koninkrijk der Nederlanden in de Tweede Wereldoorlog*. Tome 5. The Hague: Staatsuitgeverij.

De Miranda, J.
   1955   *Verkenning van de "Terra Incognita" tussen practijk en theorie in Middelbaar (Scheikunde) Onderwijs*. Groningen: J. B. Wolters.

Drenckhahn, F.
   1962   *Arbeitsbuch für den Rechenunterricht*. Tome 8. Frankfurt am Main, Hamburg: Otto Salle Verlag.

Duncker, K.
   1935   *Zur Psychologie des produktiven Denkens*. Berlin: Julius Springer.

Ehrenfest-Afanassjewa, T.
   1931   *Uebungensammlung zu einer geometrischen Propaedeuse*. The Hague: Martinus Nijhoff.

Freudenthal, H.
   1973   *Mathematics as an Educational Task*. Dordrecht, Holland: D. Reidel Publishing Company.
   1983   *Didactical Phenomenology of Mathematical Structures*. Dordrecht, Holland: D. Reidel Publishing Company.

Heikkinen, V.
   1957   *A Study in the Learning Process in the School Class Environment*. Helsinki: Suomalainen Tiedeakatemia.

Köhler, W.
   1947   *Gestaltpsychology*. New York: Liveright.

Koning, J.
   1948   *Enige problemen uit de didactiek der natuurwetenschappen in het bijzonder van de scheikunde*. Dissertation, Utrecht. Dordrecht: Retèl & Felkers.

Langeveld, M. J.
   1949   *Inleiding tot de studie der paedagogische psychologie van de middelbare-schoolleeftijd*. Groningen: J. B. Wolters.

Mallinckrodt, H. H.
   1959   *Latijns Nederlands woordenboek*. Utrecht: Het Spectrum.

Meyerson, I.
1932   Les Images. In *Nouveau Traité de Psychologie* par G. Dumas. Paris.
Mursell, J. L.
1939   *The Psychology of Secondary School Teaching.* New York: W. W. Norton & Co.
Piaget, J.
1927   *La Causalité Physique chez l'Enfant.* Neuchâtel: Delachaux & Niestlé S.A.
1941   *La Genèse du Nombre chez l'Enfant.* Neuchâtel: Delachaux & Niestlé S.A. (with A. Szeminska)
1968   *Le Structuralisme.* Presses Universitaires de France.
Popper, K. R. & Eccles, J. C.
1981   *The Self and Its Brain.* Berlin, Heidelberg, London, New York: Springer International.
Prins, F. W.
1951   *Een experimenteel-didactische bijdrage tot de vorming van leerprestaties volgens denkpsychologische methode.* Groningen: J. B. Wolters.
Pukies, J.
1979   *Das Verstehen der Naturwissenschaften.* Braunschweig: Westermann.
Roth, H.
1957   *Pädagogische Psychologie des Lehrens und Lernens.* Berlin, Hannover, Darmstadt: Hermann Schroeder Verlag.
Selz, O.
1913   *Ueber die Gesetze des geordneten Denkverlaufs.* Stuttgart.
1924   *Die Gesetze der produktiven und reproduktiven Geistestätigkeit.* Bonn: Friedrich Cohen.
1935   Versuche zur Hebung des Intelligenzniveaus. *Zeitschrift Psychologie,* Bd. 134, Heft 4 bis 6. Pp. 236–301.
Skemp, R. R.
1971   *The Psychology of Learning Mathematics.* Middlesex and Baltimore: Penguin Books.
Syswerda, A. H.
1955   *De ruimtevoorstelling bij het kind volgens J. Piaget en B. Inhelder.* Groningen: J. B. Wolters.
Turkstra, H. & Timmer, J. K.
1953   *Rekendidactiek.* Groningen: J. B. Wolters.
Van Baalen, Kees.
1981   De (onuitgesproken) vooronderstellingen van Bram Lagerwerf en van Van Hiele. In *Euclides 10 1980/81.* Groningen: J. B. Wolters.
Van Hiele, P. M.
1955   De niveau's in het denken, welke van belang zijn bij het onderwijs in de meetkunde in de eerste klasse van het V.H.M.O. In *Paedagogische Studiën XXXII.* Groningen: J. B. Wolters. Pp. 289–297.
1957   *De problematiek van het inzicht, gedemonstreerd aan het inzicht van schoolkinderen in meetkunde-leerstof.* Dissertation. Groningen: J. B. Wolters.
1973   *Begrip en inzicht, werkboek van de wiskundedidaktiek.* Purmerend: J. Muusses.
1981   *Struktuur.* Purmerend: Muusses.
1984   De ontwikkeling van wiskundige grondbegrippen, kanttekeningen bij Hans Freudenthal—Didactical Phenomenology of Mathematical Structures. In *Pedagogisch Tijdschrift, 9e jaargang, juni 1984.* Meppel: Boom. Pp. 309–314.
Van Hiele-Geldof, D.
1957   *De didaktiek van de meetkunde in de eerste klas van het V.H.M.O.* Dissertation. Groningen: J. B. Wolters.

Van Parreren, C. F.
   1951   *Intentie en autonomie in het leerproces.* Dissertation. Amsterdam: Noord-Hollandse
             Uitgevers Mij.
   1960, 1962   *Psychologie van het leren 1 and 2.* Zeist: W. de Haan, Arnhem: van Loghum
             Slaterus.
   1981   *Onderwijsproceskunde.* Groningen: Wolters-Noordhoff.
Vest, F.
   1974   Behavioral Correlates of a Theory of Abstraction. *Journal of Structural Learning, 4.*
             Pp. 175–186.

Index

A

a priori knowledge, 104, 225, 234
Abelian group, 214
abstraction, 75, 79
abstract-symbolic level, 80
action, 99
action structure, 24, 66, 127, 132, 149, 218, 224
adequacy, 24, 159
algebra, 91
animal psychology, 24, 36, 139, 151, 159, 188
anticipation, 62, 168
Archimedes, 229
argument, 109–114
arithmetic, 98
associative operations, 99
atomic model, 17
atoms, 143, 224
autoregulation, 27
axioms, 1, 218

B

Beth, Evert Willem, 163, 173
biological development, 173
biological maturation, 65, 104, 175, 186
black holes, 142
Bohr, Niels Henrik David, 141
Boltzmann, Ludwig Eduard, 237
Bos, Wim, 3
bound orientation, 97, 177, 201
Brahms, Johannes, 17
bump on the skull, 186

C

calculator, 129, 196, 215
Cattegno, Caleb, 109
causality, 235
Cavalieri, Francesco Bonaventura, 167
characteristics, 62, 64, 83

chemistry, 17, 69, 135, 143, 148
class discussion, 97, 177, 190
closedness, 228
common human knowledge, 34, 129–130
completion of the complex, 62
concept, 122
conclusion, 71, 89
conformity, 16
confrontation with the environment, 104
congruent, 123
conscious thinking, 71, 187
context, 59, 90, 95
coordinates, 122
Copernicus, Nicolaus, 16
cosmic rays, 141
counting, 118
criticism, 113
Cuisenaire, Georges, 121

D

Darwin, Charles Robert, 16
deduction, 64
deductive, 10
deductive method, 163
definition, 1, 9, 27, 123, 167, 196, 219
De Groot, A. D., 3, 187
De Jong, Lou, 30
De Miranda, Hans, 6, 40
discipline, 189
discursive, 71, 79, 89, 128
dreams, 143
Drenckhahn, Friedrich, 205
Duncker, K., 61

E

Ehrenfest-Afanassjewa Tatjana, 3
Einstein, Albert, 138, 142, 231
examinations, 161
existence, of media of structures, 137–150
expectation, 23

experiments, 146, 172, 221, 229
explanation, 10, 177, 184
explicitation, 54, 79, 97, 117, 177
exploration, 62, 67, 97, 104, 178, 186, 191

F

feeble structures, 20
Fermat, Pierre de, 237
Fibonacci, series of, 14, 20
following from, 63, 111, 147
fractions, 205–216
free orientation, 54, 97, 177, 201
Freudenthal, Hans, 3, 4, 9, 216

G

Galilei, Galileo, 16
genealogical tree, 111
gestalt, 75
Gestalt psychology, 5, 24, 49
global isomorphy, 29, 30, 35, 167
group, 124, 185
guided learning processes, 104, 175
guided orientation, 53

H

Haydn, Franz Joseph, 17
Heikkinen, Väinö, 188
Heymans, Gerard, 71
history, 90, 222
Husserl, Edmund, 61, 223

I

identification, 16
image, 60, 168
implication, 171
incidental learning process, 62, 65, 106, 117,
   175
indoctrination, 16, 56
information, 53, 96, 177, 201
insight, 24, 71, 116, 151–162
integration, 54, 67, 177, 201
intention, 24, 159, 175–186
internal ordering, 96
introductory curriculum, 166
intuition, 71–76, 115–126
inventive power, 191
irrational numbers, 142
isomorphism, 28, 29, 79, 213
isosceles triangle, 45, 75, 94, 168

J

judgment, 110, 218
junctions of a network of relations, 61, 97,
   110
Jung, Carl Gustav, 71

K

Köhler, Wolfgang, 5, 24
Kohnstamm, Philip Abraham, 64, 167
Koning, Jan, 5

L

Lagerwerf, Bram, 41
Langeveld, Martinus Jan, 4, 176
language, 9, 33, 77–81, 89–91, 96, 105, 139,
   220, 230, 236
learning intention, 175–186
Lepoeter, P. E., 3
level reduction, 46, 53, 57, 64, 87, 148, 184
levels of thought, 39–70, 83–91
Lindworsky, Johannes, 63
logic, 28, 65, 95, 100, 111, 165, 212, 233

M

Mallinckrodt, H. H., 72
materialism, 228
mathematical model, 221
maturation, 50, 65, 106, 175
media of structure, 33–37, 137–150
memorizing, 177
mental structure, 24
Meyerson, Emile, 60, 168
molecules, 17, 143
Montessori, Maria, 2, 36, 147
Montessori material, 73
Montessori school, 2, 73, 178
more inclusive structure, 214
motivation, 187–193
Mursell, J., 4

N

Napoleon, 30
network of relations, 50, 61, 97, 110
neutrino, 143
nonnatural sciences, 147
number, 93–108, 118

O

objectivity, 24, 90, 125, 217–225
operation, 99

operational norms, 218
orientation, 61, 168

P

Pascal, Blaise, 237
Pascal's triangle, 13
pattern, 13, 23
perceptive level, 79
period, 41, 63, 176
phases, 76, 176
phenomenal analysis, 59, 60, 61, 78, 163, 223
phenomenal approach, 222
philosophy, 223, 227–239
photos, 130
physics, 130
Piaget, Jean, 5, 6, 27, 36, 40, 56, 65, 73, 81, 93–108, 116, 224
pictures, 11, 19, 23
plateaus, 59
Popper, Karl Raimund, 10, 33, 227
prejudice, 72
Prins, Frans W., 159
probability, 237
problems, 154, 199–204
problem solving, 62, 67, 190
proof, 84
propaedeutic curriculum, 2
properties, 27, 28, 94
properties of a structure, 62
proportion, 196, 205–216
Pukies, Jens, 138, 146

R

rank of a matrix, 209
rational numbers, 142
ready knowledge, 203
reality, 129–130, 137–150
recommending the subject matter, 189
recognition, 74, 94, 110
reflection, 54, 118
relativity, 80
restructuring, 68, 132
reversible, 99
reward and punishment, 188
rhombus, 49, 54, 110, 168
rigid (strong) structures, 20
Roth, Heinrich, 175

S

Sand, Georg, 14
saw, 170

sciences of mind, 222
selective accentuation, 79
self-discipline, 190
self-instruction, 183
Selz, Otto, 3, 4, 5, 62, 144
semantic analysis, 78, 160, 228
series, 13
series of Fibonacci, 14, 20
set, 120
Shakespeare, William, 223
signal character, 168
signals, 61, 97, 195
similar, 83, 124
sinking and floating, 115
skeleton, 29
Skemp, Richard R., 50, 74, 81
skill, 181
slide rule, 196
social pressure, 16
Socrates, 190
Socratic teaching, 73, 178, 190
spatial insight, 90
spatial thinking, 96
square-grid paper, 13, 117
stages, 53, 99
statistics, 144, 232
stereochemistry, 143
stimulus–response, 23, 128, 188
stratification, 63
structure, 9–37, 83–88, 127–128, 131–135
Structural (Gestalt) psychology, 28
structures of space, 166
subjectivity, 217
superstructure, 233
syllogistic reasoning, 64, 173
symbol character, 168
symbolization, 115
symbols, 60, 218
system separation, 195–198
Syswerda, A. H., 102

T

technical control, 224
technical language, 54, 57, 79, 97, 126, 177
telescoped reteaching, 45, 80, 110, 162
testing, 14, 151–162, 204
textbooks, 1, 202
theory, 199–204
thinking, 9
Thorndike, Edward Lee, 159

tiled floors, 122
tiles, 13
Timmer, Jan K., 205
transfer, 195–198
transformation, 27
translating machine, 222
transstructuring, 68, 131
trapezoid, 50
trial-and-error, 24, 159
Turkstra, H., 205
typewriting, 24

U

unconscious, 71, 187
unguided learning process, 65

V

Van Baalen, Kees, 41
Van Hiele-Geldof, Dieke, 123

Van Parreren, Carel, 6, 36, 79, 181
Van 't Hoff, Jacobus Henricus, 143
vectors, 35, 77, 122, 195
verbal references, 143
verbal structures, 172
Vest, F., 80
visual structures, 16, 71, 127–128

W

Wansink, Johan, 41
Wertheimer, Max, 5
Wiersma, Dirk, 71
Worlds, 1, 2, and 3, 10, 129–130, 137–150

Z

zest for work, 191